Qualitative Health Psychology

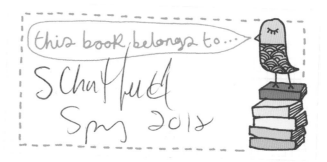

Qualitative Health Psychology

Theories and Methods

edited by
Michael Murray and Kerry Chamberlain

SAGE Publications
London • Thousand Oaks • New Delhi

First published 1999

 SAGE Publications Ltd
6 Bonhill Street
London EC2A 4PU

SAGE Publications Inc.
2455 Teller Road
Thousand Oaks, California 91320

SAGE Publications India Pvt Ltd
32, M-Block Market
Greater Kailash – I
New Delhi 110 048

British Library Cataloguing in Publication data

A catalogue record for this book is available
from the British Library

ISBN 0 7619 5660 3
ISBN 0 7619 5661 1 (pbk)

Library of Congress catalog card number 98–61737

Typeset by Mayhew Typesetting, Rhayader, Powys
Printed in Great Britain by The Cromwell Press Ltd,
Trowbridge, Wiltshire

Contents

Notes on Contributors

Helen Bryce is Research Coordinator for the Family Action Centre, University of Newcastle, Australia. The Family Action Centre is the host organization for a variety of community building programmes located in the Hunter Valley region of New South Wales, Australia. Helen facilitates and guides the action research in these programmes as well as offering consultancy services to government and third-sector organizations on innovative ways to evaluate their practices. The methods used by Helen are located in the constructivist paradigm and are an excellent tool for generating theory about what counts as effective practice.

Kerry Chamberlain is a Senior Lecturer in Psychology at Massey University in Aoteoroa/New Zealand. His research interests are centred in health psychology, and focused primarily on chronic illness and social disadvantage. He also has interests in research methodology, and specifically in varieties of qualitative research. He recently co-edited (with Michael Murray) a special issue of the *Journal of Health Psychology* devoted to qualitative research, and is co-editor (with Gary Reker) of *Existential Meaning: Optimizing Human Development across the Life Span* (Sage, 1999).

Sue Curtis has recently spent two years as Research Manager for the Action Research Program at the Family Action Centre, University of Newcastle, Australia. During this time she also coordinated the Leadership and Management Program for the University and was involved in facilitation of organizational change, change management and strategic planning. Sue is currently coordinating a programme for leading and evaluating advancements in curriculum delivery at the Centre for Educational Development and Interactive Resources, University of Wollongong. Her PhD is in action-oriented, process-based evaluation practices and her interests are in the fields of action research, participatory approaches to evaluation and organizational learning. The action researching methodology developed by Sue has been used in a wide variety of contexts. These have included higher education research and curriculum review, occupational health, safety and rehabilitation in the steel industry, and community development programmes in the third sector.

Christine Eiser is Reader in Health Psychology and Director of the Child and Family Health Research Group at the University of Exeter, UK. She has a special interest in the psychological effects of chronic illness on children and their families and has published many articles and several books in the field including *The Psychology of Childhood Illness* (Springer-Verlag, 1995) and *Growing up with Chronic Illness* (Jessica Kingsley, 1995).

Maria Jarman is currently at the Department of Psychology, University of Sheffield, UK. She has recently completed a PhD exploring health professionals' understandings and experiences of treating people with anorexia nervosa. Her other research interests are in the areas of recovery from eating disorders, women's experiences of employment in relation to psychological well-being, and qualitative methodologies.

Antonia Lyons is a Lecturer in the School of Psychology at the University of Birmingham, UK. Her main research interests are in health psychology, particularly the social construction of the 'self' during language episodes and possible physiological correlates of this process; the effects of minor daily events on physical health; and the use of qualitative methods in health psychology. She is currently conducting research into women's understandings and experiences of the menopause and hormone replacement therapy.

Cynthia M. Mathieson is an Associate Professor in the Department of Psychology at Mount Saint Vincent University in Halifax, Nova Scotia, Canada, where she teaches women's health psychology, gender differences, and human sexuality. She has a long-standing research interest in qualitative methodology as it applies to patients' issues in psychosocial oncology. More recently, she has developed a research commitment to women's health care through qualitative inquiry with lesbian/bisexual women.

Mandy Morgan is a Lecturer in critical psychology and the psychology of women at Massey University in Aoteoroa/New Zealand. Her research interests generally focus on the relationship between social constructionism, psychology and feminism. She obtained her PhD in Psychology from Murdoch University in 1992.

Michael Murray is a Professor of Psychology at Memorial University of Newfoundland, Canada. He has published books on various aspects of health psychology including *Narrative Health Psychology* (Massey University, 1997) and, with David Marks and others, *Health Psychology: Theory, Research and Practice* (Sage, 1998). He is an associate editor of the *Journal of Health Psychology* and recently co-edited with Kerry Chamberlain a special issue of that journal devoted to qualitative research.

Mike Osborn is a Clinical Psychologist working at the Royal United Hospital, Bath, UK, specializing in chronic pain and palliative care. He is also engaged in research for a doctorate at the University of Sheffield into the phenomenology of chronic benign pain. His clinical and research interests are in qualitative and dynamic approaches to the study of pain, trauma and loss.

Glynn Owens is Professor of Psychology at the University of Auckland, New Zealand. Prior to this, he was Professor of Health Studies at the University of Wales, Bangor, and Director of the Clinical Psychology Training Programme at the University of Liverpool, UK. His research interests in health psychology centre on cancer care and palliative care. He has co-authored a number of books including (with Freda Naylor) *Living while Dying* (Thorsons, 1989) and (with David Brodie and John Williams) *Research Methods for the Health Sciences* (Harwood, 1994).

Sheila Payne is Director of the Health Research Unit in the School of Occupational Therapy and Physiotherapy at the University of Southampton, UK. She is a health psychologist with a background in nursing. Her main research interests are in psychological aspects of palliative care, psychosocial oncology and health psychology. Sheila has co-authored *Psychology for Nurses and the Caring Professions* (Open University Press, 1996) and she edits (with Sandra Horn) the Open University book series in Health Psychology.

Alan Radley is Professor of Social Psychology in the Department of Social Sciences at Loughborough University, UK. His research interests include the social context of health and illness and the field of charitable giving. He is editor of the journal *Health: An Interdisciplinary Journal for the Social Study of Health, Illness and Medicine*. His book publications include *Prospects of Heart Surgery: Psychological Adjustment to Coronary Bypass Grafting* (Springer, 1988); *The Body and Social Psychology* (Springer, 1991); *Making Sense of Illness: The Social Psychology of Health and Disease* (Sage, 1994). He is editor of *Worlds of Illness: Biographical and Cultural Perspectives on Health and Disease* (Routledge, 1993).

Jane Selby's training was at the University of St Andrews, Scotland (MA) and Cambridge, UK (PhD). She adapted her work to tropical Australia after moving there in 1989, trailing her husband. Besides cross-racial research and training (the Australian Psychological Society has provided recognition for the first time of training she developed specifically for indigenous students), Jane works clinically with children and supervises practitioners from welfare as well as psychology. She has recently moved to Charles Sturt University in New South Wales.

Jonathan A. Smith is a Lecturer in psychology at the University of Sheffield, UK. His research interests are in the psychology of health, self and identity, life transitions, interpretative phenomenological analysis, and other qualitative approaches to psychology. He has written extensively in these areas and is co-editor (with Rom Harré and Luk van Langenhove) of *Rethinking Methods in Psychology* and *Rethinking Psychology* (Sage, 1995).

Mary-Jane Paris Spink is Associate Professor in the Social Psychology Post-Graduate Program of the Pontificia Universidade Catolica de São Paulo, Brazil. She has written extensively on health and illness issues concerning the health professions, organization of health services and experience of illness events, with specific attention to advances in qualitative methodology.

Carla Treloar is a Lecturer in health social science in the Faculty of Medicine and Health Sciences at the University of Newcastle, Australia. Carla has a PhD in health psychology and a growing interest and experience in qualitative research methods, including action research.

Sarah Twamley graduated from Trinity College, Dublin in 1996. She has a special interest in the psychology of health and reproduction. Since graduating she has been working on a project on diabetic risk, funded by the Medical Research Council, while completing a Masters in Psychology at the University of Exeter, UK.

Jane M. Ussher is Associate Professor of Critical Psychology, Centre for Critical Psychology, University of Western Sydney, Australia. Her publications include *The Psychology of the Female Body* (Routledge, 1989), *Women's Madness: Misogyny or Mental Illness?* (Harvester Wheatsheaf, 1991), *Fantasies of Femininity: Reframing the Boundaries of Sex* (Penguin, 1997), and *Body Talk: The Material and Discursive Regulation of Sexuality, Madness and Reproduction* (Routledge, 1997).

Lucy Yardley is Senior Lecturer in the Psychology Department at the University of Southampton, UK, and is an enthusiastic proponent of mixed methods for studying the mind/body in health and illness. Her long-standing research interests encompass all aspects of (dis)orientation and (im)balance, including qualitative analyses of the meaning of disorientation in modern society, clinical trials of exercise therapy for dizziness, and experimental investigations into the cognitive information-processing involved in monitoring and controlling orientation and balance. She recently edited *Material Discourses of Health and Illness* (Routledge, 1997).

Part I

Constructing Health and Illness Through Language

1

Health Psychology and Qualitative Research

Michael Murray and Kerry Chamberlain

Over the past thirty years, since its formal inception, health psychology has grown rapidly in popularity as evidenced by the numerous textbooks and journals dedicated to the subject, and by the size and growth of specialized societies and conferences. One problem faced by a discipline which is young and experiencing such rapid growth is that there is a tendency to adopt the standards and methods of more established disciplines as a means of gaining respectability and status within the wider scientific community. This rush for respectability can curtail debate about the relevance and legitimacy of the more dominant theoretical and methodological frameworks. Fortunately, health psychology has arrived on the scene at a time of intense debate about the nature of psychology and of science. This debate provides an opportunity to consider and reflect on the foundations of the discipline.

The purpose of this book is to contribute to that debate through an examination of the role of qualitative research within health psychology. The contributions in the book are not limited to a discussion of methods but inevitably consider broader epistemological issues. To provide a framework for this discussion it is useful to begin by considering the epistemological foundations of psychology as a discipline and the implications of the current challenges for health psychology.

Psychology as a Science

Psychology has been characterized as an archetypal quantitative science. Born in the heyday of nineteenth-century positivism it has maintained a fascination with (supposed) objective measurement and the identification of statistical associations between (so-called) psychological variables (see Danziger and Dzinas, 1997). Quantitative methods have provided a unifying feature for what was a rather diverse set of psychological perspectives. The concern for measurement and experimentation served to distinguish psychology from philosophy, religion and other attempts to explore the human psyche, such as psychoanalysis (Smith, 1997). It was through the adoption of the paraphernalia of the natural sciences, such as the laboratory and its associated equipment and white coats, that psychology paraded its self-awarded scientific status. Indeed, it could be argued that this concern for quantification reflected a certain anxiety or insecurity about the legitimacy of its position within the broader pantheon of sciences. Much research effort was expended in revising and improving psychological measurement and experimental procedures. Danziger (1990: 5), in his history of the development of psychology, suggests that 'these preoccupations with the purity of method frequently deteriorate to a kind of method fetishism or "methodolatory"'. Researchers who deviated from the strict methodological guidelines were dismissed as unscientific.

Not only was this 'scientistic' psychology (see for example Richardson and Fowers, 1997) concerned with measurement of psychological variables and the establishment of universal laws of human behaviour but it also sought to establish an applied science which could demonstrate its legitimacy and value. Rose (1996, 1997) has described how psychology justified its expansion through the advance of its applications to predict and control human behaviour. In the early days of psychology this interest in social engineering was most apparent in the concern with mental measurement and the close interweaving with eugenics. Later, the emphasis shifted to the measurement of other psychological constructs such as personality and attitudes. Such knowledge could then be used to promote the smoother working of society without critiquing its underlying ideology. Admittedly, psychology was not alone in this endeavour. As Fox and Prilleltensky (1997: 265) noted, 'the natural and social sciences have been obsessed with instrumental values of control and domination at the expense of emancipatory values such as justice, mutuality, and autonomy'.

Throughout its development, therefore, psychology has held fast to the belief that its quantitative methods gave it access to the psychological world, that the application of these 'objective' methods by the detached scientist would reveal the fundamental laws which were presumed to underlie human endeavour (Danziger, 1990), and that the use of these laws could contribute to the creation of a better world. The model of natural science was adopted as the natural model for any science, and psychology certainly considered itself to be a science.

The Place of Health Psychology

Health psychology, as a recent development, has predominantly followed the methods of mainstream psychology. The debate about epistemology that has occurred recently within some branches of psychology, in particular social and feminist psychology (for example, Gergen, 1985; Hollway, 1989), has been rather muted within health psychology. There are several reasons for this, not least being its close attachment to medical science. Medicine is an immensely powerful profession in the western world, where its standards and perspectives are broadly promoted and accepted as truth. Biomedicine is pervaded with the rhetoric of discoveries and cures. Working within the medical establishment, health psychologists have tended to follow the 'predict and control' tenets of positivist science that are dominant there. These were wedded to the methodology of physiology on the one hand and of epidemiology on the other, such that in many senses health psychology could be characterized as a blend of psychophysiology and behavioural epidemiology. The former had a particular interest in the physiological processes underlying such psychological constructs as stress, while the latter had a particular interest in topics such as psychological predictors of healthy and unhealthy behaviours. This new form of behavioural medicine was attractive to many physicians not least because it enabled them to extend their authority over other areas of human existence (Kugelmann, 1997).

Health psychology largely adopted an accommodative stance in relation to biomedicine rather than one which seriously critiqued the legitimacy of the medical model. The easiest way to do this was to introduce a new psychological dimension into the basic biomedical framework but otherwise to leave the edifice untouched. This accommodation resulted in a shift from a biomedical to a more inclusive biopsychosocial model. However, Ogden (1997) has examined this supposed challenge to biomedicine and found it to be more rhetoric than reality. She argues that, in spite of the rhetoric to the contrary, the practices of health psychology continue to privilege biological aetiology over psychological causation, serve to promote mind/body separation and interaction rather than the view of an integrated individual, and also serve to separate the bodily from the social. Modern biomedicine directs its gaze at the individual body (Foucault, 1973), and health psychology has merely extended that gaze to include the mind, defined in terms of psychological variables, with social processes often ignored or 'controlled for' in statistical analyses aimed at producing general laws.

Although health psychologists often worked as members of interdisciplinary teams, the team members all accepted the basic quantitative tenets. Each member was assumed to have specific expertise in the measurement of certain types of variables. It was expected that, in the same way as medical scientists could measure relevant aspects of particular bodily parts and functions, so health psychologists could measure the psychological variables which were relevant and held to be pre-existent and distanced from the researcher. The possibility of objectively identifying and measuring these psychological constructs was taken for granted, although there were some concerns as to how validly and reliably this could be achieved. Admittedly, this perspective on science was common throughout psychology. As Danziger and Dzinas (1997: 46) argued, throughout psychology there is 'a fairly wide-spread, though implicit and unexamined, belief that any psychologically relevant part of reality was already pre-structured in the form of distinct variables, and that psychological research techniques merely held up a mirror to the structure'. Psychological variables were

assumed to exist in reality rather than being constructed by the psychological observer. Such a view allowed health psychology to be located
within and integrated into a biomedical framework.

However, concerns about the adequacy of natural science as a model for
psychology have led to increasing criticism of the use of quantitative
methods within health psychology. For example, the experiment, the
cornerstone of classical psychology, was critiqued because it ignores both
process and context. Danziger (1990: 116) described the experiment as an
artificial construction 'in which individuals are stripped of their identity
and their historical existence to become vehicles for the operation of totally
abstract laws of behaviour'. A similar argument could be levelled against
the unquestioned acceptance of clinical trials by health psychologists in
that they ignore the social nature of the experimental procedure (Farr,
1978) and its socio-historical context. Similarly, Ibañez (1991: 195) critiqued
positivist social psychology on these grounds arguing that 'the neglect of
historicity, and, consequently, the negation of the always concrete and
singular nature of the social, obliged this research strategy to *empty the
investigated phenomena of all their social content'*. Within health psychology
this ahistoricism is reflected in the search for general laws and the ignoring
of social and cultural variability of health and illness (Landrine and
Klonoff, 1992). This debate about the adequacy of natural science methods
also had broader implications.

Challenges to Positivism

The past ten or so years has witnessed a rising critique of the legitimacy
and adequacy of quantitative methods within psychology. In view of the
centrality of measurement to psychology, this critique, which was initially
methodological, also began to question the epistemological foundations of
the discipline (for example Hollway, 1989). Whereas the positivist paradigm assumed that empirical methods gave it access to an objective reality,
critics were not so sure. Shotter (1986: 95) in his review of empirical
methods summarized the contrasting viewpoints as follows:

> We now realise that what the empirical and behavioural sciences call *data* are not
> simply given us in the phenomena we study, but are theory-laden, i.e. they only
> appear to us as the facts they are in terms of a theory constructed by us. Instead
> of being called data they could more correctly be called *capta* (Laing, 1967, pp.
> 52–53) for, rather than being simply given us by Nature, we in fact *take* them out
> of a constantly changing flux of events.

Although we do not have the space to review these debates in detail,
they have implications for how we should seek to make progress in health
psychology, especially in relation to considerations of what is available
knowledge and how it can be accessed. Shotter's argument above encap-
sulates the dilemma arising from the appeal to data as 'facts'. The rise of

social constructionsist ideas emphasized that 'reality' was more appropriately regarded as constructed in interaction between researcher and researched. The researcher was not, and could not be, value free, and facts as well as theory were necessarily value-laden. The 'subjects' of research were equally involved in this construction through the interaction of their expectations and activities with those of the researcher. Beyond this, it was argued, any piece of research was constrained to be a construction determined by the possibilities and limitations of the physical, social and historical context in which it was conducted. If this is the case, it is obviously impossible for the researcher to adopt a value-free neutral perspective and for the phenomenon under investigation to be separated from the context in which it is investigated. This presents a radically different view of the research enterprise from the one taken for granted by the positivist position. Instead of seeking accurate measurement of hypothetically related variables and assessing their relationship statistically, these alternative approaches seek detailed complex interpretations of specifically socially and historically located phenomena. As Smith, Harré and Van Langenhove (1995a) have argued, this involves a shift from measurement to understanding, from causation to meaning, and from statistical analysis to interpretation.

One of the central arguments in this critique has been concerned with the significance of language in the construction of reality. The rise of social constructionist ideas within psychology has emphasized the role of language in shaping or even creating reality (Gergen, 1985). This emphasis, and especially discursive approaches premised on it, has provided the basis for some new methods adopted recently within health psychology (for example, Stainton Rogers, 1996; Middleton, 1996). Adopting a discursive approach abandons the notion of traditional psychological variables and views them as changeable constructions, historically and socially located and serving particular functions. The discursive approach argues that psychological 'entities' such as cognitions and personality traits are not fundamental, but can be analysed as constructions to reveal why they came to be construed in a particular way by a particular group at a particular time. As Yardley (1997: 6) states, 'rather than allowing the psychosocial realm to be analysed in biomedical terms, discursive critics of the biopsychosocial model argue that we should reinterpret the biomedical realm from a psychological and socio-cultural viewpoint'.

One argument against privileging language in this way is that it denies or precludes the material dimension of life, that realm where so much of health and illness may be seen to reside. The so-called 'death and furniture' arguments (see Potter, 1996: 7) have often frustrated social constructionists who accept that while phenomena may be socially constructed in discourse this does not mean that discourse is everything (Greenwood, 1989). In the current debate surrounding embodiment, psychologists are beginning to explore further the relationship between discourse and physicality (for example, Stam, 1996) and how materialist and sociolinguistic aspects of health and illness are intertwined (for example, Yardley, 1997).

These critiques give rise to a number of concerns which specifically relate to qualitative research practice. If researchers construct their interpretations, this opens the possibility that they must choose what to interpret from amongst the detail and ambiguity of their data, and this choice will inevitably be influenced by their presuppositions and values. Their theories, therefore, can never be complete and will always be partial and value-laden. However, they can be reflective about their interpretations and offer a commentary on their position and socio-historical location in relation to the phenomena being researched. As St Maurice (1993) notes, this collapses the distinction between theory and data, and reveals how theory is a function of the way the researcher understands the world and views the data. Reflexivity offers a window on the context in which methods and theories are constructed.

The idea that our understandings are constructions also problematizes some traditional quantitative research issues such as generalizability, reliability and validity. Qualitative researchers have responded to these issues in a number of ways, from devising alternative understandings through to dismissing them as irrelevant to qualitative research. This book does not (with some specific exceptions) seek to discuss these issues explicitly, but they do form a backdrop and framework for the various chapters of the book. For instance, several of the contributors draw on the analysis of multiple paradigms offered by Guba and Lincoln (1994) as a convenient frame for providing some order to these debates, but other contributors would contest this account. Whatever claims one may make for or about qualitative research, there are always alternative views and opinions to be found. Indeed, as Becker (1993: 228) has noted, 'it is always possible to criticise how things are done if you are a different person at a different time with a different purpose'.

We have focused on constructivist challenges here because they are currently the strongest within psychology. In doing so we have not considered the debates around post-structuralist and post-modernist views which are beginning to emerge more frequently within the discipline, although minimally as yet within health psychology. We have also overlooked the possibilities of qualitative research retaining a (post-)positivist perspective, although this is a position which some qualitative researchers hold to, including some of our contributors. However, it is not the intention of this text to examine these debates in detail – if it was, this would be a very different book. Although these debates and related issues are present throughout, no final positions are offered. We do acknowledge that these issues can be a source of considerable concern for researchers, especially those beginning to use qualitative research. Although we would advocate that researchers should be as clear as possible about their assumptions in any research conducted, we note Becker's comment:

> Epistemological issues, for all the arguing, are never settled, and I think it fruitless to try and settle them, at least in the way the typical debate looks to. If we haven't settled them definitively in two thousand years, more or less, we

probably aren't ever going to settle them. These are simply the commonplaces, in the rhetorical sense, of scientific talk in the social sciences, the framework in which the debate goes on. So be it. (1993: 219)

Becker adopts a pragmatic approach here, and suggests that we can turn over concerns about philosophy of science to the specialists, the people who adopt 'philosophical and methodological worry as a profession' (p. 226). He argues that it is possible and necessary to get on and do research without becoming paralysed by these debates, but also warns that it is necessary and inevitable to have a position, even if it is implicit and inconsistent. Within the text, it is possible to identify many of these different epistemological positions in different chapters, and to locate the various contributors on these issues. Our authors are no different from other researchers using qualitative approaches – they operate from a diversity of perspectives and assumptions.

The Contributions

The contributors to this book take up and develop these and other issues. This book is not designed as a handbook but rather as a forum for ideas, opinions and debate about the methods and practices of health psychology. Although some readers may wish to use it as a handbook, they could turn to more general handbooks (for example Denzin and Lincoln, 1994; Smith, Harré and Van Langenhove, 1995b; Richardson, 1996; Silverman, 1996) for elaborated theoretical and methodological accounts of qualitative research, and to Murray and Chamberlain (1998) for a range of specific studies using these methods. The contributors to this book offer discussion and commentary on a range of selected theories and methods of qualitative research, specifically those considered relevant for health psychology. The contributions are backgrounded by the debates and challenges discussed above, and the book is intended as a contribution to the continuing debate about the nature and focus of health psychology. The contributions are divided into three broad sections.

Constructing Health and Illness through Language

The first section considers various theoretical ideas from social constructionism and discursive psychology and their relevance for an understanding of health and illness. The first two chapters by Alan Radley and Lucy Yardley centre on the role of language in the construction of health and illness. These chapters offer an alternative to the biopsychosocial model of illness. Alan Radley's chapter considers the intimate connection between illness and the social world and how the experience of illness is reflected through different social realms. It also examines the dynamic character of the qualitative interview which can provide us with insight into the human experience of illness. He stresses that the interview is not a process in which information is passively transferred from the interviewee to the interviewer but one in which the communication is conditioned by the relationship between the two parties. In the second chapter Lucy Yardley develops an alternative to the mind–body dualism which pervades health psychology. She argues that this dualism is implicit in the objectivist stance of a positivist approach. Through qualitative research we can begin to overcome it and grasp both the discursive *and* the material construction of health and illness.

As previously mentioned, it has been within social and feminist psychology that much of the debate with regard to epistemological and ontological issues has occurred. The following three chapters consider the different contributions of three social psychological perspectives; Michael Murray focuses on narrative, Mandy Morgan on discourse, and Mary-Jane Paris Spink on social representations. Michael Murray argues for the centrality of narrative in understanding meaning-making, particularly in regard to making sense of illness. His chapter introduces some philosophical and literary background to contextualize narrative accounts, arguing that narratives are personal, interpersonal and social creations through which health and illness are given meaning. Stories of illness are told and heard, are created and also create, and are inextricably linked into the social context of the teller and the hearer. Narrative, he argues, provides an important means for the investigation of health and illness. Mandy Morgan considers discursive approaches to health and illness. She takes up the question of what constitutes appropriate knowledge for health psychology, contrasting the answer from a traditional perspective with that from a discursive perspective, and noting how this entails a change in the nature and location of the object of study and the understandings provided. In this chapter she specifically represents a Foucauldian position while acknowledging other discursive positions and allowing for debate between them. Through her analysis of the field of health psychology and the use of illustrative discursive work in health, she demonstrates that it does indeed matter how we talk about health and illness. Mary-Jane Paris Spink also takes up the role and function of language in representing and making sense of health and illness. Drawing on discursive and communicative theories of the function of language, she provides an account of how the cultural-historical (discursive) level and the local-situated (intersubjective, dialogical) level of language are both involved in making sense of illness and how they can be integrated. She illustrates this with a specific example of her research on AIDS, demonstrating the complexity of such a research endeavour and, at the same time, revealing the gains to be achieved from it.

This section closes with an account of feminist approaches to health and illness by Jane Ussher. She provides an outline of the major current strands of feminist theory and epistemology, using premenstrual syndrome (PMS) to illustrate how the different positions provide different research approaches, theories and understandings of PMS. Throughout her account, she presents the case for the role of social and cultural contexts in shaping health and illness, a message common to all the chapters of this section.

Conversing about Health and Illness

This section and the following one are substantially inter-related, and their separation is somewhat artificial because it is impossible to separate methodological and theoretical concerns and discuss one in isolation from the other. None the less, this section focuses broadly on contextual issues, whereas the following section is focused broadly on methodological issues involved in collecting qualitative data about health and illness.

The chapters in this section are variously concerned with the conduct of research in different contexts, although they often include some methodological focus as well. Cynthia Mathieson covers the conduct of interviews; Christine Eiser and Sarah Twamley comment on researching children's health and illness; Glynn Owens and Sheila Payne discuss working with the terminally ill; and Jane Selby discusses the conduct of cross-cultural health research.

Cynthia Mathieson opens this section with a discussion of interviewing in the context of health and illness. The interview provides the most common source of data for qualitative health researchers and Mathieson provides a practical exposition of interviewing, which she defines as a process of story-building. She examines the form and content of several different types of interviews, and comments on issues such as developing an interview guide, the nature of interview questions, and conducting group interviews. She also discusses the context of interviews, focusing on concerns with establishing rapport, the role of the interviewer and the nature of the interview experience for the ill person. In the next chapter, Christine Eiser and Sarah Twamley discuss the special concerns involved in conducting health research with children. They make the point that this is qualitatively different from work with adults as children have different understandings and experience of illness. Eiser and Twamley discuss a range of appropriate methods for obtaining data from children, covering the expected (interviews, focus groups and case studies) and the less ordinary (play and drawing). They also comment on the value of qualitative research approaches in working with children and discuss how this work can contribute to health-care provision and health promotion for children.

Glynn Owens and Sheila Payne consider issues involved in research with people facing death. They review research from a variety of qualitative approaches in the field of death and dying, and discuss the contributions that qualitative research can make to this field. Jane Selby takes up the issues of empowerment and collaboration in her discussion of cross-cultural research practices, focusing particularly on research as intervention. She illustrates her argument with personal case studies of specific research projects, documenting how issues of power imbalance and trust, along with the definition of the problem and the ownership and use of data and findings, need to be negotiated if research in different cultural contexts is to be conducted successfully. In addition, she spells out the need for a reference group to help manage these concerns, and the emotional and relationship dynamics which are inevitably involved in research of this nature.

Transforming Talk into Text

The focus of this section is on methodological concerns in collecting and analysing data: Kerry Chamberlain discusses grounded theory approaches to health research; Sue Curtis, Helen Bryce and Carla Treloar examine action research as a means for change in health contexts; Jonathan Smith, Mike Osborn and Maria Jarman discuss data analysis processes; and Antonia Lyons considers issues involved in the evaluation of qualitative research.

Although grounded theory is widely used in health research, it has not been widely used by health psychologists. Kerry Chamberlain provides an overview of grounded theory practices and discusses the tensions and debates that have occurred around it. He argues that it offers both a viable method and a range of specific techniques that could usefully be adopted by health psychologists in conducting qualitative research. Action research provides a very different approach to researching health issues, but also has not been utilized very often by health psychologists. Sue Curtis, Helen Bryce and Carla Treloar outline this research approach, structuring their discussion around a series of critical questions, and present a case study of research on cervical screening to illustrate the research techniques. Their discussion highlights the processes involved in action research and promotes an emancipatory perspective with the researcher and participants jointly constructing findings and applications to improve health-care provision. Jonathan Smith, Maria Jarman and Mike Osborn outline a different approach to qualitative research, interpretative phenomenological analysis, and discuss its relevance to health research. Their chapter is focused primarily on the processes involved in conducting data analysis, illustrated with two different research examples, each exemplifying a different level of analysis. Their approach emphasizes the interpretive nature of all analyses, and they describe and exemplify the processes involved in taking an analysis from initial coding through to searching for themes, patterns and connections, and finally to writing up the findings. Throughout, they stress the tensions involved with the processes of analysis being difficult and demanding but simultaneously exciting and creative. In the concluding chapter, Antonia Lyons comments explicitly on the debates and tensions that underlie qualitative research. She contrasts the differing assumptions which lie behind different paradigmatic views of the research endeavour, and demonstrates how the findings and theories from each perspective are shaped by their respective assumptions, illustrating her argument with research into various aspects of women's health. She also considers the issue of how qualitative research should be evaluated, arguing that different criteria are necessary for qualitative research and that these will differ from paradigm to paradigm. The turn to language is central to this debate and

Lyons discusses how assumptions about research and the role of language function to shape the nature of our findings and our research reports. She concludes with a commentary on how the move to qualitative research has the potential to reshape the endeavour of health psychology itself.

Let the Debate Begin

Qualitative research is still at an early stage within psychology and within health psychology (Murray and Chamberlain, 1998). This book is intended to provoke more debate and not to provide finished answers. It is designed to encourage reflection on and reassessment of the quantitative approach which has dominated our discipline and to consider alternative perspectives and approaches. In his fascinating autobiography Alexander Luria (1979) contrasts the classical approach to psychology with the romantic approach (cf. Schneider, 1998) and the attempts of Lev Vygotsky to find an accommodation. Such an accommodation is also a central challenge for modern health psychology.

Qualitative researchers are often charged with throwing the baby out with the bathwater. By this is meant that they reject the contribution made to our understanding by the traditional quantitative approach. However, as Bodily (1994) retorts in his description of social constructionism, the reverse is more the case. Qualitative researchers tend to be more humble in their claims and to place emphasis on the variability of answers in contrast to the 'truth' revealed by the positivist researcher. Hence, 'if constructionism can be accused of anything, it would be of tossing additional babies into the bathwater' (Bodily, 1994: 175). We are not suggesting we dismiss the substantial contributions already made by many health psychologists working from a positivist perspective. Rather, we believe it is time to consider the relative value of that contribution and how we can further extend our understanding of the phenomena of health and illness. Luria refers to Marx's expression of 'ascending to the concrete' to describe the process whereby investigators begin to grasp the character of a phenomenon. It is through the combination of various research techniques rather than through reliance on one true method that health psychology can advance.

The chapters which follow describe some of the theories and methods, approaches and techniques of qualitative research. As we have noted, there is no one method within qualitative research. The field is varied and contested rather than agreed, codified and taken for granted. However, qualitative research has great potential to expand our understandings of health and illness, and it is through experience with the methods of qualitative research that health psychology researchers will begin to explore their value. In spite of the variety of perspectives and methods, there still remains a desire for rigour in qualitative research (for example Kvale, 1994; 1996). However, such rigour is not based upon operationalization of variables, strict experimental control, or statistical analyses but upon both theoretical and methodological clarity. Through an introduction to some of the ideas guiding qualitative research the following chapters are designed to increase that clarity.

References

Becker, H.S. (1993) Theory: the necessary evil. In D.J. Flinders and G.E. Mills (eds), *Theory and Concepts in Qualitative Research: Perspectives from the Field*. New York: Teachers College Press, pp. 218–229.

Bodily, C.L. (1994) Ageism and the deployments of 'age': a constructionist view. In T.R. Sarbin and J.I. Kitsuse (eds), *Constructing the Social*. London: Sage, pp. 174–194.

Danziger, K. (1990) *Constructing the Subject: Historical Origins of Psychological Research*. Cambridge: Cambridge University Press.

Danziger, K. and Dzinas, K. (1997) How psychology got its variables. *Canadian Psychology/Psychologie canadienne*, 38: 43–48.

Denzin, N.K. and Lincoln, Y.S. (eds) (1994) *Handbook of Qualitative Research*. Thousand Oaks, CA: Sage.

Farr, R.M. (1978) On the social significance of artifacts in experiments. *British Journal of Social and Clinical Psychology*, 17: 299–306.

Foucault, M. (1973) *The Birth of the Clinic: An Archaeology of Medical Knowledge*. London: Tavistock.

Fox, D. and Prilleltensky, I. (eds) (1997) *Critical Psychology: An Introduction*. London: Sage.

Gergen, K.J. (1985) The social constructionist movement in psychology. *American Psychologist*, 40: 266–275.

Greenwood, J.D. (1989) *Explanation and Experiment in Social Psychological Science: Realism and the Social Constitution of Action*. New York: Springer-Verlag.

Guba, E. and Lincoln, Y.S. (1994) Competing paradigms in qualitative research. In N.K. Denzin and Y.S. Lincoln (eds), *Handbook of Qualitative Research*. Thousand Oaks, CA: Sage, pp. 105–117.

Hollway, W. (1989) *Subjectivity and Method in Psychology: Gender, Meaning and Science*. London: Sage.

Ibañez, T. (1991) Social psychology and the rhetoric of truth. *Theory and Psychology*, 1: 187–201.

Kugelmann, R. (1997) The psychology and management of pain: gate control as theory and symbol. *Theory and Psychology*, 7: 43–65.

Kvale, S. (1994) Ten standard objections to qualitative research interviews. *Journal of Phenomenological Psychology*, 25: 147–173.

Kvale, S. (1996) *InterViews: An Introduction to Qualitative Research Interviewing*. Thousand Oaks, CA: Sage.

Laing, R.D. (1967) *The Politics of Experience*. London: Penguin.

Landrine, H. and Klonoff, E.A. (1992) Culture and health-related schema: a review and proposal for interdisciplinary integration. *Health Psychology*, 11: 267–276.

Luria, A.R. (1979) *The Making of Mind: A Personal Account of Soviet Psychology*. Cambridge, MA: Harvard University Press.

Middleton, D. (1996) A discursive analysis of psychosocial issues: talk in a 'parent group' for families who have children with chronic renal failure. *Psychology and Health*, 11: 243–260.

Murray, M. and Chamberlain, K. (eds) (1998) Special issue: Qualitative Research. *Journal of Health Psychology*, 3 (3).

Ogden, J. (1997) The rhetoric and reality of psychosocial theories of health: a challenge to biomedicine? *Journal of Health Psychology*, 2: 21–29.

Potter, J. (1996) *Representing Reality*. London: Sage.

Richardson, J.T.E. (ed.) (1996) *Handbook of Qualitative Research Methods for Psychology and the Social Sciences*. Leicester: BPS Books.

Richardson, F.C. and Fowers, B.J. (1997) Critical theory, postmodernism, and hermeneutics: insights for critical psychology. In D. Fox and I. Prilleltensky (eds), *Critical Psychology: An Introduction*. London: Sage, pp. 265–283.

Rose, N. (1996) *Inventing our Selves: Psychology, Power and Personhood*. New York: Cambridge University Press.

Rose, N. (1997) Assembling the modern self. In R. Porter (ed.), *Rewriting the Self: Histories from the Renaissance to the Present*. London: Routledge, pp. 224–248.

St Maurice, H. (1993) The rhetorical return: the rhetoric of qualitative inquiry. In D.J. Flinders and G.E. Mills (eds), *Theory and Concepts in Qualitative Research: Perspectives from the Field*. New York: Teachers College Press, pp. 201–217.

Schneider, K.J. (1998) Toward a science of the heart: romanticism and the revival of psychology. *American Psychologist*, 53: 277–289.

Shotter, J.D. (1986) Empirical methods in social inquiry. In R. Harré and R. Lamb (eds), *The Dictionary of Personality and Social Psychology*. Oxford: Basil Blackwell.

Silverman, D. (ed.) (1996) *Qualitative Research: Theory, Method and Practice*. London: Sage.

Smith, R. (1997) *The Norton History of the Human Sciences*. New York: Norton.

Smith, J.A., Harré, R. and Van Langenhove, L. (eds) (1995a) *Rethinking Psychology*. London: Sage.

Smith, J.A., Harré, R. and Van Langenhove, L. (eds) (1995b) *Rethinking Methods in Psychology*. London: Sage.

Stainton Rogers, W. (1996) Critical approaches to health psychology. *Journal of Health Psychology*, 1: 65–77.

Stam, H.J. (ed.) (1996) Special issue: The Body and Psychology. *Theory and Psychology*, 6 (4).

Yardley, L. (ed.) (1997) *Material Discourses of Health and Illness*. London: Routledge.

2

Social Realms and the Qualities of Illness Experience

Alan Radley

Rather than addressing the application of a specific methodology to illness experience, this chapter argues that illness experiences are qualitatively different, so that they need to be described and understood by means of what is generally termed a 'qualitative approach'. Therefore, the argument works back from the problem field to the methodology rather than from methodological preconceptions to the questions to be addressed. By making this claim I am, of course, fudging the issue, since by describing the problem and its features I shall be engaging in a loose form of qualitative practice, all the while pretending that I am just doing 'conceptual background work'. This makes the point that 'doing qualitative research', in health studies as in other areas, is always more than just using qualitative methods. Having made this admission, it is useful first to examine some historical background.

The use of qualitative methods in the study of health and illness is better established in medical sociology and in medical anthropology than it is in health psychology (Conrad, 1990). There are a number of reasons for this, including the fact that sociologists and anthropologists have been tied less closely to medicine than has clinical or health psychology. The medical model is concerned with causes and effects, using natural science methods to establish the connections between them. Psychology's contribution to this endeavour has been, if not central, then at least a major support. As a discipline that claims scientific credentials, psychology has been well placed to provide methods that render features of illness behaviour and health beliefs in quantitative form. The key aspect of this approach has been the objective specification of variables – the insistence that if anything exists, then it exists in some measurable amount. The implication of this statement is that if a thing cannot be measured then its 'existence' – its scientific legitimacy – is put in question. Psychology finds its place within the biomedical scheme by holding to the ideals of scientific experimentation and by adopting as necessary the parameters that medical practice provides for it. The questions that underlie these parameters are to do with either the clinical management of patients or the conditions that promote the onset of disease. Psychology helps medicine by, for example, joining in with its effort to specify which patients will benefit from particular treatments, what might be the (psychological) effects of carrying out certain procedures, and how psychological methods might be used to prepare patients who are to undergo surgery.

The use of quantitative methods in health psychology has grown up within a biomedical approach in which people have been regarded as patients or subjects, which is to say, objectively. This is not to say that such methods are unsuccessful, nor that this view is in itself misguided. However, it is unfortunate (for psychologists holding the natural science perspective) that the conditions which, over the last 30 to 40 years, have fostered the interest in bringing psychology into medical practice, are the same ones that have been redefining the patient-as-person. There has emerged a concern with what has been termed 'the patient's view' (Armstrong, 1984). Where previously this view was excluded, interest has been expressed in the possibility that what patients say might have a contribution to make to diagnosis and to treatment, particularly in cases where medical intervention falls short of a cure. What began in the 1960s with an interest in patients' 'lay theories' (Stimson, 1974) has progressed to a concern with patients' narratives and with their styles of life (Kleinman, 1988; Williams, 1984).

If medicine wishes psychologists to contribute their expertise on questions of motive, personality, illness behaviour, or beliefs about health, then it is to precisely these aspects of the patient's view or agency that attention is first drawn. I say 'first' drawn, because clinicians utilize an everyday language in their dealings with patients and in their understanding of the patient's role in diagnosis and treatment. So, for example, the recruitment of psychologists to the Type A Behavior Pattern (TABP) project began with descriptions of the presentation of the patient at interview, giving detailed information about his [sic] demeanour and emotional state (Rosenman, 1978). Only when the relevance and significance of the patient's psychological condition had been established in descriptive terms, did work proceed to establish quantitative measures of TABP that could be related to physiological variables by use of statistical procedures (Jenkins, Rosenman and Friedman, 1967). The apprehension of the patient-as-person – as more than an ailing physiological system – was the precondition for biomedicine to state the relevance of psychological factors and then to invite psychologists to make their contribution. A similar tale can be told about the sphere of doctor–patient communication, one that is now repeated daily in the application of psychological methods to clinical problems (Stimson and Webb, 1975).

What is important in this story is the establishment within medicine of a problem as being 'psychological'. This proceeds from describing its place in the perspective of the patient-as-person to its specification as a variable that can be entered alongside others within the biomedical paradigm. In short, what begins as something to be discussed within discourse as a problem for inquiry, is then transformed within scientific practice into the same kind of 'thing', a variable or data set that can be subject to computational analysis. Only the product of this transformation – the quantifiable object – is legitimated by this practice: the original description (if it is acknowledged at all) is restricted to informal status, bracketed outside of the scientific endeavour.

This transformation serves another important function: it raises the question of the patient-as-person, but does so in a way that limits the answer to being framed within the sphere of the 'person as patient'. Whether it be in the context of communication in the consulting room, in the diagnostics of the clinic or in the rehabilitation programmes of the hospital, the price paid for reducing descriptions to quantity is the restriction of the 'person as patient' within the sphere of medicine. In effect, and for the purposes of the analysis, the person inhabits only one psychological world – that of the individual body subject to medical thinking and practice.

A different story can be told about other social scientific disciplines that have studied health and illness. Unlike psychologists, medical sociologists and medical anthropologists have not had such a close relationship with medicine. (There are, however, important differences between countries; for example, American sociologists have a different involvement with clinical settings from that of their British colleagues.) One reason might be the absence of an existing professional structure for these disciplines such as that established by clinical psychologists. This has meant that social scientists have often tended to work outside the centres of medical power and knowledge, such as hospitals and clinics. The emergence of the patient's view, the increasing concern with the situation of people who have to live with chronic illnesses, and the need to understand the place that health matters have in people's daily lives, have meant that medical sociologists and anthropologists describe conditions in which individuals are both persons and patients. The possibility that people might become ill, or that they might recover their previous life following serious illness, has also meant that these researchers have described situations in which individuals inhabit several spheres of life simultaneously. Related to aspects of illness, this means that medical sociologists and anthropologists have studied persons when they are *not* being patients – or when they are *being more* than just patients

The fact that people are or might be both patients and mothers – or daughters, workers, homeless or immigrants – is relevant to the question of the use of qualitative methodology. It arises in a number of ways, but especially in that people can articulate their situations and express preferences and desires about these different areas of life. Of course, both sociologists and anthropologists have and still do use quantitative methods. Moreover, a significant minority of psychologists have used qualitative methods, particularly in the study of personality, and more generally where they have worked within the framework of phenomenology (Giorgi, 1992). But I submit that the study of health and illness is special in respect of the fact that people are concerned with something that potentially touches all aspects of their lives. This issues in two directions, each important to an understanding of the use of qualitative methodology in health research.

The first direction relates to the question of individuals as patients and as persons. The allocation of health states to individuals treated as 'entities' (to which variables can be attached) is inadmissible if those states are conditional upon people's occupancy of different social spheres or realms. The way that individuals understand and make attempts to affect their state of health is itself influenced by their involvement in several spheres, with all that that entails. Second, the study of health and illness often involves psychologists, like other social scientists, being in direct communication with sick individuals. This raises the question of what effect this relationship, the putative healthy psychologist on the one hand, and the sick individual on the other, might have on the kinds of information obtained. Each of these points will be addressed separately in the remainder of this chapter.

Illness and Social Realms

In this section I shall argue that illness needs to be studied qualitatively if we are to understand how people make sense of its genesis and its consequences. Underlying this argument is the claim that illness is not a stable entity, separable from other aspects of people's lives, but is always known through these other aspects, in terms of which it is acknowledged and countered. It is well established that illness, and (which is not quite the same) 'loss of health', are known through their impact upon everyday capacities and expectations (Blaxter, 1985). People's conceptions of health and of particular diseases have been shown to be framed in terms of such things as loss of fitness or the special problems that arise due to the symptoms involved. As well as this, medical knowledge concerning good or poor prognosis will also have an important role in the way that individuals think about their condition and what it means for other areas of their life (Corbin and Strauss, 1987). Only some illnesses involve incapacitating symptoms, and these are not always the most serious or life-threatening.

The argument I wish to press, however, is that becoming ill (especially chronically, or seriously ill) *colours* people's lives. The use of the word 'colours' refers to the way that everyday life is reflected through either the knowledge that one is ill, or the way that ordinary actions are affected by bodily limitations. This reflection, to use the metaphor of the mirror, may remain obscure and shifting, or else it may be given form by the person's attempts to specify what the experience is 'like'. Take, for example, this account by a man in his thirties diagnosed as having heart disease requiring surgery:

> That's the worst time after you've had a heart attack. The disappointment is when you think to yourself, 'Oh, I'm getting on the way now; another couple of

months and I'll be back at work.' And you phone up work and say, 'With a bit of luck, another couple of weeks . . .', and then something happens and you are downhill, that's the worst.

This excerpt shows how illness is reported in the context of specific spheres of life (for example work), which I shall term 'social realms'. The point is that illness does not affect life in a 'cause and effect' fashion, but that it arises within it, takes its form from the limitations and possibilities that become its vehicle of meaning. Another way of putting this is to say that the experience of illness is metaphoric (Kirmayer, 1992; Radley, 1993). The idea of metaphor is useful here because it pinpoints the way in which particular hindrances or losses can 'stand for' the illness experience as a whole. In her account of people with Parkinson's Disease, Pinder (1990) quotes a woman whose difficulties with replacing items in her handbag exemplified the 'lack of grace' that expressed her condition, something which she so resented. In this case the woman's illness was reflected through this particular problem, which was thereby made into more than a difficulty with motor movement. She reported it as happening in public places, where others could see, so that what occurred – or threatened to occur – was damaging to her presentation of herself as a competent adult person, and, perhaps more, to her self-presentation as a 'graceful woman'.

The idea of metaphor is used here, not in the sense of showing how something is like something else, but in terms of reflecting one domain (realm) of experience through another (Romanyshyn, 1982). What began as a vague ache or feeling of tiredness might be accorded meaning through medical diagnosis, but it is only elaborated as an experience of illness when reflected through realms of everyday practice. And once apprehended, it can, in turn, act as a vehicle through which can be reflected other realms of the person's social world. The excerpt given above from a man with heart disease showed the meaning of illness in terms of work and the time he was forced to spend at home. He was one of many men to whom we spoke whose experience of being 'someone with heart disease' was forced inactivity and the loss of earning power (Radley, 1988). He continued:

I buggered off and left her [his wife] not because I didn't love her – I just didn't want to be an invalid. We used to have no end of rows about what I can't do and what I can do. It would be a row who made the tea. We used to race in there. I used to literally push her out because you've got to do it.

This excerpt says explicitly that the man did not wish to be an invalid, which is a statement about his response to illness as 'inactivity producing'. Once reflected through this realm of domesticity, of his relationship with his wife, it also speaks of his loss of role as a husband, and even of his 'impotence' in the face of the events unfolding. Illness, once given form by the social realm that it metaphorically colours, can then inflect other domains of experience with new meaning. In turn, they provide another reflection upon the illness situation, so that it, too, is once more re-figured. The key point here is that these are not reflections upon a ready-made and unchanging entity called 'illness' (nor even 'disease'), but steps in the genesis of an experience which has the potential for qualitatively different outcomes.

Among these differences are what has been called 'illness behaviour', the way that the person responds to or copes with the illness. Once again, to speak in this way suggests that the illness is a stable entity, when palpably it is not. Having said that, it is quite possible for individuals to treat it precisely as such, and for no better reason than the conception of illness which they gain from biomedicine is one of objective lesions located in specific parts of the body-machine. Objectifying and specifying illness can be one way of dealing with the deep anxieties and uncertainties with which it inflects the person's life (Cassell, 1976). The use of medical talk to minimize and contain symptoms (and thereby the illness experience) is illustrated by the case of one man who spoke of coronary artery bypass surgery as like 'having a boil removed from your neck' (Radley, 1993). Whether these two surgical procedures are really similar is not the point here: the issue is that by using the analogy, not only is cardiac surgery made ordinary but illness is bounded in a way that literalizes it, defusing its metaphoric potential and making temporary its potential effects.

In those cases where illness has coloured various domains it can have a paradoxical effect. What happens is that its extensiveness, the 'sides' it reveals through its multifarious inflections, call for greater not lesser clarification and control. There might be a sense of illness as having 'taken over one's life', so that 'it' should be brought out into the open, as if 'it' could be revealed for what 'it' is. From what has been said already, it should be clear that often the best we can do, when ill, is to make illness literal, usually by means of the medical model or by quasi-medical thinking. This latter option (including the above example of 'heart surgery as boil removal') is not to be derided, as it can serve people well in the course of making sense of frightening and uncertain possibilities. However, the attempt to produce one's illness as object, to force it out from the cloak of the metaphors which give it its powers, is fraught with difficulty. The same heart patient quoted above attempted to make focal his illness in the following way:

> I used to think of it as a battle. I used to think if I walk up the hill, cut through the jetty and the bridle path and come back round the new estate, I'd see if I could do it. I suppose, if you like, you dare yourself to have another heart attack. I've walked along and I've been saying (you are chuntering to yourself, you try not to move your lips, so nobody thinks you are a nutter), and you are going along and you are saying, 'go on, if you are going to come, come now'.

This example shows that individuals are not passive in the face of illness. How they deal with symptoms is a demonstration to themselves and to others of how they have stood up to the crises or the disappointments that illness can bring. This demonstration can be private in its affirmation, as in the case of a woman diagnosed with multiple sclerosis who insisted on buying herself a new pair of shoes after each visit to the doctor; her shoe-buying affirmed her determination to be mobile and independent in spite of illness (Duval, 1984). It can also be public in the way that a woman with rheumatoid arthritis was at pains to maintain her independence by demonstrating to health visitors that she kept a clean and ordered house (Williams, 1993).

This underlines the point already made that illness does not simply affect the various realms of everyday life. Instead, it is encountered there in the individual's attempts to maintain or establish a viable identity and sense of moral worth. What might be important is not just that illness prevents a person from completing an act hitherto taken for granted (important as this might be), but that the use of one realm to signify through another is undermined. For the man with heart disease quoted above, what mattered was not just that his illness stopped him from working, that is, that it prevented him from carrying out the tasks for which he would have been paid; what was also important was that he could no longer signify in his household as the person who supported the family, but now had to depend upon his wife's salary. The quality of illness experience in the latter sphere (the home) is reflected in turn through experience of the former realm (work), so that *what appears as illness at any one time is never of that time alone.*

This brings us to an important point. Being seriously or chronically ill has an expressive quality that far exceeds the quantifiable limitations it might bring to any specific setting or sphere of social life. Because it is always reflected through social realms, and because the reflection of these realms, one against the other, is the way in which individuals display their worth and competence, then being ill is not a specific state, but an inflection of the whole of the person's being. That is why it can be so important to contain one's illness, to bear up in spite of it, to carry on as normal. What would otherwise appear as a paradox is shown to be sensible in terms of this analysis. Containing illness, perhaps by use of medical terminology, so that it impinges not at all in the various spheres of one's life, is taken by others as an expression of the affected individual. It reflects the whole just as surely as if the person had 'allowed' the illness to pervade all areas of life.

Illness, then, allows scope for expression just as it demands adjustment (Radley, 1993). In recent years this expressive potential has found voice in the narratives that patients provide about their experiences within and outside the medical system. Frank (1995) has argued that the post-modern period is characterized by a movement away from the medical account (that is, the patient) towards the establishment of the person's own story as primary. The importance of the person's own story lies not just in its content, but in its telling; this is a way of establishing for oneself and others one's moral worth in the face of serious or life-threatening illness. Telling one's story is more than a recounting of events: it is, in the act of telling, a way of reflecting upon the spheres of one's life that might have been placed in disarray. Here the act of multiple reflection is a form of narrative reconstruction (Williams, 1984) through which the person both makes sense of what has happened, and, in the course of this, re-figures himself or herself as an individual. The opportunity to tell such stories provides patients with the potential to exercise a social ethic. This means that 'finding one's voice' or 'developing one's style' is a way of reversing the diminishment of self that sufferers can experience. (Frank, 1995: 39).

I have tried to show in this section that illness and illness experience are not, *in essence*, separate entities, bounded in ways that allow them to be quantified. This is in spite of the fact that sometimes, in response to requests by researchers, people will report it as being just this kind of thing. Instead, illness always *appears* in the light of how individuals re-present their world as a result of the intrusion of disease. And the way that they reflect upon these appearances becomes enfolded in experience, so that the person is repeatedly re-figured in his or her attempts to 'deal with illness'. The fact that this is played out across a plurality of social realms is important, because it highlights how illness can come to signify in different ways and at different times. At each time, in each specific situation, what is said or done is expressive of 'a way of going on', which shows that we are concerned not with illness *per se* but with being ill, or being well. We speak of people 'bearing illness' precisely because it is something displayed, given its form through the ways that people 'show forth' what they can do in the world in spite of (or because of) their condition.

The Interview as a Demonstration of 'Healthiness'

For an ill person, being interviewed is more than being asked to 'tell one's story' or to give an account of events surrounding one's treatment. It also means having to display one's condition to the interviewer, a meeting which is invariably conducted by a healthy other. This person might also be seen to represent either the interests of medicine (if the research is cast as, for example, 'a project concerning heart patients'), or perhaps the world of psychological expertise. This matters, because what ill people feel they ought to say, can say or want to say is dependent upon the form of the interviewing relationship. I shall discuss briefly some of these points below. First, however, it is important to emphasize that the interview is precisely the kind of specific situation in which what is said and done is expressive of the person's 'way of going on', as outlined above. This means that what is said about illness is both situated *and* expressive; it draws upon the particularities of the encounter to display the world of the informant. The interview is a situation in which the ill person must exemplify the kind of person reflected in the account given. This demand arises because illness is both a bodily affair and a social condition.

The need to demonstrate one's state of health occurs in structured interviews too. A recent study, critical of using survey tools in this context, showed how elderly respondents were reluctant to speak of their health in abstract terms (that is, in terms of the questions asked). Instead, they preferred, as in the case of one woman, 'to stay within the realm of her own everyday experiences and construct her not-quite-healthy status out of two facts, i.e. lacking energy and sleeping difficulties' (Jylha, 1994: 988). By comparison with illness, good health can also be constructed in this way, so that another respondent in that study reported all three of her medical conditions – diabetes, stroke and blood pressure – in such a way as to give a picture of good, rather than poor health.

The reluctance of people outside of medical settings to talk about illness has been reported before (see particularly Cornwell, 1984). The reason often given is that 'really their health is good' and that the interviewer should find other, more suitable respondents. It is as if respondents do not recognize in their own situation the idealized notions of health or illness that they believe (with good reason) the researcher wishes to study. This point has also been made with regard to studies of the family (Backett, 1990; Silverman, 1993), where there has been a concern about the possibility of obtaining data about the 'authentic' family, given that it (like health) is regarded as a private matter. This assumes that there exists something corresponding to the idealized family under study (a realist notion), instead of recognizing that 'for sociologists [and psychologists, too] *how* we invoke the family, *when* we invoke the family and *where* we invoke the family become central analytic concerns' (Silverman, 1993: 203, emphasis in original). By substituting the word 'health' for 'family' in this quotation, we can see that these issues are also central to the study of illness experience. These are concerns which reappear in the context of the practical activities in which respondents engage in the various realms of their everyday life.

One context in which health reappears is, of course, the research interview itself. An interesting feature of health talk is the way that respondents construct their accounts so as to appear 'ordinary', so that 'the extraordinary is made ordinary' (Dingwall, 1976; Radley and Billig, 1996; Voysey, 1975). This happens because talking about one's health always runs the risk of exposing oneself as either weak or irresponsible, of having to put at risk that which should have been either protected or conserved. Where a specifiable illness might have to be reported, then the respondent must deal with any attributions that follow from revealing that she is 'someone diagnosed as suffering from X', or that he had 'previously been treated for Y'. Where the *raison d'être* of the interview is people's occupancy of the sick role, and/or their having been labelled by a diagnostic term, then being the object of such attributions is no longer a risk but an occurrence.

This picture of ordinariness is often shown to be there in spite of illness, by the mention of things that healthy people do in the course of everyday life. Or else it can be shown by virtue of illness, as in cases where the person reports achieving 'ordinary' ends by working around the constraints of symptoms (as with the elderly respondent cited above). In the early writings of qualitative researchers into health matters, this was called 'normalizing' (Davis, 1963; Strauss, 1975). What is interesting is that normalizing is achieved in talk by the use of other social realms apart from medicine (which defines the individual in terms of this or that disease), in order to reflect both the illness and the person in particular ways. Just as it was argued above that illness experience is always reflected through social realms, so the presentation of oneself at interview as 'a person with this kind of condition' involves just this sort of reflection too.

Illness, and how one deals with it, raises moral questions of right and wrong, and ethical questions about better or worse ways of living. To speak of these things requires that people abandon the neutral abstractions of the realm of medicine, and report how they live in the various social realms through which they can reflect the form of their illness, and, equally important, fashion an image of themselves as a certain kind of person. This may involve giving what Cornwell (1984) termed 'private' (as opposed to 'public') accounts, told in ways that they might use when talking to a close friend or to someone they know well. These 'private' accounts work, in part, to minimize the special features of the person's situation, those that mark them out as different because of illness. Peculiarly, then, by giving 'private' information the sick (the interviewees) can render themselves *less* exposed to the scrutiny of the healthy (the interviewer) (Radley and Billig, 1996).

What Cornwell termed 'private' accounts involves reference to what I have been calling 'social realms', the voice of the lifeworld beyond that of medicine. But just as it is possible to say something about one's formal health status by reference to such other realms, so it is possible for respondents to display their personal situation through a concern with what is considered proper in the world of medical care. The following excerpt is taken from an interview with a couple where the man had returned to work as soon as he was able, after having received surgery for the treatment of coronary disease.

Wife: [To husband] It seemed as if one week you were still feeling your way and then the next minute you decided you were fit enough for work, and to me it seemed too quick and I was a bit worried whether you were going to react at work . . .

Husband: [To wife] That I went back to work too quickly and didn't spend the end of my convalescence together with you, having a break.

Interviewer: [To both] How did you resolve this?

Husband: Well, basically by trying to make up for it, compensating by doing more now. (Radley, 1988: 138)

In this account the wife uses a question about her husband's recovery as an opportunity to reveal her feelings about their relationship. What is explicit in the wife's statement is an evaluation of the husband's speed of recovery, and a concern that he might suffer through his early return to work. This is then glossed by the husband in a way that proposes it as a reflection of another concern – to do with the time they spent together. That is, the rights and wrongs of recovery are shown to be issues in their personal relationship. There is more to it than this, however. What it also shows is that the husband's illness had not just pervaded this realm, but in doing so had coloured it in ways that were not wholly negative. His illness provided the opportunity for more time together, and also gave a new significance to the wife's role in their marriage. She made this explicit by then saying:

> I suppose because I'm rather inclined to feel, what was the point of doing things? I was so worried about his health, everything else took second place. Now it doesn't seem to be quite so important, it's very difficult to get the same enthusiasm back. (Radley, 1988: 138)

This quote makes the point that, in being reflected in the various spheres of everyday life, illness experience then becomes available as a way of reflecting upon those everyday concerns. In the course of the interview, people not only tell about the 'ordinariness' of their situation but also about the special features of their dealings with difficult situations. In the case of interviews involving the patient and others (for example spouse/partner, family member, friend), the demonstration of health status and of coping involves a joint effort at presentation. As in the case above, sometimes one party will offer, as substantive information, something which will then be taken up by the other as a mirror in which to reflect something else; and by so doing, this will throw a new light on the information originally given.

It has been pointed out that interviewing families about health involves asking them to talk about two major areas of their lives which tend to be taken for granted (Backett, 1990). This is important, as it emphasizes not only the need for informants to demonstrate ordinariness, but also the opportunity for them to display 'good coping'. (It also raises questions about differences in the data that might be collected when speaking with two (or more) rather than just one informant (Arksey, 1996)). Such 'good coping' must not only be claimed but it should be demonstrated in the accounts that the respondents jointly provide. There is scope here for both parties to display not just the good health of one of them, but their having coped well with adversity, and having achieved this together. As a result interviewees are transformed from being 'mere informants' about an objective condition, to being navigators in a world of difficulty, articulators of unusual experiences.

This last point raises an important difference between the situation of the 'mere informant' and the articulator of experience. Arthur Frank (1995), who has himself undergone treatment for cancer, argues that those with serious illness who tell their stories are engaged in something deeper than reporting facts. They are remaking their world through articulating their experience, effectively re-figuring themselves in the course of becoming storytellers of their encounters with illness. He distinguishes between 'survivors' on the one hand (passive patients who have passed through the hands of medicine), and 'witnesses' on the other:

Survival does not include any particular responsibility other than continuing to survive. Becoming a witness assumes a responsibility for telling what happened. The witness offers testimony to a truth that is generally unrecognized or suppressed. People who tell stories of illness are witnesses, turning illness into moral responsibility. (Frank, 1995: 137)

This means that what is being told are not just reports of extant events, open to proofs of truth and falsity, but are avowals of experience that are best subject to tests of sincerity. In the course of reflecting upon and about illness, the speaker con-figures himself or herself within a world that investigators can then entertain. By this I mean that the job of the researcher is not to peer behind the words to check their reality against some other ('more objective') measure, but to comprehend what it means to be ill, or to be healthy.

This is consistent with the idea that the interview is a constraint upon ill respondents to display themselves in a certain light, and yet offers the scope for this to happen in different ways. By virtue of this, what people say and do in these situations are exemplars of their lives, fragments in which are reflected the way that illness has affected them and how they, in turn, have coped with it. Interviewing people about these matters is special (though not unique) because they are obliged to show forth (that is, reflect) their health status and ways of coping with illness in the course of the exchange. It is because the interview is situated – it takes time, may involve spatial re-arrangements, perhaps includes other people, must be enacted – that it provides a fragment through which the respondent can illuminate his or her illness experience. Health reappears because it is contingent; the interview discloses because other realms are reflected through it.

Conclusion

In this chapter I have argued, first, that health and illness are not entities, but experiences that are made tangible when reflected through other realms or spheres of everyday life. This means that if health psychologists wish to know about what it means to be a patient undergoing treatment, or to suffer from a particular disease, then they must come to grips with the implications of this position. It also means that the objectification of health and illness in terms of ready-made scales or inventories will bypass entirely the way that this experience is constructed, and the way in which it is made to matter (more or less) in the lives of those concerned. I have also argued that the qualitative interview is an occasion in which this form of reflection is invited, and that the special way it does this is by enabling the respondent to be an exemplar of the position that is claimed.

What does this imply about the way that accounts are to be treated subsequently? There are different views on this point. For a phenomenologist such as Giorgi (1992), description is primary because the object of inquiry is to study the person's categories, not for researchers to interpret or categorize the account given. On the other hand, Silverman (1993) is clear that the respondent's view can never substitute for the researcher's explanation (effectively equating common sense with social science), because the researcher's view has the advantage of gathering data of various kinds from various sources. This dilemma is not restricted to health psychology; in medical sociology the question of whether categorization 'shatters' the data or is necessary to advance theory about health and illness has been stated along just these lines (Conrad, 1990).

It may be, as Frank (1995) has suggested, that the movement into a post-modern world allows the capacity for telling one's own story to be reclaimed. In the modern period medicine has had undisputed pride of place, so that it has defined reality and thereby made other realms secondary, 'alternative', 'lay' or 'folk'. It is to the realm of medicine that the natural science model of knowledge makes its application. As part of this authoritative position, the qualitative study of people's experience is made an adjunct, and remains a 'mere description' prior to the specification of variables for measurement. What has now occurred is the demand by people to reclaim what has until recently been the province of technical expertise. If this is the case, then pursuing qualitative research in health psychology is not just adopting an alternative research technique, but endorsing (perhaps unwittingly) a movement in which health and illness make a new kind of sense in people's lives.

This argument is not intended as a wholesale critique of the use of quantitative methods by health psychologists, still less a prescription for how health psychologists should conduct their research. As surely as the advance of biomedicine continues, and with it the modernist programme of specifying cause and effect, then health psychologists will undoubtedly play their part in this endeavour. On the other hand, changes in society mean that ideas of 'health and illness' are no longer bound within bio-medical categories and the practices which previously held them in check. Socio-economic differences, alternative therapies, the rationing of health care and the ethical dilemmas produced by advancing medical technology mean that we shall want to know more about how illness and health are reflected in the biographies of the individuals whom these movements touch. Even in the unlikely event that health psychologists do not care to ask such qualitative questions, then patients, carers, survivors, the chronically ill, the genetically 'at risk' and those who work at maintaining their own health will surely insist on telling them.

References

Arksey, H. (1996) Collecting data through joint interviews. *Social Research Update*, 15, Winter, (whole number), University of Surrey.

Armstrong, D. (1984) The patient's view. *Social Science and Medicine*, 18: 737–744.

Backett, K.C. (1990) Studying health in families: a qualitative approach. In S. Cunningham-Burley and N.P. McKeganey (eds), *Readings in Medical Sociology*. London: Tavistock, pp. 57–84.

Blaxter, M. (1985) Self-definition of health status and consulting rates in primary care. *Quarterly Journal of Social Affairs*, 1: 131–171.

Cassell, E.J. (1976) Disease as an 'it': concepts of disease revealed by patients' presentation of symptoms. *Social Science and Medicine*, 10: 143–146.

Conrad, P. (1990) Qualitative research on chronic illness: a commentary on method and conceptual development. *Social Science and Medicine*, 11: 1257–1263.

Corbin, J. and Strauss, A.L. (1987) Accompaniments of chronic illness: changes in body, self, biography and biographical time. In J.A. Roth and P. Conrad (eds), *Research in the Sociology of Health Care*, Vol. 6, *The Experience and Management of Chronic Illness*. Greenwich, CT: JAI Press, pp. 249–281.

Cornwell, J. (1984) *Hard-earned Lives: Accounts of Health and Illness from East London*. London: Tavistock.

Davis, F. (1963) *Passage through Crisis: Polio Victims and their Families*. Indianapolis: Bobbs-Merrill.

Dingwall, R. (1976) *Aspects of Illness*. London: Martin Robertson.

Duval, M.L. (1984) Psychosocial metaphors of physical distress among MS patients. *Social Science and Medicine*, 19: 119–145.

Frank, A.W. (1995) *The Wounded Storyteller: Body, Illness and Ethics*. Chicago: University of Chicago Press.

Frank, A.W. (1996) Reconciliatory alchemy: bodies, narratives and power. *Body and Society*, 2: 53–71.

Giorgi, A. (1992) Description versus interpretation: competing alternative strategies for qualitative research. *Journal of Phenomenological Psychology*, 23: 119–135.

Jenkins, C.D., Rosenman, R.H. and Friedman, M. (1967) Development of an objective psychological test for the determination of the coronary-prone behavior pattern in employed men. *Journal of Chronic Disease*, 20: 371–379.

Jylha, M. (1994) Self-rated health revisited: exploring survey interview episodes with elderly respondents. *Social Science and Medicine*, 39: 983–990.

Kirmayer, L.J. (1992) The body's insistence on meaning: metaphor as presentation and representation in illness experience. *Medical Anthropology Quarterly*, 6: 323–346.

Kleinman, A. (1988) *The Illness Narratives: Suffering, Healing, and the Human Condition*. New York: Basic Books.

Pinder, R. (1990) *The Management of Chronic Illness: Patient and Doctor Perspectives on Parkinson's Disease*. Basingstoke: Macmillan.

Radley, A. (1988) *Prospects of Heart Surgery: Psychological Adjustment to Coronary Bypass Grafting*. New York: Springer-Verlag.

Radley, A. (1993) The role of metaphor in adjustment to chronic illness. In A. Radley (ed.), *Worlds of Illness: Biographical and Cultural Perspectives on Health and Disease*. London: Routledge, pp. 109–123.

Radley, A. and Billig, M. (1996) Accounts of health and illness: dilemmas and representations. *Sociology of Health and Illness*, 18: 220–240.

Romanyshyn, R.D. (1982) *Psychological Life: From Science to Metaphor*. Milton Keynes: Open University Press.

Rosenman, R.H. (1978) The interview method of assessment of the coronary-prone behavior pattern. In T.M. Dembroski (ed.), *Coronary–Prone Behavior*. New York: Springer, pp. 55–69.

Silverman, D. (1993) *Interpreting Qualitative Data: Methods for Analysing Talk, Text and Interaction*. London: Sage.

Stimson, G. (1974) Obeying doctor's orders: a view from the other side. *Social Science and Medicine*, 8: 97–104.

Stimson, G. and Webb, B. (1975) *Going to See the Doctor: The Consultation Process in General Practice*. London: Routledge and Kegan Paul.

Strauss, A.L. (1975) *Chronic Illness and the Quality of Life*. St Louis, MO: Mosby.

Voysey, M. (1975) *A Constant Burden: The Reconstitution of Family Life*. London: Routledge and Kegan Paul.

Williams, G.H. (1984) The genesis of chronic illness: narrative reconstruction. *Sociology of Health and Illness*, 6: 174–200.

Williams, G.H. (1993) Chronic illness and the pursuit of virtue in everyday life. In A. Radley (ed.), *Worlds of Illness: Biographical and Cultural Perspectives on Health and Disease*. London: Routledge, pp. 92–108.

3

Understanding Embodied Experience

Beyond Mind–body Dualism in Health Research

Lucy Yardley

This chapter considers how qualitative research can be used to develop a more intricate and sophisticated understanding of the interdependence of mind and body. In order to do this, it is necessary to move beyond the limitations of our traditional, 'dualist' way of thinking, which creates a sharp distinction between mind and body, viewing the body as an objective, physical entity and the mind as a subjective, private realm of ethereal thoughts. As an alternative to studying mind and body as separate (albeit interlinked) phenomena, a variety of 'material-discursive' approaches (Yardley, 1996, 1997a) can be employed to investigate simultaneously the psychosocial and physical dimensions of health and illness as different aspects of a unitary embodied experience.

Quantitative research is not always dualist, and a dualist approach can be adopted in qualitative research. Nevertheless, the theoretical rationale for most quantitative research is quite different from the theoretical foundation for much qualitative research, and provides a very different basis for comprehending the relation between mind and body. The sharp distinction between mind and body is closely associated with a 'realist' conception of our knowledge of the world. Realist theories of knowledge assume that there is a stable reality which is independent of the observer, and propose that an accurate understanding of this reality is best achieved by means of precise, controlled, objective observation. It is for this reason that quantitative measurement and statistics are often employed to maximize the precision and objectivity of the analysis. In this kind of research, the aim is to obtain measures of objective, physical reality which are uncontaminated by subjective, mental processes – whether these are the investigator's or the research subject's 'biases' in perception or reporting. However, when the research is concerned with phenomena which are viewed as partly subjective, such as perceptions of pain or beliefs about illness, this approach can lead to difficulties. For example, researchers are continually confonted by the problem of how the 'bodily' component of pain (the physiological sensation) can be distinguished from the 'mental' component (subjective perception), and how such private, subjective experiences can be objectively measured.

In contrast, much qualitative research takes a quite different approach to gaining knowledge, based on the idea that the 'reality' of any individual is created by an interaction between his or her beliefs, goals and activities, and the constraints and possibilities of the physical, socio-historical and linguistic background and context. Since this applies not only to the beliefs and perceptions of the 'subjects' who are being studied but also to the views of reality of the scientists and psychologists who investigate them, it is unrealistic to attempt to attain a neutral, objective perspective. A more practical and useful objective is to develop a detailed, multi-layered, insightful interpretation of a phenomenon, and to consider explicitly the way in which the context, the participants and the researchers have jointly contributed to the understanding acquired in the course of the investigation.

From this perspective, there is no sharp distinction between subjective and objective, mental and physical, mind and body. Instead, there is an acceptance that all our experiences and our knowledge are both substantial *and* symbolic – our beliefs have real, material roots and consequences, while our experience of physical embodiment cannot be isolated from our perceptions and interpretations of the meaning of physical states. Hence, an expression of pain is not a public report of a subjective interpretation of a private physical event. Pain complaints can instead be understood as one verbal element of a changed relationship to the world, which may also entail restriction of physical and social activity, appeals for assistance from healers, family and friends, and an emotional revaluation of identity and purpose. And while physiological status contributes very significantly to this changed relationship, it is not the only or even the most 'real' element. Physical trauma elicits an entirely different psychophysiological, perceptual and socio-behavioural reaction depending upon whether it occurs in the context of a battle, religious ritual, medical operation, or sexual act. In different situations pain may be experienced as an ecstatic transcendent state or as a debilitating affliction. Moreover, it is important to note that the 'subjective' processes (attention, appraisal, expectations) which modify the experience of pain are not ethereal psychic forces, but are themselves instigated by bodily enacted social practices. For example, the analgesic placebo response is fostered partly by a system of healing-related beliefs and relationships which are realized and reinforced by the demeanour and discourse of the doctor, and partly by conditioned psychophysiological reactions to features of the physical environment, such as the hypodermic needle or hospital ward, which previous experiences have imbued with meaning.

While it is entirely possible to analyse the influence of expectations and socio-cultural context on pain perception within a dualist theoretical framework, the differences between dualist and non-dualist approaches to embodied experience comprise subtle but important shifts in the objectives of the research enterprise and the interpretation of research findings. In the first half of this chapter I will examine the origins of dualist thinking and the way in which it has influenced our understanding of health and illness, drawing attention to some of the problems posed by this way of conceptualizing human existence. In the second half I will describe some alternative theoretical perspectives which may allow us to integrate research into the psychosocial and physical aspects of health and illness. The practical problem of dizziness will be used to exemplify the character, advantages and limitations of dualist and non-dualist approaches. Persistent dizziness (although somewhat neglected by health psychologists) has many similarities with better known conditions such as chronic pain or fatigue, and can serve to illustrate how dualism affects our understanding and management of a wide variety of health problems.

The Dualist View of Mind and Body

The origins of mind–body dualism, the belief that the mind and body are qualitatively distinct and separate entities, can be traced back at least as far as the ancient Greek philosophers. Plato perpetuated this early dualism, distinguishing between the rational, immortal soul, which was located nearest to the heavens in the head, and the bestial body (Averill, 1996). Whereas thought was conceptualized as self-contained, the body was portrayed as open to external influences, through its desires and emotional reactions.

The conceptualization of the mind–body relationship which remains most influential today was formulated in the seventeenth century by Descartes, and has hence become known as 'Cartesian' dualism. His famous statement 'Cogito, ergo sum' ('I think, therefore I am') summed up the view that the only certain knowledge we can have consists of the contents of our own mind. We must therefore derive our impressions of the external world through observation and inference (Hocutt, 1996). Descartes equated the mind with the soul, which was viewed as immaterial, self-contained, rational, and unique to humans. The body was seen as a part of the physical world, subject to the laws of mechanics. This distinction between private, rational mental processes and external, physical processes gave rise to a number of related dualist dichotomies: mind–body; perception–action; subjective–objective; internal–external; rational–irrational; human–inhuman. In addition, the Cartesian depiction of the mind as isolated from an external physical reality led to a conception of knowledge acquisition as the process whereby the rational, individual mind could, through systematic observation, deduce the nature of the material world and thereby gain the ability to predict and control physical events. This perspective can be seen as part of the ideological development of modern western capitalism and industrialization, which advanced the ideals of individual autonomy and choice, rational decision-making, and the attainment of mastery over physical processes (Hollinger, 1994).

Descartes himself stated that his primary intention was to develop an epistemological foundation for the development of scientific medicine, declaring that:

I have resolved not to employ the time which remains to me in life in any other matter than in endeavouring to acquire some knowledge of nature, which shall be of such a kind that it will enable us to arrive at rules for Medicine more assured than those which have yet been attained. (cited in Leder, 1990: 139)

The way in which the modern, rational approach to the body he instigated later transformed medical practices has been vividly described by Foucault (1989). Previously the body had been regarded as a constituent of the person rather than as a physical mechanism, and the religious prohibition of dissection (as well as the one-to-one financial relationships between patients and their doctors) made it difficult to investigate diseases as physical entities, and encouraged a holistic approach to healing. However, once the sacred mind was dissociated from the physical body, and publicly funded clinics for the treatment of the poor had been established (which enabled physicians to compare and experiment), doctors were able to regard bodies in a new light and investigate them both mentally and physically as 'cases' of material malfunction rather than as unique individuals.

It is evident that the theoretical framework offered by Cartesian dualism had many advantages, especially for Descartes' expressed purpose of furthering scientific exploration of physical processes. Nevertheless, it created an ambiguity about the mind–body relationship which is particularly awkward for health psychologists. Cartesian dualism depicts the body as a lifeless object which must be animated by the mind, but provides no plausible explanation as to how the two might be connected, since the mechanical body and immaterial mind are portrayed as qualitatively entirely dissimilar. Indeed, the distinction between mind and body is associated with opposing philosophies of knowledge; 'empiricists' and 'materialists' stress the essentially physical basis of existence, while 'constructivists' and 'idealists' emphasize the central role of the mind in structuring perceptions and creating meaning. Since there is no way of actually proving whether or not there is a world independent of our awareness of it, adherence to one or other of these views, or to any of the compromise positions which lie between these extremes, must be based on theoretical and ideological rather than empirical grounds (Potter, 1996). However, the conceptualization of animals as physical mechanisms proved so useful for anatomical and physiological research that Descartes' original notion that *human* bodies were animated by the mind came to be replaced by a purely materialist approach to physical functioning (Carrier and Mittelstrass, 1995). This in turn led to a biomedical model of health and disease in which the status of psychological factors became precarious and problematic.

Dualist approaches to Dizziness

Many people suffering from dizziness find that the Cartesian distinction between mind and body does not map easily on to a condition in which mental and physical factors seem to interact in a complex manner.

Sufferers are often unsure to what extent their feelings of disorientation and malaise are due to physiological processes or emotional reactions, and are aware that there is a variety of ways in which their symptoms may be triggered or exacerbated by certain situations or activities, and by subjective states such as anxiety or fatigue. But the traditional biomedical model does not allow for such interactions, and assumes that the primary task for the doctor is to undertake 'differential diagnosis' – to decide whether the problem is due to a particular physical cause such as vestibular dysfunction, or to a mental cause such as anxiety, so that the patient can be managed by the appropriate specialist, either in physical disorientation or in mental disturbance.

The differential diagnostic approach clearly has important benefits, especially in the case of conditions with a single physical cause and specific physical remedy, as in these circumstances it is both feasible and important to locate the physical malfunction. The dualist approach in medicine thus works well when the body does indeed behave like a machine, isolated from the mind. But owing to the complexity of the balance system (which comprises the visual, vestibular and somatosensory systems and their interconnections in the brain), causes of dizziness often are difficult to identify or are multifactorial, and are seldom easily treated by medication or surgery. There is no simple test to confirm an organic cause for dizziness, and so doctors must often make a subjective judgement as to whether the dizziness has a physical or 'psychogenic' (mental) basis. Such judgements naturally take into account the level of anxiety exhibited by the patient – yet this is actually a dubious strategy, since dizziness can *cause* anxiety. Hence it is impossible to attain the ideal Cartesian situation, in which the medical scientist directly observes evidence of low-level physical lesions, and instead both doctor and patient must struggle to interpret the meaning of subjective sensations and higher-level perceptual-motor dysfunction.

Whereas differential diagnosis seeks to attribute cases of dizziness to *either* mental *or* physical dysfunction, strong evidence for an association between the two (for example Eagger et al., 1992; Sullivan et al., 1993) led clinicians and researchers to begin to explore the nature of the mind–body link between balance system dysfunction and anxiety. Initially, two alternative hypotheses were proposed. Either the link must be somato-psychic (in other words, a physical disease was causing psychological problems) or it must be psycho-somatic – psychological problems were causing the development of physical disease. Clinical experience amply supported the theory that attacks of dizziness could provoke anxiety, panic and agoraphobia (Pratt and McKenzie, 1958). However, it proved much more difficult to find good evidence of psychosomatic causation of disease. Although there were indications that people with certain balance disorders had abnormal personality profiles or elevated stress levels, it was unclear whether the balance dysfunction was caused by or had itself caused these higher levels of reported stress and psychological dysfunction. This led to the development of more complicated 'transactional' models of the possible relationships between psychological and physical factors. For example, several researchers proposed that pre-existing vulnerability to anxiety, whether due to personality or stress, might lead to a worse reaction to dizziness, resulting not only in more complaints from people who were both dizzy and anxious, but also in more handicap, distress, and secondary autonomic symptoms such as nausea and sweating (Eagger et al., 1992; Hallam and Hinchcliffe, 1991; Yardley, 1994b; Yardley et al., 1992).

These investigations into the relationship between mind and body in dizziness have undoubtedly contributed valuable insights into the factors which can hinder or support recovery from disorientation. Nevertheless, although these studies acknowledge a variety of ways in which mind and body might *interact*, they are still cast within a dualist framework which continues to pose problems for dizziness sufferers.

One difficulty concerns the supposed qualitative difference between mind and body. Whereas physical matters are regarded as amenable to objective verification, mental phenomena are deemed private and subjective. The result is that psychological causative factors in disorientation tend to be viewed as less 'real' than organic factors, and are therefore perceived (by both doctors and patients) as undermining the legitimacy of complaints of illness. This is particularly ironic, since a common biomedical response to the mind–body problem has traditionally been to assert the pre-eminence of the physical nature of human functioning, thus reducing mind to matter – for example, by proposing that mental disturbances such as anxiety are due to biochemical imbalances, and should be treated with medication. However, where psychological factors are suspected in dizziness, the dizziness seems to lose the status of real illness, since it is then seldom treated by drugs or any other means (Clark et al., 1994).

Pollock (1993) has noted that it is common for invisible, mental problems to be viewed as due to a failure of will rather than a physical defect; people who are unable to maintain control or to 'cope' by applying 'mind over matter' are seen as socially weak or inadequate. This attitude has its roots in the dualist view of the spiritual mind as the essence and pinnacle of humanity, and the belief that the rational mind should be able to subdue the vulnerable body. Indeed, Descartes explicitly expressed the opinion that both emotional and physical distress (which were both depicted as originating in the body) could be overcome by a dispassionate mental outlook:

> there might be a person with genuine reasons for distress but who took such pains to direct his imagination that he never thought of them . . . [or] he would look on them without passion. Moreover, I do not doubt that this by itself would be capable of restoring him to health, even if his spleen and lungs were already in a poor condition because of the bad temperament of the blood produced by sadness. (cited in Gaukroger, 1995: 15–16)

Consequently, people whose loss of control has an emotional element are seen to some extent as human failures – an attitude which can itself be a source of considerable anxiety and distress to people complaining of uncontrollable disorientation due to ambiguous or mixed causes (Yardley, 1994a).

A related difficulty is that the responsibility for mental coping or weakness is attributed principally to the sufferer, and his or her personal efforts or characteristics. This individualistic perspective emanates from the Cartesian view of the mind as an isolated, almost asocial entity. The problem with individualistic analyses of the effects of beliefs, personality or coping strategies is that they fail to take into account the context of the individual's behaviour and beliefs, which constrains the way in which sufferers can make sense of illness and create viable roles and lifestyles for themselves (as discussed below). Such research may therefore simply repeat the conventional exhortations for the individual to exert control over the illness.

A further limitation of this kind of dualist research is that the techniques of accurate statistical measurement used to assess the mind–body relationship in most of these studies are taken from the realist paradigm for research into observable physical phenomena. Indeed, the 'biopsychosocial model' (Engel, 1982), the framework within which mind–body interactions are often conceptualized by health psychologists, is itself based on an approach to the control of mechanical systems developed within the discipline of engineering (Stam, 1988). But while the reproducibility and precise quantification afforded by questionnaires may *simulate* the objective measurement of observable properties, it is doubtful whether the ambiguous and compound psychosocial considerations which lead to a particular response to a questionnaire can actually be so easily specified. In the following section I hope to explain how qualitative approaches may offer a rich, contextualized and linguistically sophisticated alternative to the pre-defined and restricted range of responses necessitated by questionnaire research. In addition, the explicitly interpretive nature of qualitative studies, and the attention to diversity and change, promotes an appropriate awareness of the variability and indeterminacy of people's motives and meanings which cannot be as readily pinned down as numerical quantification by questionnaire may sometimes imply.

Material-discursive Approaches to the Mind–body Relationship

The unequal weight assigned to the psychosocial compared with the physical aspects of illness within the biomedical model led some qualitative researchers to attempt to redress the balance by focusing almost exclusively on subjective experiences or health-related discourse. But this itself still constitutes a dualist approach, since it downplays or neglects the role played by the body, and the material dimension of our lives and our environment. It is for this reason that 'material-discursive' approaches are needed, which can embrace the physical side of existence in a non-realist

manner, thus sidestepping some of the unwarranted or exaggerated distinctions between the subjective and objective, mental and physical, mind
and body.

A non-dualist appreciation of the material dimension can only be
achieved by putting aside assumptions which are so integral to our modern
western culture that they appear to be simply 'common sense'. The change
in perspective entailed is perhaps nearly as great and as disturbing as
when, several centuries ago, westerners had to adjust to the idea that the
earth was round and circled the sun, despite its seemingly obvious flat and
stable properties! Indeed, the appeal of dualist theories may be partly
attributable to a similar foundation in everyday perception. In an intrigu-
ing analysis of the possible phenomenological basis for dualist beliefs,
Leder (1990) points out that the brain is a particularly self-effacing organ.
While we can view the activities of our trunk and limbs, we cannot observe
ourselves thinking. Consequently, whereas we have perceptual evidence
for the external dimension of our world, including our bodies, we have
none for the subjective dimension, and hence can more easily come to
regard it as immaterial. Moreover, the distinction between subject and
object has a genuine phenomenological basis. The object is the thing to
which attention is directed, whereas the subject is the outward-looking
agent – the perceiving eye, reaching hand or processing brain, which
we remain unconscious of *because* of our absorption in the object. Consequently, although eyes, brains, spoken and written words are all physical
entities which *can* become the object of attention, in the course of our
activity we are seldom aware of our gaze, mind, or thoughts as an
embodied part of the world – in the same way that when reading we
simply experience the transmission of ideas, and necessarily overlook
the physical process whereby physical marks on pieces of paper convey the
meaning of the author.

Once we become aware of ourselves as subjects (and hence also objects)
it becomes clear that the Cartesian ideal of 'objectivity' – a neutral,
independent description of the world – is unattainable, since the only
knowledge we can acquire must be filtered through our minds and bodies,
our outlook and preconceptions, our activities and interpretations. Hence,
one consequence of recognizing the constructed nature of experience is that
the dualist distinction between subjective and objective knowledge starts to
break down. All knowledge can be seen to be experiential, and hence
perspectival (Lakoff, 1987). The dualist notion of a disembodied, neutral
rational mind can be replaced with an acknowledgement that the views of
different people – men and women, people from different countries and
continents, doctors and patients – represent different but equally authentic
perspectives (Sampson, 1993).

However, this does *not* mean that all views are equally valid in all
contexts. The meaningfulness of any view or statement depends upon the
degree to which it makes symbolic *and* practical sense in the context of a
particular way of life. For example, patients' knowledge of their illness will
not necessarily be as valid as a doctor's in *medical* terms. The context which

legitimizes doctors' statements consists of the body of scientific beliefs which have been shown to be effective in relieving physical ailments. This context provides a situated, practical guarantee of the 'truth' of, for example, a diagnosis – not 'truth' as a timeless, universal, objective certainty, but rather as an assurance that the diagnosis is consistent with contemporary, local 'best practice' in the art (or science) of healing, drawing on the tools of modern biotechnology which vastly extend our capability to physically observe disease processes, and based on the understanding and experiences of many thousands of doctors and patients.

In our society medical interpretations of physical status have such immense intellectual and social authority, and such far-reaching practical and social significance, that medical views often come to be regarded as objective truths whereas patients' views may be characterized as 'lay beliefs'. However, non-medical interpretations of physical dysfunction can have important and equally valid implications. For instance, doctors tend to view deafness as a physical impairment which needs to be corrected, and sometimes have difficulty understanding why many deaf adults are opposed to the implantation in deaf babies of 'cochlear implants', a form of hearing aid. These deaf people have generally had painful personal experience of unsuccessfully attempting to become a 'normal' hearing/speaking person, sometimes spending their whole childhood and education trying to master elementary speech, and meanwhile missing out on the culturally vital process of easy, intimate and informal communication and information exchange. They would therefore rather be accepted as different rather than deficient, and supported in a more viable identity and congenial community which uses sign language (Yardley, 1997b). While the doctors' understanding of deafness as deficiency is valid in terms of a medical model of normal physical functioning, deaf people's desire to communicate freely using sign rather than be forced to communicate with difficulty by speech is valid in terms of a social model of the rights of minorities with differing needs, desires and abilities.

In modern science the Cartesian goal of achieving an exhaustive, objective knowledge of an unchanging reality has been superseded, and it is now accepted that simply 'observing' a process is an activity which has an impact on the event, that the behaviour of complex multifactorial dynamic systems cannot be reduced to or predicted by simple causal models, and that the 'laws' which allow scientists to manipulate matter very successfully are none the less partial, relative truths which are operative only within a carefully constructed and controlled setting. These observations in no way detract from the power and utility of scientific modes of thought, but they do lead to a view of 'reality' as an active, changeable, constructed relationship with an enigmatic and mutable environment, rather than as a stable and controllable set of external objects and forces which can be examined from a neutral perspective. Acknowledgement of the constructed nature of experience has radical implications for our understanding of mind and body, as it undermines the distinction between what is mental and internal and what is physical and external.

Many of the mental qualitites which were considered to be private and ethereal can be seen to have material, external manifestations. Instead of regarding thoughts as internal mental events, and language as a means of passing these bits of information to other equally isolated minds, the language and activities which structure, inform and support our 'private' thought can be seen to be concrete forms of embodied human endeavour (Lakoff and Johnson, 1980; Leont'ev, 1978). Consequently, the dualist distinction between physical reality and its representation in ideas or language can also be seen to be artificial. Our shared concepts are manifested in talk, education and debate, and our knowledge, skills and social relations are manifested in tools and technologies (Ibañez, 1994). Indeed, it is possible to conceptualize not only human activities and socio-cultural artefacts but also biological organisms themselves as a form of embodied knowledge – a physical expression of an accurate rapport between organism and environment, manifested in appropriate structures, instincts and capabilities (Maturana and Varela, 1987).

Since the socio-cultural dimension is grounded in the material world and has material consequences, and all material forms and activities have symbolic and social implications, the concrete, social and allegorical aspects of our own bodily states are often intermingled in a subtle and complicated manner. The early social constructionists, Berger and Luckmann, noted that 'Biological factors limit the range of social possibilities open to any individual, but the social world, which is pre-existent to each individual, in its turn imposes limits on what is biologically possible to the organism' (1966: 201–202). Socio-economic status influences our height, intelligence and lifespan (Wilkinson, 1996), while the region and culture in which we were brought up becomes imprinted in our physical tastes and postural habits – a predilection for a certain kind of food (Bourdieu and Wacquant, 1992), or a certain style of movement (Mauss, 1979; Sherlock, 1993). These are not superficial, voluntary alterations to our physique, but profound and often ineradicable differences in embodiment. Even our skeletons are shaped by society – in cultures where squatting is the normal form of repose, the kneecap becomes notched (Ingold, 1996). The non-western conceptualizations of health and illness as reflecting social rather than purely physiological processes can hence be seen to have a certain validity. For example, it seems plausible to attribute the epidemic of obesity-related health problems to a society in which physical exertion is no longer necessary and high-calorie food is ubiquitously promoted, rather than to individual bodily dysfunction or mental weakness.

However, the human body is not simply a passive object upon which socio-cultural practices impinge, but itself constitutes a powerful expression of social meaning and site of social negotiation and contest. The bodies of anorexics and drug addicts are living symbols of protest and despair, while acts such as illegal drug-taking can physically convey (perhaps more powerfully than words) contempt for social norms or regulations, assertion of autonomy, and even acceptance of mortality (Lupton, 1995). Indeed, the physical and social aspects of deviance are so closely intermixed that the two are often conflated. Lupton (1994) records that in the 1830s the victims of cholera epidemics were considered to have deliberately weakened their bodies by unseemly behaviour and vices, such as 'debauchery' and failure to observe the Sabbath. In contemporary society, physical self-harm contracted as a result of socially accepted activities, such as horse-riding, driving or overwork, is sanctioned as unfortunate accidental damage, whereas physical self-harm incurred as a result of less widely approved activities, such as boxing, smoking or unconventional sexual behaviour, tends to be viewed as predictable retribution. The rationale for this pattern of unequal blame is the dualist distinction between forces perceived either as external, physical, uncontrollable or as internal and voluntary, and so this partiality can be overcome by acknowledging that *all* bodily states have psychosocial as well as physical origins and implications.

New bodily conditions can arise as the socio-cultural and physical aspects of existence feed into one another. For instance, conflicting social pressures to eat and stay slim, together with the increasing 'medicalization' of diverse forms of behaviour, produce new eating 'disorders' such as bulimia. Similarly, repetitive strain injury may be created by the combination of muscular strain and the stress and ennui which often result from working on a factory assembly line (Hopkins, 1989). In the penultimate section of this chapter, I will illustrate a material-discursive approach to embodiment by considering how the contemporary experience of persistent disorientation can be viewed as the outcome of an interaction between the material and psychosocial attributes of the sufferer and his or her environment. This description of the origins and meaning of disorientation looks beyond dualist explanations in terms of mental or physical deficits, or some interaction between the two, and seeks particularly to understand how the material and social context affects the sufferer's activities.

A Material-discursive Analysis of Disorientation

While dualist analyses attempt to pinpoint unitary physical or psychosocial causes of disorientation in the individual or in the environment, disorientation actually results from a combination of the individual, their behaviour, and the context of their activities. Disorientation occurs whenever there appears to be ambiguity or incongruence in the perceptual information about orientation or self-motion detected by the visual, somatosensory and vestibular systems. Someone who feels disoriented is, by definition, uncertain about his or her relationship to the environment, and disorientation can thus *only* arise in the course of some kind of interaction between individuals and their surroundings. Without accurate knowledge of orientation it is impossible properly to control posture or accomplish any kind of coordinated activity, and so disorientation can lead to staggering or falling. The fear which can accompany this state of existential uncertainty about self–world relations has been compared with the 'primal terror' associated with early experiences of sexual or destructive urges (Shaffer, 1979).

Even if the disorientation is associated with physiological dysfunction, such as impairment of one of the vestibular organs, the activities of the individual are crucial to provocation and recovery. Following vestibular damage, acute symptoms of dizziness gradually subside as the brain becomes accustomed to the new pattern of signals generated by the damaged organ during routine head orientations and movements. However, as soon as the sufferer undertakes a less familiar movement, disorientation will again occur – until the brain also adjusts to this motion. Alternatively, disorientation may be provoked by some perceptually confusing attribute of the physical environment, such as the unusual vertical motion of the 'ground' on board a ship or in an elevator. But again, this is a matter of individual–environment interaction, since environments which may not be disorienting for most people can be disorienting for those with poor balance function. For instance, large-scale movement of the visual scene (for example at the cinema, or when watching passing traffic or moving crowds) can cause feelings of unsteadiness in people who have come to rely more on visual than vestibular input for balance.

Since activities and environments are central to the generation and amelioration of disorientation, then the psychosocial aspects of these activities and environments must clearly have an important influence on the experience of disorientation. The Cartesian emphasis on mental control of the body tends to inspire negative attitudes towards admissions of feeling unsteady or confused, and behaviour such as swaying and staggering. People prone to disorientation are very aware of these normative expectations for control, and consequently learn to fear particularly and avoid any situation in which their weakness might be betrayed (Yardley, 1994b). However, since experience of the movements and environments which provoke disorientation is essential in order to allow the brain to adjust to the perceptual input associated with these activities and situations, this strategy can actually prolong the sufferer's susceptibility to disorientation indefinitely.

Unfortunately, the dualist conceptualization of illness prevalent in western society tends to encourage this self-handicapping behaviour. According to the dualist biomedical model, a body which threatens the immaterial self, brutally interfering with the accomplishment of desired objectives, should ideally be controlled by the rational power of scientific medicine (Kirmayer, 1988). Both doctors and patients are therefore committed to a model of illness regulation in which the scientific expert takes responsibility for defining and managing the illness. In order to persuade doctors, family, friends and colleagues that they are 'really' ill, sufferers may also feel impelled to depict themselves as physically incapacitated, since admission of any psychological aspect to their condition might undermine its status as illness (Yardley and Beech, 1998). Moreover, the dualist model portrays the body as a machine, illness as physical malfunction, and disorientation as a sensation with no intrinsic meaning.

This theoretical framework cannot provide sufferers with the terms in which they might be able to make sense of their own experience of disorientation as an altered state of being which fundamentally transforms both their inner lives and their relationships to the physical and social world (Yardley, 1997c). The way in which sufferers typically reconcile this position of helplessness with society's requirement that they attempt to cope with their illness is therefore to avoid any theorizing concerning the problem, and simply try to conceal, avoid or suppress attacks of dizziness, and adopt the inactive, resigned role of the good patient (Yardley and Beech, 1998). This is not simply a matter of self-presentation or impression management – lacking the vocabulary and the opportunity to approach their illness in any other way, their experience is genuinely one of passive bewilderment.

It is interesting that in many of the modern constructed environments which people prone to disorientation find most problematic, the physical factors which provoke disorientation and social pressures to conceal it are combined in a pernicious fashion (Yardley, 1997c). Early analysts of modern capitalism, such as Walter Benjamin, have noted how modern spaces and technologies frequently produce both physical and social dislocation. Benjamin observed that forms of mass transport such as trains, and mass gatherings such as the world exhibitions and the Parisian arcades, created a new kind of social situation in which the individual becomes a passive body which is transported under the gaze of numerous strangers. The self-consciousness and alienation caused by proximity to strangers, together with the bright colours, constant movement and novelty, are designed to induce a heightened level of autonomic arousal, which may be experienced as either excitement or anxiety. Moreover, these situations are often characterized by unusual and perceptually disorienting spatial layouts or motions, produced by mirrors and split levels, escalators and lifts, rapid movement and flashing lights. It is therefore unsurprising that people who are vulnerable to disorientation often feel particularly uneasy in public places such as airports and shopping malls, or on underground railway systems and motorways.

From a material-discursive perspective, the experience of disorientation in modern western society can hence be understood not simply as the consequence of individual defects of mind or body, but as the product of contemporary circumstances. In previous eras, when human lives inevitably involved a great deal of physical activity just to gather food, collect water, and create warmth and shelter, the inactivity which deprives the balance system of the chance to adjust and recover would simply not be an option. Other key components of the modern experience of persistent disorientation – the exposure to disorienting situations while under scrutiny by strangers, the need to demonstrate control, the dilemma concerning the 'reality' of the disorientation, the compulsion to relegate all responsibility for defining and managing the problem to the scientific expertise of medicine – can be traced to our dualist western culture. The chronic impotence which is such an important feature of disorientation can therefore be viewed as a phenomenon which is perpetuated partly by the norms, beliefs, activities, institutions and environments which shape the physical and the psychosocial dimensions of sufferers' lives.

Beyond Dualism: Implications for Qualitative Health Research

As I mentioned at the outset of this chapter, it is perfectly possible – indeed it is not uncommon – for qualitative research to be conducted within a realist, dualist theoretical framework. But in such cases the use of qualitative methodology simply yields a more detailed and elaborate descriptive complement to quantitative research. In this chapter, I have attempted to outline some of the advantages to be gained from employing a non-dualist, non-realist qualitative approach. By relinquishing the unattainable ideal of an objective viewpoint, and recognizing that all views are from the per-spective of a particular, embodied situation, it is possible to overcome the Cartesian dualist bias towards over-privileging the supposedly pure and rational 'scientific' opinion. It then becomes clear that there is no single correct view of the world, and that phenomena genuinely have different meanings and implications for different people in different contexts. This respect for diverse opinions frees us to explore the value and significance of a variety of perspectives, thus enriching our own understanding of the topic of research. In addition, by abandoning the idea that individuals' minds are somehow isolated or independent from their embodied physical and social experiences and context, we can begin to appreciate how supposedly private mental phenomena – ideas, perceptions, intentions – are rooted in physical and social constraints and possibilities. At the same time, we can start to investigate the symbolic meanings and socio-cultural functions of physical states and actions, objects and procedures. And perhaps most importantly for health psychologists, we can begin to comprehend the material force and substantive implications of our conceptualizations and discussions of health and illness.

References

Averill, J.R. (1996) An analysis of psychophysiological symbolism and its influence on theories of emotion. In R. Harré and W.G. Parrott (eds), *The Emotions: Social, Cultural and Biological Dimensions*. London: Sage, pp. 204–288.

Berger, P.L. and Luckmann, T. (1966) *The Social Construction of Reality*. Penguin: London.

Bourdieu, P. and Wacquant, L.J.D. (1992) *An Invitation to Reflexive Sociology*. Cambridge: Polity Press.

Carrier, M. and Mittelstrass, J. (1995) *Mind, Brain, Behavior: The Mind–Body Problem and the Philosophy of Psychology*. New York: de Gruyter.

Clark, M.R., Sullivan, M.D., Fischl, M., Katon, W.J., Russo, J.E., Dobie, R.A. and Voorhees, R. (1994) Symptoms as a clue to otologic and psychiatric diagnosis in patients with dizziness. *Journal of Psychosomatic Research*, 38: 461–470.

Eagger, S., Luxon, L.M., Davies, R.A., Coelho, A. and Ron, M.A. (1992) Psychiatric morbidity in patients with peripheral vestibular disorder: a clinical and neuro-otological study. *Journal of Neurology, Neurosurgery and Psychiatry*, 55: 383–387.

Engel, G.L. (1982) The biopsychosocial model and medical education. *New England Journal of Medicine*, 306: 802–805.

Foucault, M. (1989) *The Birth of the Clinic*. London: Routledge.

Gaukroger, S. (1995) *Descartes: An Intellectual Biography*. Oxford: Clarendon Press.

Hallam, R.S. and Hinchcliffe, R. (1991) Emotional stability: its relationship to confidence in maintaining balance. *Journal of Psychosomatic Research*, 35: 421–430.

Hocutt, M. (1996) Behaviourism as opposition to Cartesianism. In W. O'Donohue and R.F. Kitchener (eds), *The Philosophy of Psychology*. London: Sage, pp. 81–95.

Hollinger, R. (1994) *Postmodernism and the Social Sciences*. London: Sage.

Hopkins, A. (1989) The social construction of repetitive strain injury. *Australian and New Zealand Journal of Sociology*, 25: 239–259.

Ibañez, T. (1994) Constructing a representation or representing a construction? *Theory and Psychology*, 4: 363–381.

Ingold, T. (1996) Situating action: the history and evolution of bodily skills. *Ecological Psychology*, 8: 171–182.

Kirmayer, L.J. (1988) Mind and body as metaphors: hidden values in biomedicine. In M. Lock and D.R. Gordon (eds), *Biomedicine Examined*. Dordrecht: Kluwer Academic, pp. 57–93.

Lakoff, G. (1987) *Women, Fire and Dangerous Things*. Chicago: University of Chicago Press.

Lakoff, G. and Johnson, M. (1980) *Metaphors We Live By*. Chicago: University of Chicago Press.

Leder, D. (1990) *The Absent Body*. Chicago: University of Chicago Press.

Leont'ev, A.N. (1978). *Activity, Consciousness and Personality*. Englewood Cliffs, NJ: Prentice Hall.

Lupton, D. (1994) *Medicine as Culture: Illness, Disease and the Body in Western Societies*. London: Sage.

Lupton, D. (1995) *The Imperative of Health: Public Health and the Regulated Body*. London: Sage.

Maturana, H.R. and Varela, F.J. (1987) *The Tree of Knowledge: the Biological Roots of Human Understanding*. London: New Science Library.

Mauss, M. (1979) *Sociology and Psychology Essays*. London: Routledge.

Pollock, K. (1993) Attitude of mind as a means of resisting illness. In A. Radley (ed.), *Worlds of Illness*. London: Routledge, pp. 49–70.

Potter, W.J. (1996) *An Analysis of Thinking and Research about Qualitative Methods*. Mahwah, NJ: Lawrence Erlbaum.

Pratt, R.T.C. and McKenzie, W. (1958) Anxiety states following vestibular disorders. *Lancet*, 2: 347–349.

Sampson, E.E. (1993) Identity politics: challenges to psychology's understanding. *American Psychologist*, 12: 1219–1230.

Shaffer, M. (1979) Primal terror: a perspective of vestibular dysfunction. *Journal of Learning Disabilities*, 12: 89–92.

Sherlock, J. (1993) Dance and the culture of the body. In S. Scott and D. Morgan (eds), *Body Matters: Essays on the Sociology of the Body*. London: Falmer Press, pp. 35–48.

Stam, H.J. (1988) The practice of health psychology and behavioral medicine: whither theory? In W.J. Baker, L.P. Mos, H.V. Rappard, and H.J. Stam (eds), *Recent Trends in Theoretical Psychology*. New York: Springer-Verlag, pp. 313–325.

Sullivan, M., Clark, M.R., Katon, W.J., Fischl, M., Russo, J., Dobie, R.A. and

Voorhees, R. (1993) Psychiatric and otologic diagnoses in patients complaining of dizziness. *Annals of Internal Medicine*, 153: 1479–1484.

Wilkinson, R.G. (1996) *Unhealthy Societies: The Afflictions of Inequality*. London: Routledge.

Yardley, L. (1994a) *Vertigo and Dizziness*. London: Routledge.

Yardley, L. (1994b) Contribution of symptoms and beliefs to handicap in people with vertigo: a longitudinal study. *British Journal of Clinical Psychology*, 33: 101–113.

Yardley, L. (1996) Reconciling discursive and materialist perspectives on the psychology of health and illness: a re-construction of the biopsychosocial approach. *Theory and Psychology*, 6: 485–508.

Yardley, L. (ed.) (1997a) *Material Discourses of Health and Illness*. London: Routledge.

Yardley, L. (1997b) The quest for natural communication: language, technology and deafness. *Health*, 1: 37–56.

Yardley, L. (1997c) Disorientation in the (post) modern world. In L. Yardley (ed.), *Material Discourses of Health and Illness*. London: Routledge, pp. 109–131.

Yardley, L. and Beech, S. (1998) 'I'm not a doctor': deconstructing accounts of coping, causes and control of dizziness. *Journal of Health Psychology*, 3: 313–327.

Yardley, L., Masson, E., Verschuur, C., Luxon, L. and Haacke, N.P. (1992) Symptoms, anxiety and handicap in dizzy patients: development of the Vertigo Symptom Scale. *Journal for Psychosomatic Research*, 36: 731–741.

4

The Storied Nature of Health and Illness

Michael Murray

If poets' verses be but stories
So be food and raiment stories;
So is all the world a story;
So is man of dust a story.

> St Columba (sixth century)

According to narrative psychology (for example Sarbin, 1986; Mair, 1989) we are all storytellers and we live in a storied world. Narratives or stories permeate our everyday life such that we interpret the world and define ourselves through stories. The past decade has seen an increased interest among a wide range of social scientists in the use of narrative as an analytic and interpretive framework (for example Plummer, 1995; Polkinghorne, 1988). Admittedly, the study of narrative has a substantial history within psychology although its potential within health psychology has yet to be developed (Murray, 1997a). In this chapter, the aim is to introduce some of the philosophical and literary background to the use of the concept of narrative. In particular, the work of the hermeneutic philosopher Paul Ricoeur and the literary critic Peter Brooks will be considered. Their ideas will be used to explore a range of examples taken from various contexts.

Time and Narrative

Paul Ricoeur, who describes his work as philosophical anthropology, has made an immense contribution to our understanding of narrative particularly through his three-volume work entitled *Time and Narrative* (Ricoeur, 1984a, 1985, 1988). Even for the trained philosopher this can be a difficult work (Reagan, 1996), mixing analytic philosophy with French and German literary theory and historiography. Fortunately, he has also written a large number of more concise articles which have been collected (for example Valdes, 1991) and to which I will mostly refer.

We can begin with reference to Ricoeur's discussion of time as one of the defining characteristics of life. All around us things come into being, exist and then fade away. We ourselves exist in chronological time – we are born, we live and we die. We cannot separate ourselves from time. Since the essence of time is its changeability how can we capture and describe it? This was the philosophical conundrum posed by Saint Augustine. 'What then is time?' he asked. 'I know well enough what it is, provided that nobody asks me; but if I am asked what it is and try to explain, I am baffled' (cited in Ricoeur, 1984a: 7). Ricoeur suggests that narrative provides a means of overcoming this problem. It is the process by which we organize our experience of time. Prior to narrative there is no sense of order. Narrative organizes and in doing so gives time meaning. Time and narrative are interwoven. 'Time becomes human to the extent that it is articulated through a narrative mode, and narrative attains its full meaning when it becomes a condition of temporal existence' (Ricoeur, 1984a: 52).

Ricoeur contrasts the disorder of Augustine's definition of time with the order provided by Aristotle's concept of *muthos* or emplotment which brings order to our interpretation of the constantly changing world. Whereas life consists of a myriad of events which occur over time and which may often be conflictual and contradictory, narrative brings a sense of order. This is the contrast between 'the discordance of time (*temps*) and the concordance of the tale (*récit*)' (Ricoeur, 1984b: 466). Admittedly, concord is never completely achieved since time does not stop. Rather the tension between order and disorder is part of life. We are always encountering new situations that require us to reassess our storyline. In particular, life crises, such as the onset or diagnosis of an illness, can become turning points when we begin to reassess who we are and where we are going.

Much of health psychology has ignored the temporal nature of health and illness. Certain forms of qualitative research have also ignored this central characteristic preferring to abstract pieces of text/discourse from both their social and temporal context.[1] This is contrary to the narrative approach which 'does not fragment the text into discrete content categories for coding purposes but, instead, identifies longer stretches of talk that take the form of narrative – a discourse organized around time and consequential events in a "world" recreated by the narrator' (Riessman, 1990: 1195). This means not only allowing the research participants to tell their stories, but also ensuring that the researcher does not then proceed to dismember them.

The central process in narrative is emplotment. This is the process by which we derive 'a configuration from a succession' (Ricoeur, 1987: 427). Emplotment provides order and meaning to the previous chaotic flow of events. It is the 'synthesis of heterogenous elements' (ibid.: 426); the process by which 'we provide "shape" to what remains chaotic, obscure, and mute' (Ricoeur, 1979: 115). Emplotment is not a finished event but an ongoing process. As new information arises the plot is accordingly adjusted.

Reading for the Plot

The basic modernist narrative has a beginning, a middle and an end. The beginning introduces the participants, the middle describes the main action sequences and the end describes the consequences. Admittedly there are many twists and turns in this basic structure. The literary critic Northrop Frye (1957), who actually coined the term emplotment in his review of fictional plots, identified four archetypal plot structures, namely comedy, romance, tragedy and satire. Although these were derived from an analysis of literary texts they have wider currency. Kevin Murray (1985) has discussed the application of these plots in everyday life. He argues that, at least in terms of Goffman's (1959) dramaturgical perspective, these plots can not only apply to the actions of actors in the theatre but to humans in everyday action. When there are dramatic occasions in our lives the salience of such plot lines becomes more apparent. For example, in discussing the sudden death of Princess Diana it was commonplace to talk about a tragedy. In their commentaries people frequently made reference to classic narrative plots in which different members of the Royal Family were cast in the roles of heroes or villains. Earl Spencer's speech in Westminster was compared with that of Mark Antony in Shakespeare's *Julius Caesar*. Indeed, the very setting of his speech encouraged the television viewer to make these connections.

There is substantial interweaving of literary imagery and everyday life such that we frequently make reference to such images and plots to help understand our world. Plummer (1995), in his discussion of sexual narratives, describes how publicly told stories, such as those told through television, films, newspapers and magazines, feed back into everyday discourse such that people begin to define themselves and their lives with reference to these public stories. The narratives move from the level of the personal to that of the public and political, and back to that of the personal.

Peter Brooks has explored further the nature of the plot both within fiction and everyday life. Probably his most influential work is *Reading for the Plot: Design and Intention in Narrative* (Brooks, 1984). In this he argues that the creation and exchange of narrative is an intrinsic feature of the human condition. He describes the human as 'a fiction-making animal, one defined by fantasies and fictions' (Brooks, 1994: 108). That is, we both create narratives and are created by them. Narratives are part of our very being since 'the structure of literature is in some sense the structure of mind' (ibid.: 24). We cannot avoid this interpenetration since the temporal nature of life requires that we organize our interpretation of the world in narrative form. In everyday conversation we make use of literary terms. For example, not only do we tell stories but we also open and close chapters and turn over new pages. Brooks went further in examining the connections between literature and psychoanalysis. Both can be considered as forms of narrative which have a central role in providing meaningful order to the 'flux of temporal existence' (Rickard and Schweizer, 1994). This narrative re-reading of psychoanalysis rescues it from the mechanistic interpretations which have been more commonplace (see also Schaffer, 1992). Subsequently, we can see the value of this re-reading for a narrative understanding of illness.

Although the bringing of order to disorder is implicit in narrative construction, in the late modern era there is a cynicism about the degree of closure which the plot can attain. As Brooks argues: 'we have, in a sense, become too sophisticated as readers of plot quite to believe in its orderings' (1984: 314). Despite this scepticism there is still a need for meaning which the even partially completed narrative can provide. We can still obtain meaning through narrative although we may maintain suspicions as regards the adequacy of our interpretation. Indeed, it could be argued that it is this unfinishedness which is part of the character of our era – this difficulty of reaching agreement about the nature of reality.

We not only arrange events in the narrative but we also assign different values to the same events. Events which were inconsequential or almost forgotten can assume central importance and, conversely, events which were at one time perceived as important can be relegated. Which events are recalled and which story is told depends upon a variety of factors. These factors include who is telling the story, why the story is being told at that particular moment, where and to whom it is being told, and what medium is being used to convey the story (Murray, 1997b). Some of these factors will be considered further in our exploration of illness narratives.

Illness and Narrative

Health and illness are part of life and hence exist in time. They are not static elements which can be extracted from time but are in constant flux. Let us consider an example. In August 1989, Anatole Broyard, an editor of the *New York Times Book Review*, was diagnosed with prostate cancer. The initial prognosis was positive and the medication he received seemed to be controlling the cancer. He continued to write his book reviews and articles including one entitled 'Intoxicated by my illness'. In this article he describes his reaction to the disease. In April 1990 he gave a talk at Chicago Medical School describing his experience. A revised version of this talk was published as two articles entitled 'Toward a literature of illness' and 'The patient examines the doctor'. Subsequently he began to deteriorate physically. Despite the nausea he experienced as a result of the medication he continued his writing until shortly before he died in October 1990. These later writings were more journal entries than coherent narratives. His writings were subsequently collected by his wife and published with an introduction by Oliver Sacks in 1992. His short account of his illness provides a fascinating example of the role of narrative in making sense of illness.

In Broyard's case the disease was life-threatening. The diagnosis of cancer led him to a meditation on time: 'I realized for the first time that I don't have forever. Time was no longer innocuous, nothing was casual anymore' (1992: 4). He recalled the disconnectedness of his initial experience of cancer. Indeed, it was an attempt to remove this disconnectedness and the associated distress that drove him to transform it into a narrative. In 'Toward a literature of illness' he describes how he strove to make sense of his existential crisis:

> My initial experience of illness was a series of disconnected shocks, and my first instinct was to bring it under control by turning it into a narrative. Always in emergencies we invent narratives. We describe what is happening, as if to confine the catastrophe . . . story telling seems to be a natural reaction to illness. People bleed stories, and I've become a blood bank of them. (1992: 19)

Admittedly, Broyard was a literary critic and attuned to narrative concepts. He was also writing for a literary audience, many of whom were familiar with his earlier work. His account needs to be read with reference to this context. However, the less literary-minded person also has recourse to narrative to grasp the meaning of illness.

Let us take another example. This one is an account of the experience of Lupus provided by a woman we will call June. A large part of this account describes her repeated visits to a series of specialists all of whom suggested that there was nothing wrong with her and indeed that her complaint was psychological in nature. Finally, she was diagnosed with Lupus. Although she recognized the serious nature of the disease, obtaining the diagnosis was a relief: 'I felt as if a load was lifted from me.' In June's narrative the diagnosis was a turning point. Her narrative revolved around this point. Now she was diagnosed as having Lupus she recounted her life with reference to this diagnosis. In that sense, it was partly the end which determined the structure of the story. June described her earlier life especially her family life. She had had a drunken and abusive husband who provided her with little support in raising six children. One of her daughters miscarried and she felt very distressed. It was after the miscarriage that she began to experience a range of symptoms which were eventually diagnosed as Lupus. Tying these events together, she stated: 'I honestly feel that my Lupus was stress-induced.'

From the present, after the diagnosis of Lupus, June created a narrative. Although she did not make explicit reference to narrative terms, her account was narrative in the way she linked together the various experiences early in her life with her current condition and the prospects she perceived for the future. The family problems she had endured now assumed a new importance as the cause of her disease. Her life had been transformed by the diagnosis. She was now a Lupus patient. She attended meetings of the support group and discussed ways of helping fellow patients. Admittedly, her narrative was unfinished in the sense that her prognosis was uncertain.

Good and DelVecchio Good (1994), in their study of Turkish people with epilepsy, also commented on the unfinished nature of their narrative accounts. When a disease is chronic its future character remains uncertain. For this reason, they described their narrators as being 'situated in the midst of the accounts. Endings were often hypothetical; outcomes which were feared were juxtaposed against those desperately hoped for. Beginnings and previous experiences were subject to re-evaluation, as events unfolded, revealing the nature of the illness and its response to treatment' (Good and DelVecchio Good, 1994: 837).

Despite the variability and apparent contradictory nature of these epilepsy narratives, Good and DelVecchio Good felt they provided psychological order through 'subjunctivizing reality'. This is a term taken from Bruner (1986) to describe the process whereby the author draws the reader into the indeterminacy of reality and suggests alternative endings. Good and DelVecchio Good identified several subjunctivizing elements in their stories. The first was the use of multiple perspectives which provided the potential for multiple readings. 'Each story casts doubt on the others, or provides a potential alternative interpretation of the illness and of other stories about it. New experiences call for reinterpretation of past experiences and suggest new possibilities for the future, in life as in reading' (1994: 839). The second subjunctivizing element was the use of stories which included reference to encounters with the mysterious. These stories offer the hope that mysterious alternative forces exist which may provide healing. Although the medical establishment may offer little hope, there was always the prospect of recovery through the intervention of these other non-scientific forces.

Besides uncertainty and conflicts in her story about the future, June's illness narrative also contained conflicting elements about her past. Initially, her story was bound up with personal crises and conflict with the medical establishment. She recalled that she began to question her sanity. She entertained a variety of conflicting plots:

> I've seen more doctors in the past years. I've been told it's my nerves, my age, menopause, its all in my head, yet I was feeling sicker all the time. I kept thinking this must be how one feels in the late 50s or early 60s.

But now that she had the diagnosis she was able to reorder her life-history and her self-definition. She was a woman who, despite the disease or even because of the disease, was beginning to assert control over her life. Where previously there had been disorder and a sense of confusion about self, the diagnosis allowed her to develop a more coherent narrative and sense of self.

These examples are of individuals who were still in the midst of their illnesses. Murray (1997b) reported an analysis of a selection of the published accounts of women whose illness was behind them, at least in medical terms. These were the narratives of women who had had breast cancer. These women explicitly referred to the disorganization of their lives they had experienced as a result of having had cancer and how the writing of their narratives was a means of restoring order. Some of the women referred to this ability to consign disorder and confusion to the past. For example, Betty Rollins (1976: vii) says: 'I wrote it to make myself seem better, to tidy up the mess in my head and it worked. When I was done I felt right side up again, different than before, but okay – in some ways better'. The very process of constructing the narrative enabled these women to, as it were, move forward.

These women's accounts had a progressive rather than a regressive or a stable structure (Gergen and Gergen, 1986). The beginning described their lives before the diagnosis of cancer. In describing this phase the women emphasized the carefree nature and innocence of their lives. This section closed with the diagnosis of cancer and the initial reactions of the women. The middle portion of their accounts focused on the medical treatment and the final portion concerned their current situation. In writing these accounts the women were constructing them from the end to the beginning. They had survived cancer and now they were recasting their lives with reference to this success. Looking back, the women select and order the incidents from their past. Mark Freeman (1993) distinguished between a chronicle of past events and a history. Whereas the former is simply a listing of past events, the latter requires the narrative reconstruction of those events. He reflects on the word 'recollection': 'while the "re" makes reference to the past, "collection" makes reference to a present act, an act . . . of gathering together what might have been dispersed or lost' (p. 47). The narrator organizes the narrative from a particular moment in time. Similarly, Cheryl Mattingly in her discussion of illness narratives dwells on the selective and organizing nature of narrative. She says (1994: 812): 'When we tell stories, we intensify and clarify the plot structure of events as lived, eliminating events that, in retrospect, are not important to the development of that plot – which do not, as we say, contribute to the ending'. This process of selection and organization is done from the present and within a certain social context. In the case of the women who had had breast cancer the fear and anguish which they felt at initial diagnosis is placed firmly in the past. Instead they emphasize the positive features of having had cancer.

Illness gains meaning through the stories we tell about it. On diagnosis, during its course, and after the illness has ended or at least subsided, we attempt to bring order to the crisis by constructing a story. This story integrates material from our life history with information about the current situation and future prospects. It is a dynamic construction which is rooted in the social and cultural context.

Telling Stories

Narratives do not, as it were, spring from the minds of individuals but are social creations. We are born into a culture which has a ready stock of narratives which we appropriate and apply in our everyday social interaction. Ricoeur recognized this: 'There can be no praxis which is not already symbolically structured in some way. Human action is always figured in signs, interpreted in terms of cultural traditions and norms. Our narrative fictions are then added to this primary interpretation of figuration of human action; so that narrative is a redefining of what is already defined, a reinterpretation of what is already interpreted' (1984b: 469).

Narratives are situated and created within both the broader socio-cultural and more immediate interpersonal context. They cannot be abstracted from this context. Recent investigators of language have empha-sized its social nature. Markova (1990), in her critique of traditional linguistic analysis, characterized it as 'monologism'. She emphasized the communicative nature of language, the sense of which cannot be abstracted from its expressive context.[2] Similarly, Burkitt (1996) and Wortham (1996) in their critique of Mancuso's (1996) discussion of personal construct psychology emphasized the social context of construing. Burkitt stressed the importance of the broader socio-cultural context within which personal constructs are developed. He noted that 'the persons who construe are themselves constructs of a broader cultural and historical system and are locked in the interdependence of joint discursive practice' (1996: 72).

Much previous work on health beliefs has failed to consider the social and cultural context within which they are embedded. Garro (1994), in her study of the stories people with temporomandibular joint (TMJ) disorder used to describe their condition, noted how people relate their individual accounts to broader cultural and shared models. The people she inter-viewed used a similar narrative framework to characterize their illness. In attempting to make sense of their illness people draw upon broader, culturally-shared narratives. In western society, the dominant biomedical narrative is infused with a message of success, of an ability to cure. DelVecchio Good et al. (1994) have described how American oncologists have a cultural mandate to encourage a narrative of hope in their engage-ment with their patients. They achieve this by focusing on the immediate treatment plan rather than on the longer term and through this encourage the patient to invest energy in frequently arduous treatment programmes. Popular medical books are also filled with this message of hope. Broyard commented on the popular books by Norman Cousins who, he says, 'advises the patient to regard the diagnosis of critical illness not as a threat or a prophecy but as a challenge' (1992: 16). Naturally, in particular cases this optimistic narrative can jar with the evidence that medical intervention is failing.

The telling of stories is not only influenced by but also contributes to a social representation about a particular disease. This is illustrated in the work of Farmer (1994). In the early 1980s, he conducted interviews about AIDS with residents of a Haitian community. Initially, there was little evidence of a shared representation of the disease. However, in the following years this silence gave way to considerable discussion as actual contact with individuals who had the disease increased. Informants began to recount specific stories about individuals who had died of AIDS. Increasingly there was evidence of a sharing of these stories which

Farmer took as an indication of the development of a collective model of AIDS. In an earlier study in Ireland, we (Murray and McMillan, 1988) found evidence of a similar sharing of stories about cancer in interviews we conducted with people about that disease. Frequently, they referred to similar stories of people who had either died of the disease or had survived. These stories were drawn both from their immediate community and from the national media illustrating how both local and national stories combine in shaping a community's representation of a disease.

Narratives are also constructed in an interpersonal context. There has been much debate recently about the frequent ignorance of the inter-personal context in psychological research. Leudar and Antaki (1996) have suggested the use of Goffman's (1979) concept of 'footing' as a means of discussing how the different participants in a research project occupy shifting positions which need to be taken into consideration. This is an important point which emphasizes the social and active nature of discourse and, in our case, of narrative telling. In telling their stories, the narrators shape their narratives to their audience. For example, they can exaggerate certain aspects and downplay certain other aspects. Thus the sick person will tell one version of a story about illness to one person and another to a different person. In the same way, Cornwell (1984) distinguished between public and private accounts of illness, the character of which depend upon the interpersonal context in which they are produced. Radley and Billig have provided an extended commentary on interpersonal contexts within which stories are told. They raise the important point of the health status of the interviewer in the research study. Since the interviewer is usually healthy the sick interviewee feels 'the need to legitimate [their] position'. The stories are generated in 'a rhetorical context of justification and criticism' (1996: 226; see Chapter 2 for more detail).

Brooks (1994), in his narrative re-reading of psychoanalysis, focuses on the dialogic nature of the analyst–analysand interaction. While originally Freud was concerned with extracting, almost like a dental surgeon, the supposed psychic cause of the analysand's distress which was revealed during analysis, subsequently he began to consider the dialogic character of the narrative constructed in the interaction. In his 'Constructions in analysis' Freud (1937) writes: 'The analyst finishes a piece of construction and communicates it to the subject of analysis so that it may work on him; he then constructs a further piece out of the fresh material pouring in on him, deals with it in the same way and proceeds in this alternating fashion until the end' (cited in Brooks, 1994: 56). The analyst is not a passive observer or listener but someone who plays an active role in the thera-peutic session. He engages with the analysand who develops his narrative account within that context.

The character of the relationship between the two partners in the dialogue is of vital importance. Brooks adds: 'the relation of teller to listener inherently is part of the structure and the meaning of any narrative text, since such a text (like any text) exists only insofar as it is transmitted, insofar as it becomes part of a process of exchange' (1984: 50). Both partners have a particular perspective which they want to advance. In telling his or her story, the storyteller is conveying a particular viewpoint and trying to convince the other of that viewpoint. For example, Broyard states: 'Like a convert who's had a vision, I wanted to preach it, to tell people what a serious illness is' (1992: 21). The story told not only conveys a message about the person and the disease but also reflects the context within which it is told. Patients will tell one story to their partners and, in some ways, another to their physician.

Reading Stories

Stories are not only told but they are heard or read. The process of reading is not a passive process but an active one. As Ricoeur says: 'the process of composition, of configuration, is not completed in the text but in the reader and, under this condition, makes possible the reconfiguration of life by narrative' (1991: 25). Thus the listener transforms the story told. This is an important issue for researchers. Although the research participant may tell a particular story, which s/he may or may not agree with subsequently, the researcher then has to interpret that story. We can distinguish the process of interpretation from the more traditional process of explanation. Whereas explanation as proposed by positivist scientists is the result of a supposed objective assessment of the information available, 'interpretation has specific subjective implications, such as the involvement of the reader in the process of understanding and the reciprocity between text-interpretation and self-interpretation. This reciprocity is usually known as the hermeneutical circle' (Ricoeur, 1974: 303).

Interpretation of the narrative requires the process of appropriation which Ricoeur (1972: 89) defines as the ability 'to make one's own what was initially "alien"'. He borrows from the hermeneutic philosopher Hans-Georg Gadamer the concept of play to explore further the process of appropriation. 'We play with a project, with an idea; we can equally "be played". What is essential is the "to and fro" of play. Play is thereby close to dance, which is a movement that carries away the dancer' (ibid.: 90).

Monica Rudberg has used this analogy to help her understand the process of interpreting young people's accounts of their relationships. 'The text invites one to dance – which means that the interpreter is both actively involved as well as responding to the movements of the partner – the dance has a logic of its own, you are not just dancing, you are danced with.' Further, she adds that 'just like dancing, any interpretation of a text involves being seduced into following the text itself'. Of course, the researcher has to be careful not to be taken in by fantastic tales. 'It is in the dialectics between "letting go" and "holding on" that interpretation works' (1997: 8).

Through the process of appropriation the researcher comes to know more not just about the research participant but also about herself. Admittedly, the more convincing narrators will be able to transport the reader more easily into their worlds. In everyday life we can often be taken in by fantastic tales which are told by convincing narrators. It is the task of the critical reader to challenge such tales. It is for this reason that Ricoeur (1972) talks of the 'hermeneutics of suspicion'. A critical reading requires a constant process of checking the adequacy of the story told.

No matter how sophisticated the narrator, s/he does not provide all the details of any event but merely an outline. The reader needs to make sense of that outline. As Brooks writes: 'The process of listening to a story or reading a text is essentially constructive, a filling-in of gaps, a building of fragments into a coherent whole: a conquest of the non-narrative by the narrative, of non-sense by the semantic' (1994: 57). The reader must enter into the narrative if s/he is to understand it. Unlike the traditional positivist reading of texts which tends to impose a fixed model, the critical reader engages with the text. Brooks suggests that we

> think in terms of an interference of two systems, where you start from two different places, one in the literary text, the other in theoretical considerations, and try to see what their merger looks like, and what happens as they start to contaminate one another, as you create a sort of effect of superimposition of one on the other (and vice versa), which is what I try to do particularly in the use of psychoanalysis. (ibid.: 105–106)

But what then is the standing of competing narratives? What criteria can we use to judge the value of one story over another? Consider the everyday situation where you are presented with competing narratives. In assessing the narratives you consider such contextual factors as who is telling the tale, to whom and why (see Murray, 1997b). You also consider to what extent the narrative not only 'fits' with what you already know about the issue but provides you with increased insight. It was these issues that led Brooks to describe narrative truth as

> a matter of conviction, derived from the plausibility and well-formedness of the narrative discourse, and also from what we might call its force, its power to create further patterns of connectedness, its power to persuade us that things must have happened this way, since here lies the only explanatory narrative, the only one that will make sense of things. (1994: 59)

As an alternative to a positive truth Brooks proposes a transferential truth which emphasizes the process of negotiation and exchange within the dialogue. 'The truth of narrative is situational, the work of truth reciprocal. Wisdom comes from conviction, however you construct it' (p. 101).

Narrative and Life

A recurring question is whether human life, health and illness exist outside of narrative and whether narratives can be lived as well as told. Ricoeur argues that 'a life is no more than a biological phenomenon as long as it has not been interpreted' (1987: 432). We can never have access to life except through narrative. While we can refer in an abstract sense to the pre-narrative quality of human experience, once we begin to think and talk about it we transform it through narrative. We live in a material world but it is one which we must interpret. Admittedly, it could be argued, as does Ricoeur, that the world already has a type of structure which we organize into a narrative. He writes that 'the configuration effected by narrative is not grafted onto something figureless, faceless, but upon a life in which narration structure is "prefigured"' (Ricoeur, 1984a: 87). Admittedly, we can tell fantastic stories which have no connection with reality, but it is the task of the reader to distinguish between fantastic and realistic accounts although the distinction can often blur.

Although life and narrative remain distinct, they interpenetrate. Ricoeur argues that the distinction 'is in part, abolished through our capacity to appropriate in the application to ourselves the intrigues we received from our culture, and our capacity of thus experimenting with the various roles that the favourite personae assume in the stories we love best' (ibid.: 437). Life and narrative are closely intertwined. While we live lives we simultaneously live within narratives although we may not be aware of these. As we previously mentioned we can take on the personae of the characters we read about or have heard about.

Narrative is constructed within a personal and social context. It not only draws meaning from that context but dialectically gives meaning to it. While disease exists in physical terms we interpret and transform it through narrative (see Sedgwick, 1982). Narrative makes sense of disease within a personal and social context. It gives disease a personal history and places it within a particular social order. Consider how Broyard constructed his personal history of prostate cancer:

> It's not unusual for the patient to think that it's sex that is killing him and to go back over his amatory history for clues. And of course this is splendid material for speculation, both lyrical and ironical. My first reaction to having cancer was lyrical – irony comes later. . . . I'm tempted to single out particular women and particular practices that strike me now as more likely to be carcinogenic than others. (1992: 26)

In telling his personal story Broyard is projecting a certain image of himself to his audience. Human identity is not something which is fixed but something which is created and recreated through the very process of narration. The sense of identity which defines the individual is derived from the very process of story-telling. As Ricoeur states: 'it is by trying to put order on our past, by retelling and recounting what has been, that we acquire an identity' (1984b: 467).

Although such an identity has a certain constancy it is not fixed. This is because 'we do not cease to re-interpret the narrative identity that constitutes us in the light of stories handed down to us by our culture' (Ricoeur,

1987: 437). One problem which emerges here revolves around the change-ability or variability of narrative identity (see Gergen, 1991). Does this imply that we are simply storytellers but have no fixed viewpoint? Riessman (1990) makes a similar point with reference to the lack of self in Goffman's (1959) concept of impression management in social situations. If we can always change our story to match the situation then what is left behind the mask? However, this is to abstract the individual from the context. The two remain in constant interaction. Not only are we social beings but all stories emerge in dialogue. At all times they convey a certain image of the narrator. For example, the women with breast cancer in recounting their cancer stories convey an image of themselves as women who were not, as it were, defeated by cancer. Rather they were women who 'defeated' cancer, at least temporarily. The essence of the person lies in this social engagement.[3]

Admittedly, in telling our stories certain metanarratives have greater power than others. Ricoeur (1987) refers in particular to the role of literary, scientific and political modes of representation. These different modes of narration condition the way we think about life such that 'we learn to become the narrator of our own story without completely becoming the author of our life' (p. 437). This proposal allows the maintenance of a sense of personal identity and selfhood but one which is situated within social discourse. When Brooks states: 'We constitute ourselves as human subjects in part through our fictions' (1994: 36) he was talking about the role of literature in our society. But we can add, it is also through the everyday exchange of stories by real living beings that we reaffirm our humanity and individuality.

Narrative, Health and Illness

While health and illness exist outside narrative we can only begin to under-stand them through narrative. Admittedly, certain illness narratives could be described as more healthy than others. Indeed, it is through narrative reconstruction that the personal character of illness can be changed. Consider the classic case history of Dora which was reported by Freud (1905) in his 'Fragment of an analysis of a case of hysteria'. This case illustrates the centrality of narrative within the therapeutic process. At the outset Freud asks Dora to tell him 'the whole story of his life and illness'. Instead, he receives a confusing mixture of information which lacks any clear structure. Freud writes: 'The connections – even the ostensible ones – are for the most part incoherent, and the sequence of different events is uncertain. . . . The patients' inability to give an ordered history of their life in so far as it coincides with the history of their illness is not merely characteristic of the neurosis. It also possesses great theoretical signifi-cance.' Freud argues that it is through therapy that these discontinuities are sorted out such that 'it is only toward the end of the treatment that we have before us an intelligible, consistent, and unbroken case history' (in Brooks, 1994: 48). It is through the process of constructing a more ordered narrative that the analysand begins to improve psychologically. Brooks summarizes this argument as follows: 'Mens sana in fabula sana: mental health is a coherent life story, neurosis is a faulty narrative' (ibid.: 49).

Ricoeur also comments specifically on the narrative character of psycho-analysis. He considers 'the client who turns to a psychoanalyst to present him with bits of lived histories, dreams, "primitive scenes", conflicting episodes; one can indeed say that the goal and effect of the analytic sessions is that the person analyzed draws out from these bits and pieces a story that is both intelligible and more bearable' (1987: 435). It is this disconnectedness to which Broyard referred which is the source of psy-chological distress. It is through the creation of a more coherent and non-threatening narrative that this distress can be alleviated. Broyard felt that the ability to transform his experience into narrative was beneficial: 'Just as a novelist turns his anxiety into a story in order to be able to control it to a degree, so a sick person can make a story, a narrative, out of his illness as a way of trying to detoxify it' (1992: 21). Broyard continued that, at least in phenomenological terms, the construction of a narrative account brought order and meaning to the illness. It rescued him 'from what Ernest Becker called "the panic inherent in creation" or "the suction of infinity"' (ibid: 20–21).

Through narrative the sick person begins to bring order to time. Broyard continues:

> all cures are partly 'talking cures,' in Freud's phrase. Every patient needs mouth-to-mouth resuscitation, for talk is the kiss of life. Besides talking himself, the doctor ought to bleed the patient of talk, of the consciousness of his illness, as earlier physicians used to bleed their patients to let out heat or dangerous humors. (ibid.: 54)

Admittedly, the individual does not require analysis to obtain the thera-peutic benefits of narrative. This can occur in everyday social interaction as we exchange and revise narrative accounts (Murray, 1997a).

This does not mean that narrative offers the promise of some miracle cure to disease. Rather it can be transformed psychologically. Broyard illustrates this process vividly. He recalls the autobiography of the British psychoanalyst D.W. Winnicott which begins with the statement 'I died', and then continues five lines later with 'Let me see. What was happening when I died? My prayer had been answered. I was alive when I died. That was all I had asked and I had got it.' Broyard continues: 'Though he never finished his book, he gave the best reason for writing one, and that's why I want to write mine – to make sure I'll be alive when I die' (1992: 30). It was narrative which gave his life coherence and the creation of narrative which maintained his hold on life. Conversely, as Robinson (1990) found in his study of the written narratives of patients with MS, people can be said to be dead before they physically die. Their story has ended. While these examples may seem melodramatic, they illustrate the linkage between narrative, illness and life. We are narrative beings. The stories we tell or are encouraged to tell can be either life-enhancing or threatening. Through qualitative research health psychology can begin to understand the character and evolution of the various narratives which we use to order illness in our societies.

Acknowledgements

Thanks to Ed Drodge and Peter Trnka for their critical comments on an earlier version of this chapter.

Notes

1. Admittedly, many medical sociologists and anthropologists have adopted temporal and narrative perspectives in their studies of health and illness (for example Becker, 1997; Charmaz, 1991; Frank, 1995).
   2. I was reminded of this when reading the article by Paula Nicolson (1999).
   3. This leads into discussion of the dialogical self. The interested reader should consider Bakhtin (1981), Hermans, Kempen and van Loon (1992) and Shotter (1993).

References

Bakhtin, M.M. (1981) *The Dialogical Imagination*. Austin, TX: University of Texas Press.

Becker, G. (1997) *Disrupted Lives: How People Create Meaning in a Chaotic World*. Berkeley, CA: University of California Press.

Brooks, P. (1984) *Reading for the Plot: Design and Intention in Narrative*. New York: Alfred A. Knopf.

Brooks, P. (1994) *Psychoanalysis and Storytelling*. Oxford: Blackwell.

Broyard, A. (1992) *Intoxicated by my Illness and Other Writings on Life and Death*. New York: Fawcett Columbine.

Bruner, J. (1986) *Actual Minds: Possible Worlds*. Cambridge, MA: Harvard University Press.

Burkitt, I. (1996) Social and personal constructs: a division left unresolved. *Theory and Psychology*, 6: 71–77.

Charmaz, K.C. (1991) *Good Days, Bad Days: The Self in Chronic Illness and Time*. New Brunswick, NJ: Rutgers University Press.

Cornwell, J. (1984) *Hard-earned Lives: Accounts of Health and Illness from East London*. London: Tavistock.

DelVecchio Good, M.-J., Munakata, T., Kobayashi, Y., Mattingly, C. and Good, B.J. (1994) Oncology and narrative time. *Social Science and Medicine*, 38: 855–862.

Farmer, A. (1994) AIDS-talk and the constitution of cultural models. *Social Science and Medicine*, 38: 801–810.

Frank, A.W. (1995) *The Wounded Storyteller: Body, Illness, and Ethics*. Chicago: University of Chicago Press.

Freeman, M. (1993) *Rewriting the Self: History, Memory, Narrative*. London: Routledge.

Freud, S. (1937) Constructions in analysis. In *Standard Edition of the Complete Psychological Works of Sigmund Freud, vol. 23*. London: Hogarth Press, 1953.

Freud, S. (1905) Fragment of an analysis of a case of hysteria. In *Standard Edition of the Complete Psychological Works of Sigmund Freud, vol. 7*. London: Hogarth Press, 1953.

Frye, N. (1957) *Anatomy of Criticism*. Princeton, NJ: Princeton University Press.

Garro, L.C. (1994) Narrative representations of chronic illness experience: cultural models of illness, mind, and body in stories concerning temporomandibular joint (TMJ). *Social Science and Medicine*, 38: 775–788.

Gergen, K.J. (1991) *The Saturated Self: Dilemmas of Identity in Contemporary Life*. New York: Basic Books.

Gergen, K.J. and Gergen, M.M. (1986) Narrative form and the construction of psychological science. In T. Sarbin (ed.), *Narrative Psychology: The Storied Nature of Human Conduct*. New York: Praeger.

Goffman, E. (1959) *The Presentation of Self in Everyday Life*. New York: Anchor Press.

Goffman, E. (1979) Footing. *Semiotica*, 25: 1–29.

Good, B.J. and DelVecchio Good, M.-J. (1994) In the subjunctive mode: epilepsy narratives in Turkey. *Social Science and Medicine*, 38: 835–842.

Hermans, H.J.M., Kempen, H.J.G. and van Loon, R.J.P. (1992) The dialogical self: beyond individualism and rationalism. *American Psychologist*, 47: 23–33.

Leudar, I. and Antaki, C. (1996) Discourse participation, reported speech and research practices in social psychology. *Theory and Psychology*, 6: 5–29.

Mair, M. (1989) *Between Psychology and Psychotherapy: A Poetics of Experience*. London: Routledge.

Mancuso, J.C. (1996) Constructionism, personal construct psychology and narrative psychology. *Theory and Psychology*, 6: 47–70.

Markova, I. (1990) Introduction. In I. Markova and K. Foppa (eds), *The Dynamics of Dialogue*. London: Harvester Wheatsheaf, pp. 1–22.

Mattingly, C. (1994) The concept of therapeutic 'emplotment'. *Social Science and Medicine*, 38: 811–822.

Murray, K. (1985) Life as fiction. *Journal for the Theory of Social Behaviour*, 15: 173–187.

Murray, M. (1997a) A narrative approach to health psychology: background and potential. *Journal of Health Psychology*, 2: 9–20.

Murray, M. (1997b) *Narrative Health Psychology*. Palmerston North, New Zealand: Massey University.

Murray, M. and McMillan, C. (1988) *Working Class Women's View of Cancer*. Belfast: Ulster Cancer Foundation.

Nicolson, P. (1999) The In-depth Interview: Reflexivity, Intervention and the Construction of Post-natal Depression. In press.

Plummer, K. (1995) *Telling Sexual Stories: Power, Change, and Social Worlds*. London: Routledge.

Polkinghorne, D.E. (1988) *Narrative Knowing and the Human Sciences*. Albany, NY: SUNY Press.

Radley, A. and Billig, M. (1996) Accounts of health and illness: dilemmas and representations. *Sociology of Health and Illness*, 18: 220–240.

Reagan, C.E. (1996) *Paul Ricoeur: His Life and Work*. Chicago: University of Chicago Press.

Rickard, J.S. and Schweizer, H. (1994) Introduction. In P. Brooks, *Psychoanalysis and Storytelling*. Oxford: Blackwell, pp. 1–19.

Ricoeur, P. (1970) What is a text? Explanation and understanding. In M.J. Valdes (ed.), *A Ricoeur Reader: Reflection and Imagination*. Toronto: University of Toronto Press, pp. 43–64.

Ricoeur, P. (1972) Appropriation. In M.J. Valdes (ed.), *A Ricoeur Reader: Reflection and Imagination*. Toronto: University of Toronto Press, pp. 86–98.

Ricoeur, P. (1974) Metaphor and the main problem of hermeneutics. In M.J. Valdes (ed.), *A Ricoeur Reader: Reflection and Imagination*. Toronto: University of Toronto Press, pp. 303–319.

Ricoeur, P. (1979) The human experience of time and narrative. In M.J. Valdes (ed.), *A Ricoeur Reader: Reflection and Imagination*. Toronto: University of Toronto Press, pp. 99–116.

Ricoeur, P. (1984a, 1985, 1988) *Time and Narrative*, vols. 1–3. Chicago: University of Chicago Press.

Ricoeur, P. (1984b) The creativity of language. In M.J. Valdes (ed.), *A Ricoeur Reader: Reflection and Imagination*. Toronto: University of Toronto Press, pp. 463–481.

Ricoeur, P. (1987) Life: a story in search of a narrator. In M.J. Valdes (ed.), *A Ricoeur Reader: Reflection and Imagination*. Toronto: University of Toronto Press, pp. 425–437.

Ricoeur, P. (1991) Life in quest of narrative. In D. Wood (ed.), *On Paul Ricoeur: Narrative in Interpretation*. London: Routledge, pp. 20–33.

Riessman, C.K. (1990) Strategic uses of narrative in the presentation of self and illness: a research note. *Social Science and Medicine*, 30: 1195–1200.

Robinson, I. (1990) Personal narratives, social careers and medical courses: analyzing life trajectories in autobiographies of people with multiple sclerosis. *Social Science and Medicine*, 30: 1173–1186.

Rollins, B. (1976) *First, You Cry*. New York: HarperCollins.

Rudberg, M. (1997) *To Study Gender in Love – Revealing Passions of Research*. Paper presented at the Fifth European Congress of Psychology, Dublin.

Sarbin, T. (ed.) (1986) *Narrative Psychology: The Storied Nature of Human Conduct*. New York: Praeger.

Schaffer, R. (1992) *Retelling a Life: Narration and Dialogue in Psychoanalysis*. New York: Basic Books.

Sedgwick, P. (1982) *PsychoPolitics*. London: Pluto Press.

Shotter, J. (1993) *Cultural Politics of Everyday Life*. Toronto: University of Toronto Press.

Steffen, V. (1997) Life stories and shared experience. *Social Science and Medicine*, 45: 99–111.

Wortham, S. (1996) Are constructs personal? *Theory and Psychology*, 6: 79–84.

Valdes, M.H. (ed.) (1991) *A Ricoeur Reader: Reflection and Imagination*. Toronto: University of Toronto Press.

5

Discourse, Health and Illness

Mandy Morgan

By Way of a Preface

Discursive psychologies are relatively new approaches within psychology. They are wide-ranging and often complex in their challenges to more traditional, quantitative approaches. The task of introducing areas which are far-reaching, complex and relatively recent is difficult. Some writers choose to divide discursive psychologies into different types. Parker (1997), for example, relies on the historical traditions of debates in other disciplines to present two varieties of discursive work, and Lupton (1992) uses the concepts of 'macro' and 'micro' approaches to present a similar division. I have taken a somewhat different approach by focusing on the ways in which discursive work challenges psychology's traditional objects of study and notions about the nature of psychological knowledge. In doing this I have not explicated the historical traditions of different approaches to knowledge nor created a typography based on different conceptualizations of the object of study. There is little agreement or continuity within discursive psychologies about the grounds for such typography. Instead, I have used examples of discursive work in health-related areas to foreground the differences between traditional and discursive approaches, while leaving open, as far as possible, the debates within the field. In the section on the object of study, I have focused on the work of psychologists who take social processes rather than the individual as their object of study. In the section on psychological knowledge, I present a more detailed introduction to the work of Foucault (1970, 1973, 1979, 1981, 1982).

When I first started thinking about writing this chapter I was struck by the complexity of relationships between discourse, health and illness. It seemed that even within the context of psychology the possibilities for an introduction to the field were many. So, to begin, I searched for a framework to delimit the possibilities. In the processes of this search, a particular question occurred to me: What does it matter how we speak about health and illness?

In general, discourse refers to speaking and writing in all its forms, so a question that focuses on 'how we speak' is a question about discourse in its broadest sense. This question has guided this chapter – although not as if I have been looking for its definitive answer. Rather, it has provoked my thinking about discourse, health and illness in particular ways. It has framed my aims and my choice of reference material and enabled me to find a place to start.

Finding a Place to Start

It seems to me that our speaking about health and illness will matter, at least in part, according to how we construe speaking. If speaking is seen as a vehicle for expressing ourselves it may be taken as a (more or less) valid indicator of how we feel, and useful for assisting diagnosis or measurement. It might be seen as somehow loaded with our feelings or experiences and useful as a symptom in its own right. Or it might be construed as a fundamentally physiological behaviour and examined for its pathologies and normalities.

In the context of health psychology, speaking will also matter differently depending on how we understand the field itself. I want to begin by exploring the possibilities of locating discourse within the field of health psychology.

In 1980 Matarazzo offered an initial definition of health psychology as a stimulus to further discussion about the nature of the field. This definition has become widely influential. It suggests that the field consists of the

> aggregate of the specific educational, scientific, and professional contributions of the discipline of psychology to the promotion and maintenance of health, the prevention and treatment of illness, and the identification of etiological and diagnostic correlates of health, illness, and related dysfunction. (p. 815)

An understanding of the location of discourse within this field concerns the meaning of that term 'contributions'.

Of course, it is entirely possible to view discourse as simply another of the objects of study about which we may make contributions to promotion, maintenance, prevention, treatment, identification and diagnosis. For example, we might study scales or measures and find that some ways of speaking about risk-taking behaviours are more effective for collecting data than others. For the moment, I want to leave this possibility aside and explore the idea that there might be differences between a standard view (John, 1984) and a discursive approach of the contributions themselves.

Matarazzo's (1980) definition divides our contributions to health psychology into three components: educational, scientific and professional. Each of the components is associated with the discipline of psychology and

with the activities of promotion, maintenance, prevention, treatment, identification and diagnosis. It would be easy to suggest that these contributions
are the collective of research findings, theories and models, as well as
procedures for intervention, education and evaluation. This collective has
been derived from the current state of psychological knowledge so that
health psychology is a form of psychological knowledge.

For some time psychological knowledge has been construed as scientific.
Even professional and educational activities have privileged science
through the model of the scientist practitioner. The procedures for deriving
scientific knowledge are often regarded as satisfying requirements for
technical, objective, valid and reliable statements about the nature of
reality. It is these procedures which make scientific knowledge qualitatively different from everyday knowing or subjective understandings of the
world. John calls this view of psychological knowledge the 'standard or
empiricist view' (1984: 29).

According to this standard view, psychology uncovers, discovers and
exposes aspects of our reality as human subjects. We are taken as objects of
study which are made up of empirical facts of nature or perhaps, in the
more social fragments of psychology, facts of culture and social
relationships. From this viewpoint, Matarazzo's (1980) notion of contributions would be construed as representations of the reality of health and
illness for human subjects. These representations are more reliable and
valid than everyday or common-sense representations. They are expert
representations derived from a system of knowledge production which
ensures their objectivity.

Within this standard view discourse might be taken to be the means
through which various aspects of the reality of health and illness are
represented. How we speak might be important in terms of how reliable
and valid our representations are, of how well discourse performs as a
vehicle for the transmission of information. Where it is studied it may well
be in the context of examining problematics, for example: What goes wrong
with communications when patients misunderstand the doctor's instruc-
tions? or, Is there some form of communication that might decrease a
patient's resistance to a doctor's advice? In these cases we would not be
studying discourse *in its own right* but in terms of its performance in
relation to other problems with which we are concerned. Such an approach
might include discourse within the realms of health psychology, but would
not substantially change the standard view of the contributions
psychological knowledge might make to the field of health.

A discursive approach to the contributions of psychological knowledge
would make somewhat different assumptions about the nature of the
object of our study and about the relationship between discourse and
knowledge. By way of introducing such a view, I want first to present the
'different object' that concerns discursive psychology. Then I want to make
use of Foucault's (1973, 1979, 1981) notion of discourse and his work on its
place in relation to scientific knowledge to explore more fully the implications of a discursive approach to psychological knowledge.

Discourse and the Object of Study

Within the last decade, discursive psychologists have reconceptualized a number of psychological constructs, including the self and attitudes (Potter and Wetherell, 1987), attributions (Edwards and Potter, 1992), the mind (Harré and Gillett, 1994) and emotions (Harré, 1986) as discursive phenomena. That is, they are taken to be the effects of active social processes which are historically and culturally specific, rather than 'internal' attributes or individual variables.

The traditional object of study in psychology is the individual. Ogden (1995) points out that health psychology shares this tradition. She also raises questions about the adequacy of this object, particularly when it is conceptualized as a discrete unit composed of measurable parts. While particular conceptions of the individual have altered from time to time, variously construing people as passive responders or as 'inter-' or 'intra-' active, the focus of attention has remained on an entity both separated from its environment and composed of palpable 'internal' variables. Such a conceptualization poses problems for incorporating an account of social processes into health psychology.

Spicer (1995) has noted serious attempts to include social processes related to health and illness in recent theorizing. He suggests that a substantial contribution to the continued strength of the notion of the individual as a bounded entity comes not from theoretical conceptualizations but from methodological constraints. A continuing focus on statistical analysis of the relationship between variables, no matter whether they are regarded as social or intra-personal, requires attention to characteristics which have the bounded and measurable qualities of discrete entities.

From these accounts it is possible that traditional conceptualizations and methodological prescriptions have worked together to make it difficult to address issues of social context, except through notions of 'interaction' between the individual and the social. Ogden (1995) advocates a discursive approach to enable these difficulties to be addressed.

When the object of study in health psychology is taken to be a bounded individual entity, speaking is often construed as either the neutral transmission of information or as representation biased by subjectivity. In both cases, speaking is neither construed as a social process nor studied in its own right. A discursive approach takes speaking as an active social process and in doing so it challenges the traditional view of the object of study as a bounded individual.

Within this approach traditional constructs such as emotion, for example, are no longer taken as measurable individual attributes. Rather, they are construed as embodied processes lived in particular cultural contexts. How these processes are experienced will depend, in part, on the discursive resources available within those contexts to make them sensible and intelligible. The units of analysis in this approach are linguistic resources, not individuals. Various speakers may make use of these resources, to produce a variety of constructions of their experiences, but they are not 'individual' resources and the functions they serve are not characteristics of a particular person.

Like emotion experiences, experiences of health and illness may be understood as embodied processes lived in particular cultural contexts. Backett and Davison (1995: 629) point out that it is

> axiomatic to the social sciences that health and illness are not simply matters concerning human bodies and their function. Rather these states and the transition between them represent a complex interplay of physiological conditions, the cultural structures which give them meaning, and the social organizations and interactions within which they are situated.

Discursive psychologists focus their attention on this complex interplay, assuming that the experience of health and illness will be different in different social contexts. Social contexts are neither singular nor unified, but multiple and heterogeneous, so that experience will vary between and even within different local contexts. The analysis of the resources available within a particular locality, and of the uses to which those resources are put, enables discursive psychologists to account for the diversity and complexity of individual experience without separating that experience from the social context in which it is lived.

While discursive psychology is a relatively new approach, it has already been proposed and taken up by health researchers (Stainton Rogers, 1996), particularly in relation to health policy and education. Lupton (1992) advocates discourse analysis to address the inadequacies of traditional measures of attitudes and behaviour in relation to health risk perception. She suggests that discourse analysis 'is a valuable way of understanding the underlying assumptions inherent in health professionals' communication with their clients, lay health beliefs and the messages and meanings about health issues disseminated in the popular media' (1992: 149).

An example of this kind of research is Balshem's (1991) study of conflict between health educators and community members during a cancer education programme. As part of a larger study she interviewed community members about heart disease and cancer and identified variations in the way that her respondents made sense of these illnesses. One result of her analysis was the recognition that, within this particular working-class locality, discourse on the nature of cancer was 'fundamentally different from that propounded by scientific medicine' (1991: 161), while discourse on heart disease was far more similar. Using this analysis Balshem shows how the cancer discourse of this community functions as an active resistance to scientific authority and suggests that its effects cannot be overcome simply by 'more' or 'better' education practices.

Another focus of attention for discursive researchers is professional diagnostic practice. Harper (1994) reports a study of the diagnosis of paranoia which illustrates the ways in which diagnosis is accomplished in practice. His findings suggest that any particular diagnosis is influenced by a wide range of contextual information, which is considerably more variable and flexible than the criteria for diagnosis themselves. For example, it is possible for professionals to make use of notions like 'typical' and 'atypical' diagnoses. These rhetorical categories allow professionals to introduce new criteria into a diagnosis which does not fit the standard criteria. So, diagnosticians may introduce the logic of a particular attitude to argue that it fits the diagnosis of paranoia, even though that logic is not a standard criterion. In this way, they make flexible use of categories and criteria to bring forth paranoia as a phenomenon.

Harper (1994) also describes a study which demonstrates similar flexibility and variation in the diagnosis of physical illness. He stresses that the results of these studies do not merely indicate variation in the perception of the facts on which diagnosis is based, but that the facts themselves are constructed within specific social contexts.

It is apparent from these examples that discourse analysts construe all speakers as embedded in social contexts, making use of social resources to constitute their experiences, whether these are experiences of health, illness or professional practice. This involves transforming the conceptualization of the speaker from an individual who is communicating or representing a more or less accurate portrayal of some aspect of themselves, to a culturally embedded subject actively using shared social resources to perform various and diverse functions.

Within this framework, our contributions to the field of health psychology concern the various and diverse means through which health and illness experiences are made meaningful, not only by those who experience health or illness but also by health 'experts'.

To explore more fully how a discursive approach may take account of the contributions of experts to the field of health psychology, I want to turn now to a more detailed introduction to the work of Michel Foucault. Foucault's conceptualization of 'discourse' specifically addresses the relationship between social processes and knowledge. It takes account of the operations of social power and provides a challenge to our traditional ways of understanding ourselves as producers of psychological knowledge.

Discourse and Knowledge

Michel Foucault (1982: 208) described the objective of his work as creating 'a history of the different modes by which, in our culture, human beings are made subjects'. Foucault's notion of discourse emerges initially in historical accounts of the ways in which scientific disciplines formulated standards of validity and objectivity. He described his approach as 'archaeological' to distinguish it from more traditional approaches to the history of ideas. Foucault's (1970, 1973) concern was not only with ideas and their development, but with the social relationships and political changes which made certain ideas more possible at particular historical moments.

One of Foucault's (1970) archaeological studies, *The Order of Things*, excavates the conditions which made it possible for the human sciences, including psychology, to emerge within the European tradition. He challenges the view that the social sciences appeared as a result of a *natural progression* of scientific knowledges. Instead, he traces the emergence of the human sciences to a *transformation* in the field of knowledge. This transformation enabled the possibility of the social sciences by breaking with classical conceptions of the nature of knowledge, and creating the space for a different kind of science. Classical knowledge is marked by a number of characteristic assumptions: things in the world are ordered and their true order can be determined by the presence or absence of particular characteristics; properties are quantifiable and knowledge can take the form of a mathematical system; reliable identification of properties can (in principle) lead to certainty. An ideal outcome of classical knowledge is something like a table which represents categories of things with each thing in its proper place.

The human sciences, including psychology, concern themselves with human subjects as living beings rather than merely as biological entities that take a particular form in relation to other biological entities. So, it was necessary for the classical preoccupation with tables of order and identification of properties to be transformed before the social sciences could exist. This transformation heralds what Foucault (1970) calls the modern episteme.

In the process of tracing the emergence of the human sciences, Foucault challenges the standard view of scientific knowledge which construes it as representing reality. He refers to the human sciences as a body of discourse with the qualification that the term knowledge is 'perhaps a little strong' (1970: 344). This challenge is based on recognizing that a body of knowledge is made up of statements, of discourse, and that these statements can be studied in their own right.

Gutting (1989) points out that there are two ways in which statements have traditionally been studied in their own right: grammar and logic. Grammar concerns the rules of order through which meaningful statements can be made and logic concerns the rules of order through which statements may be consistently linked to each other. Gutting also points out that there are many more statements permitted by grammar and logic than are actually admissible as statements of knowledge within any given domain. In psychology, for example, neither grammar nor logic would prohibit psychologists from speaking of the 'health of the spirit' or a 'sickness of the soul'. Yet such statements are not usually admissible as psychological discourse.

Foucault's (1970, 1973) archaeological work was concerned with identifying the rules of order which govern the formation of admissible statements: statements that are granted the status of knowledge within a given domain and which also define the domain. He named these rules of order *discursive formations* and identified four elements of which they are composed: the objects about which the statements are made, the status and authority of the statements, the concepts associated with the statements, and the theories or viewpoints that the statements develop.

Within this framework, statements may be organized into particular groups which are consistent or coherent with regard to their rules of formation. It is these groups or unities of statements which constitute the specific notion of discourse developed from Foucault's work. Such groups of statements construct and define particular objects of study.

Although the term discourse is used to challenge the connotations of the standard view of statements of scientific knowledge, this challenge is not a denial of the relationship between discourse and knowledge. Neither is it an attempt to replace the term knowledge with the term discourse so that we can say, for example, 'psychological discourse' instead of 'psychological knowledge'. Rather, Foucault (1970, 1973) presents discourse as the means of stipulating what is known, what can be known and what statements count as knowledge at any particular time (Ramazanoglu, 1993). Knowledge and discourse are intimately related but not isomorphic.

By way of illustrating this relationship between discourse and knowledge I want to introduce Foucault's (1973) second major project, *The Birth of the Clinic*. This study comprised an archaeology of medical knowledge and its transformation towards the end of the eighteenth century. In *The Birth of the Clinic* Foucault challenges the commonly held view of medical history in which the 'discovery' of pathological anatomy led to the development of clinical medicine. For Foucault, clinical medicine emerges from a discursive transformation, rather than a discovery.

In classical medicine, diseases are conceptualized as abstract essences. A disease is 'recognized' by its qualities, and diseases are ordered and classified according to the similarities and differences of their properties. Neither the body of the diseased person, nor relationships of cause and effect, are important to classical medicine. Diagnosis is a matter of identifying which qualities are present. Their location, or the sequence of their appearance, is irrelevant (Gutting, 1989). The task of the medical practitioner is to return the diseased body to health.

Classical medicine dominated medical practice and knowledge in Europe until the end of the eighteenth century. At that time notions of knowledge were transformed by a revaluing of education which became seen as a way of discovering: a 'bringing to light' of the previously unknown (Foucault, 1973: 63). Simultaneously, a number of social concerns converged in the transformation of medical knowledge and practice: spreading epidemics, poorly trained or untrained medical practitioners, and a lack of funding for hospitals contributed to social pressures from which arose the institution of the Clinic.

The Clinic refers to both the physical institution of the teaching hospital and the discursive practices of clinical medicine. The transformation enabled by practices of the Clinic was discursive in the sense that the teaching hospital became the site of a new form of status and authority for statements of medical knowledge, a new mode of 'perceiving' the objects of medical knowledge, and new concepts and theories about illness and health.

The new status and authority for statements of medical knowledge involved a shift from the university lecture theatre to the teaching hospital ward as the location of expertise. This 'move' was closely aligned to a shift from classification to observation as the principal mode of 'perceiving' disease and illness. Objects of scientific medical study also changed. Instead of studying similarities and differences in disease characteristics, medical practitioners studied patients in hospitals.

The teaching hospital also enabled a transformation in what Foucault (1973) calls 'the medical gaze' (*le regard*). This gaze is particular to the kind of observation which can be made when the medical expert is at the bedside of the patient *and* the new institution of the teaching hospital is being used to survey the health of the national population (Sarup, 1993). The knowledge produced from this form of observation was very specific to its context and was based on a set of assumptions about what was able to be seen: it was not the view of a 'clear and unbiased empirical eye' (Gutting, 1989: 4).

So it is that Foucault (1973) presents pathological anatomy, the form of knowledge made possible by the new medical gaze, as an effect of a break with classical conceptions of medical practice and disease, rather than as an outcome of progress towards a better 'map' or 'picture' of the human body. This break is a discursive transformation: it involves changes to the rules concerning how medical knowledge could be produced and legitimated; changes in what would be admissible as statements of medical knowledge; and changes to the nature of the objects of medical inquiry.

Alongside the development of pathological anatomy, then, there is the development of new ways of speaking about the body, health and illness. These new ways of speaking allow, for example, that fever is no longer construed as an essence of disease but is 'no more than an acceleration in the flow of blood' (Broussais, 1808, cited in Foucault, 1973: 189). Such a shift demonstrates a fundamental transformation in a known object. This transformation is produced with and through a particular configuration of changes in perception, conception and theory made possible by the practices of the Clinic. These practices enable fever to be seen and spoken about differently, and for these different statements to be granted status as knowledge.

It is possible to imagine that Foucault (1973) is merely describing something that is more or less taken for granted in many contemporary views of scientific knowledge: that knowledge is produced in a social context which inevitably affects our interpretations of reality. Such an insight might mean very little to the contributions which we can imagine making to health and illness. However social their character, it is still possible that some of our statements about 'bodies', 'health' and 'illness' will be better representations than others, of what is happening to us when we are well or ill. And if the relationship of discourse to knowledge was simply a matter of transformations which allowed different standards for admitting statements as knowledge, it might be the case that some standards provided better grounds for representation than others. From a Foucauldian perspective, though, the relationship is not quite so simple, for the account has not yet considered the relationship between knowledge and power.

Discourse, Knowledge, Power

The standard view of psychology often dissociates knowledge from regimes of social power through a commitment to objectivity. The discipline is presented as a 'free floating body of knowledge detached from wider society' (John, 1984: 29). To the extent that there is any presumption of a relationship between power and knowledge it is most likely to encompass the view that by discovering reality we provide the means to do that which we could not do without the knowledge. This relationship between power and knowledge suggests liberation. Knowledge as a representation of reality may be used to develop interventions for the improvement of the human condition, for emancipation in the face of overwhelming and uncontrolled natural and social phenomena. This view would be consistent with interpreting Matarazzo's contributions as knowledge which can be used to promote health and prevent illness. This is emancipatory in the sense that our knowledge produces the means through which individuals may be increasingly liberated from sickness and disease, and increasingly able to control their health and well-being.

Foucault (1979, 1981) challenges the notion of knowledge as emancipatory. In his view, rather than knowledge producing the means of emancipation, it is involved in systems through which individuals are subjected to particular practices of surveillance and discipline. He contrasted the notion of *disciplinary power* with monarchical power. Monarchical power is modelled on the relationship of kingship and government to the general population. Power is the possession of the monarch, embodied in the person of government and exercised over the population. Disciplinary power is modelled on monitoring systems in which each person is able to act as his or her own supervisor (Sarup, 1993). In principle, disciplinary power enables individuals to be conscious of themselves as permanently visible to others, as subject to the norms of behaviour acceptable within their social context and as accountable for themselves in terms which are understood by others. Such consciousness involves a form of self-surveillance that 'is permanent in its effects, even if it is discontinuous in its action' (Foucault, 1979: 201).

In tracing the shift from monarchical power to disciplinary power, Foucault suggests that the operations of power are transformed. The conception of monarchical power as embodied in a particular person involves power operating negatively through the judicial authority to limit, prohibit or censor. Instead, disciplinary power operates positively in as much as it works to bring into the social realm the technical and strategic means for constructing new capacities and activities. It does not merely limit or control pre-existing possibilities (Sarup, 1993).

An excellent example of the operation of disciplinary power within the framework of psychology is Foucault's (1981) interpretation of the practice of confession. The practice is predicated on the notion of a 'truth' residing within a person which will be 'revealed' by speaking it. While the psychoanalytic practice of the talking cure is the paradigmatic form of psychological confession, other psychodynamic practices, and even practices of measurement and diagnosis which involve confidential 'disclosure' on the part of the client, may be construed as forms of confession; as inner truths revealed in speech. The practice of confession is supported by groups of statements, admissible as knowledge, that enable the individual to perceive a buried inner problem and articulate it. Parker (1989: 61) comments that through these discourses 'deep-felt needs are produced, and are actually experienced as "real"'. As a psychological practice, then, confession enables a particular reality to come into being through the disciplinary power of self-examination, self-disclosure, and the accompanying surveillance of an 'inner world' for the purpose of revealing hidden mysteries.

Rose (1989, 1990) uses Foucault's notion of modern power to analyse the ways in which psychology contributes to the operation and effects of 'human technologies'. We are most familiar with technologies as material objects seen as applications of our scientific knowledges; weaponry and satellites; microwave ovens and stereo systems; electrocardiograms and electron microscopes. These technologies inhabit our world, giving it meaning and organizing our lifestyles and experiences. Human technologies may also be seen as applications of our scientific knowledge. They consist of both devices and practices which give meaning to and organize our personal and social experiences (Gavey, 1992). In Rose's analysis the devices through which psychology inscribes and calibrates the human psyche and through which it becomes possible to identify both the normal and pathological are examples of human technologies. From this perspective when psychologists contribute a measuring instrument, like the MMPI, to the field of medicine, we are not merely contributing an application of our expertise which will allow the reality of various personalities to be viewed. Rather, we are contributing a technology which will structure and order the experience of human subjects in such a way that it produces categories and kinds, and eventually, perhaps, diagnoses. The objects of our measurement are not simply there and represented to us through the instrument but are, rather, produced through the use of the instrument. In health psychology, for example, the construct of 'self-efficacy' operates technologically to produce theories and models, general and specific measuring instruments, proposals for interventions and a particular kind of knowledge about the relationship between the person and his or her health-related behaviours.

Rose (1990) also attends to the configuration of human technologies which brings together not only instruments like the MMPI, but also the institutions and practices which support and reproduce the discourses within which such an instrument is sensible. Such a configuration may involve professional practices, training and pedagogic theory, architecture, writing and publishing, networks of communication, regimes of experimentation and replication, evaluations and applications, treatments and interventions, timetables and schedules, equipment and statements. Altogether, they produce a network in which the operation of power is threaded throughout. Such technologies and strategic practices may be generally construed as produced within, and productive of, particular forms of knowledge. Exercised, these techniques and strategies yield knowledge of a specific kind.

Power and knowledge are thus interdependent, and complicitous with the discourses of a particular episteme which specify the rules for the formation of objects, concepts, perceptions and theories. Power/knowledge/discourse are neither each the same nor each separate and distinct. Intertwined, they operate to produce reality and 'truth statements' at particular historic sites. In as much as human subjects are subjected to the technologies and strategies through which discourses constitute objects, they are also produced in and through discourse. Under the gaze of medical and psychological 'perceptions' and within the parameters of medical and psychological concepts and theories, persons come into view. They are seen and acted upon through various technologies and strategies which themselves are both produced by and enable medical and psychological knowledge.

Intertwined with power and discourse, knowledge is no longer a matter of representation, in which it may be possible that some representations are better than others to indicate what is really happening to us when we are well or ill. For example, no matter how well refined the MMPI as a measuring instrument, it will not 'represent' the inner world of the individual subject. Instead, it will produce that inner world by enabling both experts and their clients to perceive, and speak about, the human subject in a particular way. The MMPI itself is also produced through certain ways of knowing and speaking about human subjects.

So, a Foucauldian discursive perspective of Matarazzo's 'contributions' differs from a 'standard' view. The contributions are less like valid and reliable research findings, theories, pedagogic and intervention practices developed by psychological science and professional practice, and more like particular technologies and statements through which health and illness are constituted in specific places and times, with specific effects on human subjectivity.

What are the implications of this shift from knowledge as representation to discourse/power/knowledge and technologies as productive of reality? By way of addressing this question I would like to introduce some examples of 'contributions' to the field of health and medicine which have taken something of a Foucauldian perspective. Of course, each of these examples has been taken out of its context of publication for use here. They are neither summarized nor reviewed. Instead they have been fragmented – even torn apart – for the purpose of illustration. I make no claim to a comprehensive representation of the 'work' these particular contributions might do.

Contributions to a Discursive Health Psychology

For no other reason than because it follows most closely on Foucault's (1973) conclusions concerning the 'Birth of the Clinic', I will start with an article by Nettleton and Burrows (1994) which provides a Foucauldian analysis of some of the effects of shifting the focus of health care from hospitals to communities. It outlines some important Foucauldian notions, and introduces the work of Armstrong (1983) who elaborated the notion of a dispensary regime of disciplinary power.

According to Armstrong (1983) the Dispensary mediated between the community and the hospital. Like the Clinic, the Dispensary is more than a building, or even an institution; it is also a new perceptual structure. It involved a new way of construing illness and health which was accompanied by new practices and technologies. In the Clinic, the medical gaze was turned upon the interior of a docile body and the patient was construed primarily as a body in which disease and illness resided. This gaze and the body which became its object, enabled pathological anatomy as a body of knowledge and simultaneously produced particular pathological and normal objects of study.

The Dispensary was founded to facilitate the screening, diagnosis and treatment of patients with tuberculosis. The gaze enabled by the Dispensary saw beyond the body to the social relations of the patient, and beyond the patient to those who might potentially become ill. Nettleton and Burrows (1994) pursue the implications of this shifted gaze in terms of the human technologies it implicates and the kind of object it produces. The shift produces a distinction between pathological anatomy and pathological lifestyle. The object of Dispensary medicine is not a docile body but a whole person who is not simply examined for the interior functioning of anatomical objects, but is encouraged to speak about their health and illness, and the practices of their life and relationships. Practitioners of Dispensary medicine are not simply engaged in protecting healthy bodies from disease or treating ill bodies so that they regain health. They are engaged in supporting people to live healthy lives. Medical encounters are transformed, as are the agents of medical practice: not only the doctor, but the whole health-care team, as well as lay educators, are now engaged in helping people to monitor their own health and illness.

Taking examples from mental health and dentistry, Nettleton and Burrows (1994) articulate specific transformations in objects and human technologies of health. Their account enables readers to consider various possibilities. For example, the mental health focus on behaviour enabled a flourishing of sites for the practice of psychological intervention including therapeutic communities and self-help groups as well as more conventional psychotropic medications. Pressure to deinstitutionalize patients did not simply involve a more liberated approach to treatment. The psychological population became increasingly differentiated. A new range of target subjects came into view, for example, alcoholics, anorexics, bulimics, and battered wives. Attention turned from mental disorder and specific pathologies, to mental health. The creation of new practices and technologies of mental health care was not simply the result of criticisms of institutionalization. It involved a complex interplay between forms of disciplinary power concerning mental health, and resistance to those forms of power. Nettleton and Burrows (1994) invite us to consider that the effect of this interplay is not a straightforward liberalization or emancipation of psychological subjects, but a transformation in both the objects of the psychological gaze and the effects of new technologies of mental health care. It is not a demise of power but a transformation in its regime and operation.

The second example, drawn from medical anthropology, explores three discourses on illness, paying particular attention to what is called the 'mindful body' discourse (Di Giacomo, 1992). Mindful body discourse names the group of statements which are concerned with empowering the ill and giving due consideration to experiences which are often excluded from discourses which separate the mind and the body.

Di Giacomo (1992) locates her argument as Foucauldian with reference to the manner in which the medical gaze was authorized as expertise, and medical discourse became hegemonic during the transformation from classical to modern epistemes. However, the hegemonic authority of medical discourse is not absolute and resistance enables transformation. In particular, Di Giacomo (1992) traces recent resistance to biomedical discourse which involves transforming symptoms of illness from 'biological entities' to 'metaphors'. In the work of Scheper-Hughes and Lock (1986) she identifies a theoretical shift in which symptoms are construed as metaphors for unspoken conflict in social life, unvoiced emotion and thoughts that must be concealed. This perception of the objects of medical inquiry sees codes and forms of signifying social and emotional matters in place of signs and symptoms of pathological anatomy. The conceptualization of illness as metaphor links individual suffering with political, social and economic systems. It encourages the development of human technologies which take account of the experience of the 'ill person' and challenge the hegemonic discourse of biomedical expertise.

Using the illustration of cancer, Di Giacomo (1992) opens up the possibility that the transformation of symptoms from the realm of the material body to the realm of signifying codes, although emerging through resistance to a hegemonic discourse of medical expertise, may still support asymmetrical relations of power that silence the voices of the ill. Tracing the technologies that accompany this new perception of illness, Di Giacomo finds reference not only to cancer-prone cultures but also cancer-prone personalities; self-help books which speak of illness as an escape from responsibility for unmet emotional needs and interpersonal conflicts; a therapist who asks clients why they need their cancer; and, the constitution of a new civic duty – individual responsibility for health. Di Giacomo concludes that:

> reading illness as a text on unmastered emotions (or on the social disorder that produced them) yields up a moral economy of illness that silences the voices of the afflicted . . . as effectively as biomedicine, in which the sick person fades out of the picture, like the Cheshire Cat, except for a single defining feature, the diseased body part. (1992: 133)

It would seem that while the mindful body discourse provides the resources for resisting biomedical discourse, it does not necessarily give voice to the experience of the ill person, or challenge the authority of experts. Di Giacomo's analysis enables readers to consider how transforming biomedical discourse implicates power relations. By reflecting on the implications of a particular discourse she opens up discursive transformations to critical scrutiny.

The third example, Haraway's (1991) study of immune system discourse, begins with a conception of the power of biomedical discourse which is resonant of Foucauldian notions of power. For Haraway, biomedicine structures and orders experiences of illness with its 'stunning artefacts, images, architectures, social forms, and technologies' (p. 204). The power of biomedical human technologies is dynamic and elusive, is everywhere yet difficult to pin down.

Haraway assumes that scientific discourses, biomedicine included, are 'lumpy' rather than 'smooth' and seamless. They are heterogeneous, their boundaries with non-scientific discourses are permeable and they involve disputes over meanings and practices. None the less, they are caught up in the work of constituting objects, and it is the 'preeminently twentieth-century' object – the immune system – with which Haraway is concerned.

Haraway's contention is that the immune system is an icon and a map. As a map, the immune system 'guides' contemporary understandings of the differences between 'self' and 'other' and of the processes of recognition and misrecognition that such differences entail. As an icon it speaks for the dominant organization of symbolic and material difference in late twentieth-century industrialized culture. Haraway's text weaves an intricate enmeshing of the immune system within multiple discourses of contemporary culture. The complexity of her argument entirely escapes reproduction here but I would like to point to three of the interconnections between discursive fields which she suggests so as to illustrate the scope of her analysis.

The first interconnection is a site where myth and scientific practice are interwoven. In tracing the historical progression of images 'representing' the theories of immunology, Haraway notices this interconnection in the obituary for Richard K. Gershon, the immunologist responsible for identifying the suppressor T cell. Gershon is described as having 'had what the earliest explorers had, an insatiable desire to be the first person to see something, to know that you are where no man has been before' (1991: 205). As Haraway notes, it would not be unreasonable to assume that for readers raised in a television era, the 'ringing tones' of the voice-over introducing Star Trek echo through the text. The mythology of science as heroic quest, as probing the landscapes of the unknown, saturate the image of the scientist. The interweaving of myth and science, the constitution of the scientist as hero, reproduce the dominant organization of differences, including differences between 'experts' and their 'subjects'.

Another interconnection of discursive fields is identified when Haraway maps a particular shift in the construction of the immune system. In this case the interconnection concerns the images of the immune system and theories of communication and information processing. Haraway notices that the immune system had been imaged according to a thematics of co-operation and control in which a master system controlled information flow. This imaging has shifted to a thematics of pastiche in which there is conflict among multiple centres of interpretation and the integrity of the whole system is threatened. Haraway notes that this shift is very like recent transformations in theories of language in which language is no longer considered as a natural system, controlled by a master/author, but as a system of differences, with little integrity as a whole and no clearly located 'centre'. Through this interconnection, Haraway draws attention to the way in which images of the immune system are related to images of other systems, and to the way our knowledge of these systems relies on historically specific discourses.

In yet another example of interconnections between discursive fields, Haraway traces a move in more general conceptualizations of the body. She identifies different sets of practices and different technologies emerging from the mid-twentieth century through which the body has been transformed from an object characterized as highly organized, hierarchical and organic to an object more like a semiotic system, a 'complex meaning producing field' (1991: 211). And again, Haraway draws connections between these shifts and others. She notices that within the same period of history, decolonization, multinational capitalism, high-tech militarization, and the emergence of political organizations grounded in previously marginalized identities have destabilized simple notions of 'liberation' and humanist conceptions of the substantive unity of 'human' interests. Differences, in the field of politics, are no longer simply given by the reality of human life, but rather they are multiply produced through the interplay of local interests in complex and diverse fields of meaning-making. In the field of the body, differences between the normal and the pathological are no longer simple 'givens' either. The body is conceived as a strategic system in which disease is a type of information malfunction or a mis-recognition of the self.

Haraway also poses the question of how post-modern, biotechnical, biomedical discourse constitutes an individual. This is not necessarily a simple question since 'even the most reliable Western individuated bodies . . . neither stop nor start at the skin, which is itself something of a teeming jungle threatening illicit fusions, especially from the perspective of a scanning electron microscope' (1991: 215). She considers how images of immunology inform the question – images of battlefields and inner 'space', imaging as therapeutic practice and as critical visual technology in the conduct of post-modern science (as well as in business and war). From her analysis of images and imaging, and of the parallels and connections between the 'lumpy' discourses of immunology, politics, economics, bio-medicine and more, Haraway suggests that what is at stake in contemporary transformations and shifts is precisely the kind of collective and personal selves that will be enabled as human subjects.

Tending Towards a Conclusion

From biomedicine to dentistry, psychotherapy to cancer prevention, psychologists use techniques and strategies which order human experience and make it meaningful in particular ways. The sites at which technologies of health operate are multiple and diverse. In exemplifying the kind of contributions to health psychology which are enabled by a Foucauldian approach, there is little by way of organizing principles which enable them to be seen as coherent or as unified. The field of Foucauldian contributions is as fragmented as the field in and through which power/knowledge/discourse operates. Each contribution may be said to construe a particular site at which technologies of health operate idiosyncratically in the enabling and constraining effects of medical power/knowledge/discourse. Simultaneously these sites resonate with connections to the hegemonic discourses of the modern episteme. From such a perspective, there could be no single answer to the question: what does it matter how we speak about illness and health? A Foucauldian approach to discursive health psychology suggests there could only be a diversity of answers, each specific to particular sites where technologies of health and illness are operating. This implies that a unified or consistent answer across sites will fail to address the specific effects of power. Psychologists' traditional concern with generalizing findings and discovering universal laws will, perhaps unwittingly, continue to reproduce hegemonic discursive formations.

In as much as the examples I have introduced make a 'common contribution' to the field of health psychology, they share a concern with reflexivity. Each, differently, 'makes visible' the discursive field within which health psychology makes its contribution to the constitutions of health and illness. In making the discursive field visible, in bringing it into the 'analyst's gaze', each of these writers contributes to bringing psychological discourse into the realm of 'knowable objects'. As psychologists and patients, as practitioners and clients, as researchers and students, whether healthy or ill, the discourses we speak, the knowledge we produce, the technologies we use and the power which enables and constrains us, all operating at diverse sites, become potential objects of study. Through the constitution of these objects, a Foucauldian discursive psychology is able to take a 'different' account of social context, of the relationship between mind and body, healthy living and the experience of illness. It is not an account which seeks to represent the reality of these phenomena. Rather, it seeks to perform a kind of self-examination, proposing possible symptomatic relationships between the technologies of health we are subjected to, the moral, political and ethical effects of these technologies and the kinds of persons any of us are able to be – whether ill or healthy.

Acknowledgements

I would like to thank Leigh Coombes for her careful, thorough reading and suggestions.

References

Armstrong, D. (1983) *Political Anatomy of the Body: Medical Knowledge in Britain in the Twentieth Century*. Cambridge: Cambridge University Press.

Backett, K.C. and Davison, C. (1995) Lifecourse and lifestyle: the social and cultural location of health behaviours. *Social Science and Medicine*, 40: 629–638.

Balshem, M. (1991) Cancer, control, and causality: talking about cancer in a working class community. *American Ethnologist*, 18: 152–172.

Di Giacomo, S.M. (1992) Metaphor as illness: postmodern dilemmas in the representation of body, mind and disorder. *Medical Anthropology*, 14: 109–137.

Edwards, D. and Potter, J. (1992) *Discursive Psychology*. London: Sage.

Foucault, M. (1970) *The Order of Things*. (A. Sheridan, trans.) New York: Random House.

Foucault, M. (1973) *The Birth of the Clinic*. (A. Sheridan, trans.) New York: Vintage.

Foucault, M. (1979) *Discipline and Punish*. (A. Sheridan, trans.) London: Penguin.

Foucault, M. (1981) *History of Sexuality*. (R. Hurley, trans.) Harmondsworth, Middlesex: Penguin.

Foucault, M. (1982) The subject and power. In H. Dreyfus and P. Rabinow (eds), *Michel Foucault: Beyond Structuralism and Hermeneutics*. Chicago: University of Chicago Press, pp. 208–226.

Gavey, N. (1992) Technologies and effects of heterosexual coercion. *Feminism and Psychology*, 2: 325–351.

Gutting, G. (1989) *Michel Foucault's Archaeology of Scientific Reason*. Cambridge: Cambridge University Press.

Haraway, D. (1991) *Simians, Cyborgs and Women: The Reinvention of Nature*. London: Free Association.

Harper, D.J. (1994) The professional construction of 'paranoia' and the discursive use of diagnostic criteria. *British Journal of Medical Psychology*, 67: 131–143.

Harré, R. (1986) An outline of the social constructionist viewpoint. In R. Harré (ed.), *The Social Construction of Emotion*. Basil Blackwell: Oxford, pp. 2–14.

Harré, R. and Gillett, G. (1994) *The Discursive Mind*. London: Sage.

John, I.D. (1984) Science as a justification for psychology as a social institution. *Australian Psychologist*, 19: 29–37.

Lupton, D. (1992) Discourse analysis: a new methodology for understanding the ideologies of health and illness. *Australian Journal of Public Health*, 16: 145–150.

Matarazzo, J.D. (1980) Behavioral health and behavioral medicine: frontiers for a new health psychology. *American Psychologist*, 35: 807–817.

Nettleton, S. and Burrows, R. (1994) From bodies in hospitals to people in the community: a theoretical analysis of the relocation of health care. *Care in Place*, 1: 93–103.

Ogden, J. (1995) Changing the subject of health psychology. *Psychology and Health*, 10: 257–265.

Parker, I. (1989) Discourse and power. In J. Shotter and K. Gergen (eds), *Texts of Identity*. London: Sage, pp. 56–69.

Parker, I. (1997) Discursive psychology. In D. Fox and I. Prilleltensky (eds), *Critical Psychology: An Introduction*. London: Sage, pp. 284–298.

Potter, J. and Wetherell, M. (1987) *Discourse and Social Psychology: Beyond Attitudes and Behaviour*. London: Sage.

Ramazanoglu, C. (1993) Introduction. In C. Ramazanoglu (ed.), *Up against Foucault: Explorations of Some Tensions between Foucault and Feminism*. London: Routledge, pp. 1–25.

Rose, N. (1989) Individualizing psychology. In J. Shotter and K. Gergen (eds), *Texts of Identity*. London: Sage, pp. 119–132.

Rose, N. (1990) *Governing the Soul: The Shaping of the Private Self*. London and New York: Routledge.

Sarup, M. (1993) *An Introductory Guide to Post-structuralism and Post-modernism*. Hemel Hempstead: Harvester Wheatsheaf.

Scheper, N. and Lock, M.M. (1986) Speaking "truth" to illness: Metaphors, reification, and a pedagogy for patients. *Medical Anthropology Quarterly*, 17 (5): 137–140.

Spicer, J. (1995) Individual discourses in health psychology. *Psychology and Health*, 10: 291–294.

Stainton Rogers, W. (1996) Critical approaches to health psychology. *Journal of Health Psychology*, 1: 65–77.

6

Making Sense of Illness Experiences

Integrating the Cultural-historical and Local-situated Levels for Understanding Meaning

Mary-Jane Paris Spink

Making sense of illness events is a process that integrates two levels of socially constructed contents: the *collective level* associated with the circulation of ideas and socially instituted practices, and the *inter-subjective* level of dialogical interchanges in daily life. Making sense is fundamentally a linguistic phenomenon, although it may also rely on non-verbal signals. Language is here addressed essentially as action, and more specifically as situated language-use. As such, focus is placed on the communicative function of language, rather than its grammatical and stylistic aspects. This approach to language draws heavily on some of the tenets of Bakhtin's work (Emerson and Holquist, 1994; Holquist, 1994), especially on his views on utterances and addressivity (Bakhtin, 1994).

Many authors – Austin (1962) and Searle (1969) among them – stress the importance of speech exchanges. However, Bakhtin brings to the discussion two aspects that are central to the integrative approach developed in this chapter: the *dialogical overtones* of all utterances – even when they are expressed in a monological format (such as in a scientific text); and the *primacy of context over text*, that makes an utterance 'specially social, historical, concrete and dialogical' (Holquist, 1994: 433).

Any utterance, as Bakhtin repeatedly tells us, is a link in a chain of communication that highlights a 'ceaseless battle between centrifugal forces that seek to keep things apart, and centripetal forces that strive to make things cohere' (Holquist, 1994: xviii). The centripetal forces encompass the pull towards cultural permanencies, among them unitary language systems. The centrifugal forces, scenario for the 'polyphony'[1] of our speech communications, are, according to Holquist, more powerful and ubiquitous because 'theirs is the reality of actual articulation' (1994: xix).[2] In Holquist's words:

> This extraordinary sensitivity to the immense plurality of experience more than anything else distinguishes Bakhtin from other moderns obsessed with language.

> I emphasize experience here because Bakhtin's basic scenario for modeling variety is two actual people talking to each other in a specific dialogue at a particular time and in a particular place. But these persons would not confront each other as sovereign egos capable of sending messages to each other through the kind of uncluttered space envisioned by the artists who illustrate most receiver–sender models of communication. Rather, each of the two persons would be a consciousness at a specific point in the history of defining itself through the choice it has made – out of all the possible existing languages available to it at that moment – of a discourse to transcribe its intention in this specific exchange. (1994: xx)

Thus, understanding meaning in everyday life requires a double effort: focusing on the concrete chain of utterances that take place in *local-situated contexts*, in order to understand the here-and-now specificity of dialogue; and mapping the more general *cultural-historical context* that shapes the various social languages and speech genres.

The Cultural-historical Context of Meaning

Mapping the cultural-historical context is above all an incursion into the history of ideas. It implies the development of a historical sensibility (rather than being an exercise in history making) with the aim of apprehending the possibilities of meaning at the collective level.

Meaning at the collective level is a particular configuration resulting from the triangulation between the contents of the social imaginary, of the scientific enterprise and of the cumulative social experiences in our daily lives, as shown in Figure 6.1.

The social imaginary is here understood in Castoriadis' (1987) frame of reference. The imaginary, Castoriadis tells us, has nothing to do with a mirror-like image of reality, nor with the Freudian notion of 'fantasy'. Rather than being an 'image of', 'it is the unceasing and essentially *indeterminate* (social-historical and psychical) creation of figures/forms/images on the basis of which it is possible to talk about "something"' (p. 3). In other words, what we call reality and rationality are basically the sub-products of the imaginary, rather than its determinants.

The imaginary, therefore, is neither pure function, nor pure symbol; it is instituted meaning expressed through symbols and functions. It is the *sine qua non* of social organization and in no manner reducible to 'pure ideas'. The social imaginary, in Castoriadis' version, does find anchorage in corporeality; the world that presents itself to our senses is indeed articulated by biological necessities such as eating and sexual reproduction. However, it is not the fact that humans have eaten or produced children that gives us clues to social organization. It is the meanings articulated around eating and producing children that generate specificity to each social organization.

The foundational aspect of the social imaginary can best be understood when thought of as the 'cumulative web of meanings' that interpretative

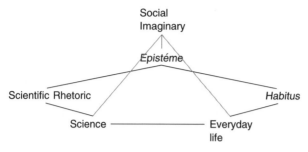

Figure 6.1   *Meaning at the Collective Level*

anthropologists call culture (Geerz, 1973). Conceived as a web, its contents are nowhere specifically and yet are everywhere, deposited as they are in all manner of cultural artefacts with which we come into contact in our daily life: traditional songs and rhymes ('Sugar and spice and all things nice, that's what little girls are made of'), proverbs (Early to bed, early to rise . . .), iconography (such as the variety of representations of women and babies) and all forms of written texts.

The contents of the social imaginary are pervasive but not binding, for new arrangements are always possible and new contents can disturb established patterns and configurations. Different arrangements emerge because access and interpretation are bound by our experiences as situated subjectivity – the systems of durable, transposable dispositions called *habitus* by Bourdieu (1994).

The notion of *habitus* was developed by Bourdieu with the difficult aim of introducing a generative principle of structuration of social practices and representations – with a strong resonance of Chomsky's generative grammar – but sufficiently flexible to account for the active participation of the subject and thus avoid the pitfalls of structuralism. *Habitus* is 'structured structures predisposed to function as structuring structures' (1994: 96), thus, integrating all past experiences forms the basis of perception and appreciation of all subsequent experience.

> It ensures the active presence of past experience, which, deposited in each organism in the form of schemes of perception, thought and action, tends to guarantee the 'correctness' of practices and their constancy over time, more reliable than all formal rules and explicit norms. (ibid.: 98)

Anchored in socialization processes, *habitus* has heuristic value for understanding both the differences in world views that emerge from the diversity of social positions within society, and the experience of a consensual world. In Bourdieu's words: 'The homogeneity of *habitus* that is observed within the limits of a class of conditions of existence and social conditionings is what causes practices and works to be immediately intelligible and foreseeable, and hence taken for granted' (ibid.: 102).

However, being a 'matrix generating responses adapted in advance to all objective conditions identical to or homologous with the (past) conditions of its production' (ibid.: 110), it is also open to re-signification in the light of new experiences and new contents. Understanding meaning at the collective level, especially when the reference model is modernity (or post-modernity), urbanity and global society, must inevitably take into consideration the informational disruption associated with the advances of science (here including the technological developments that exponentially increase the spread of information derived from all manner of scientific endeavours).

Modern consciousness is undoubtedly fed by the products of science. Science has become a commodity. Moscovici, in his major work on the social representations of psychoanalysis (1961), warns convincingly that the angle through which the relationship between scientific contents and modern consciousness should be seen is not that of diffusion or distortion of contents, but of its socialization effects.

> The appearance of a science or a new technique has a similar effect. The relationship with the world, the hierarchy of values, the relative valuation of behaviours, all that is disturbed. Norms are simultaneously changed: what used to be permitted reveals itself as prohibited, what used to be irrevocable seems revocable and vice versa. The microbe theory of illness institutionalized hygiene. The rites of cleaning, isolation, the prescriptions for avoiding contact with certain people, certain animals, certain objects, of a search for a purified environment, gave origin to the sequence of medicaments that prevent rabies, tuberculosis, venereal disease, etc. Vaccination received the force of law and disinfection received the authority of rule. Little by little everyone assimilated these rites, these prescriptions, forced them upon others and became, so to speak, their own doctors, each and everyone equipped with their own medical science. (1961: 23)[3]

Science generates new possibilities of meaning and the close surveillance by media – because science is always 'news' – makes the circulation of new ideas, or new configurations of previous contents, spin progressively faster. Examples in the AIDS arena are plentiful: from nomination ('gay cancer' to female holocaust), to hope (from certain death in a short time to an expensive chronic disease); from non-civilized (the perverse sexuality in the simian or homosexual origin theories) to a consequence of civilization (the breakdown in the immune system).

However, as many sociologists of science have been showing (Knorr-Cetina, 1981; Latour and Woolgar, 1986, among others), science itself is a social practice bounded by the rules of the scientific game that are in operation in a given historical moment, and that are equally fed by the contents of the social imaginary, whenever there are gaps in the meaning text.

The intertextuality of science, mingling scientific texts with a variety of contents derived from the social imaginary, is seen whenever the rule-bounded discourse gives way to the meaning imperative of daily practices. Research carried out on a clinician's view on essential hypertension patients (Spink, 1994a) illustrated the recourse to lay theories whenever medical explanation was not sufficient to account for the everyday practice in the consultation room. Thus, while talk about hypertension was based on medical textbook repertoires, talk about the patients frequently resorted to repertoires stemming from many different vocabularies: psychological, gender and environmental talk. For example, stress was seen as central to the development of essential hypertension, but its meaning was derived from very different gender-based experiential spheres: work relationships for men, sexual-familial experiences for women.

What constitutes legitimate science is bound by rules stemming from the scientific rhetoric dominant at a given historical period. These rules serve as filters in the complex relationship between social imaginary and organized social enterprises, just as *habitus* structures the potentially 'polysemic'[4] nature of repertoires during our socialization process. However, the model presented in Figure 6.1 incorporates yet another filter: the *epistéme*

> We suspect, perhaps, that *epistéme* is something like a world view, a slice of history common to all forms of knowledge and that would impose on each one of them the same norms, the same postulates, a general stage of reason, a certain structure of thought from which people of a specific period would not know how to escape – broad legislation written, most definitively, by an anonymous hand. (Foucault, 1969: 217)[5]

Thus, understanding meaning at the collective level implies necessarily an understanding of the rule-bound circulation of ideas described in Figure 6.1. The inclusion of cultural and social contexts increases the complexity of research procedures in that an immersion into the historical, anthropological and sociological contexts of meaning productions becomes necessary. It also increases complexity because it brings to the fore the 'polyphonic' nature of meaning in modern society. Under the impact of global media there is both an acceleration and proliferation of contents. The acceleration stems from the increasingly present media resulting in the immediacy of events – hot news! Proliferation is a by-product of the increased availability of information sources (TV, Internet). The result is both cacophony and the imperative of making choices. Cacophony because there is no linearity: old and new contents, whether contradictory or not, can live side by side. Choice because the cafeteria aspect of post-modern information implies navigating through diversity and contradiction. Discussing processes of individualization in modern society and its implication for love and intimacy, Ulrich Beck and Elisabeth Beck-Gernsheim comment on the new imperative of choice:

> Everywhere we look in our private lives we see new openings and find ourselves forced to make decisions. . . . The option to take no decision at all is vanishing; having the chance to choose puts one under pressure to do so. So there is no evading going through the mills of weighing up our feelings, our problems and the possible consequences. (1995: 35)

Making Sense as a Day-to-day Imperative

Although the collective level gives us access to the repertoires available to us in a particular place and time, making sense is necessarily a local and situated process. It is a powerful and perhaps inevitable force shaping human social practices. In fact, we would go as far as proposing that our daily life is a continued process of production of meaning, and that meaning is the result of an active – or more precisely, interactive – process of elaboration of social knowledge.

The expression 'social knowledge' is here used to emphasize the dimension of knowledge as social practice, as opposed to knowledge as mere information content, devoid of its historical and situational characteristics. The expression 'common-sense knowledge' is purposely avoided because inherent in its use is the acceptance of a polarization between common sense and scientific knowledge. Explicitly or implicitly, this polarization introduces a hierarchy based on a rhetoric of truth which is 'articulated around scientific reason and around the scientific criteria used to warrant the validity of descriptive or explanatory assertions' (Ibañez, 1991: 7). In contrast, the notion of 'social knowledge' brings to the fore the socially constructed nature of knowledge, the diversity of possibilities within the social language/genre continuum and the dialogical characteristic of our exchanges in everyday life.

Coherent with this perspective, making sense is here taken to be a social practice, essentially dialogical and frequently based on sharing linguistic signs. Central to this view is the concept of *discursive practices*. Following Davies and Harré (1990), the term discursive practices is used to refer to all the different ways in which people, through their discourses, actively produce psychological and social realities. Discourse, 'in this context, is to be understood as an institutionalized use of language and language-like sign systems' (p. 45).[6] According to Davies and Harré, institutionalization can occur both at the macro level of political and disciplinary systems and at the more restricted level of specific social groups. Therefore, 'discourses can compete with each other or they can create distinct and incompatible versions of reality' (ibid.).

Discourses, thus defined, bear similarity to *social languages* in Bakhtin's conception. For Bakhtin (according to Holquist, 1994: 427) a social language is 'a discourse peculiar to a specific stratum of society (professional, age group, etc.) within a given social system at a given time'. These various languages, as will be discussed later in this chapter, constitute the collective repertoires that are available for making sense.

Discursive practices are phenomena at the level of interaction and can be apprehended empirically, in Bakhtin's perspective, through the concepts of 'utterance' and 'addressivity'. The *utterance* is the point of departure for understanding speech communication. Although constructed from language units (words, phrases and sentences), its main constitutive feature is the 'change of speaking subject'. The ensuing sequentiality frames each utterance by the introduction of clear-cut boundaries, thus 'creating for it a stable mass that is sharply delimited from other related utterances' (Bakhtin, 1994: 76).

Although configured by the change of speaking subjects, utterances have definitive and rather stable forms of construction: the *speech genres*, 'a horizon of explanations brought to bear on certain classes of text types' (Holquist, 1994: 428) such as rejoinders of everyday dialogues, military commands, business documents, scientific texts, novels and many others. There is a rich repertoire of genres that we use confidently and skilfully 'in practice', but might not even suspect their existence 'in theory'. However, using repertoires freely and creatively is not the same as creating a genre from the beginning; they must be fully mastered in order to be freely manipulated (Bakhtin, 1994: 80), a typical Bakhtinian statement that serves as a reminder of the need to integrate the cultural-historical context when working with meaning.

Any utterance is a link in a chain of speech communication. The very boundaries of the utterance are determined by the change of speaking subjects: 'every utterance must be regarded as a response to preceding utterances of the given sphere' (Bakhtin, 1994: 91). However monological they might seem – as in a scientific text – they 'cannot but be, in some measure, a response to what has already been said about the given topic, on the given issue, even though this responsiveness may not have assumed a clear-cut external expression' (p. 92).

Therefore, a constitutive marker of the utterance is its quality of addressivity. In Bakhtin's words, 'the utterance has both an author . . . and an addressee' (p. 95).

Every utterance is expressed from a particular point of view: a subject position, his or her conceptual horizon, intentions, and world view. This point of view is the subject's 'voice'. However, for Bakhtin this voice does not exist in isolation because, as aptly formulated by Wertsch (1993: 52), 'meaning can come into existence only when two or more voices come into contact: when the voice of a listener responds to the voice of a speaker'.

In this manner, understanding is always a confrontation of two or more voices, even when these voices are temporally and spatially distant. They may even be, as pointed out by Wertsch, 'the voice of an indefinite, unconcretized other' (1993: 53). The obvious consequence of such formulation is that discursive practices are always dialogical (or at least have dialogical overtones): the utterances of a person are always in contact with, or are addressed to another person and these voices are in a permanent process of inter-animation, even if the dialogue occurs as an inner speech.

The concept of *dialogical inter-animation* allows for the introduction of the concept of *positioning* (Davies and Harré, 1990) and, hence, for proposing that making sense is always concomitantly a discursive production of the self. In other words, when we focus discursive practices we are also faced with identity constructions. To position oneself (or accept being positioned by others) implies navigating through the multiple narratives with which we come in touch and that are articulated in our discursive practices. In the words of Davies and Harré (1990: 46):

> Who one is is always an open question with a shifting answer depending on the positions made available within one's own and others' discursive practices and, within those practices, the stories through which we make sense of our own and

others' lives. Stories are located within a number of different discourses, and thus vary dramatically in terms of the language used, the concepts, issues and moral judgments made relevant and the subject positions made available within them. In this way poststructuralism shades into narratology.

Integrating Levels: Cultural Permanency and 'Polysemy'

Although the appropriate scale for understanding meaning is the level of face-to-face interaction, the repertoires used for making sense are derived from the level of collective consciousness. The concept of collective consciousness here utilized does not imply homogeneous consensual contents. To the contrary, it brings forth the 'polysemic' nature of the repertoires available as a direct consequence of our experiences with various social languages that result from our many affiliations within society: the language of our primary socialization; those associated with our professional worlds; the languages specific to our various leisure activities, and so on.

These various languages are learned in the context of our lived-in time. *Context*, as proposed in earlier papers (Spink 1994a, 1994b), is defined not only by the social space in which the action takes place; it is also defined by a temporal perspective. Not time measured by the clock or by the rolling of days, months and years, but rather the internal time that results from the relationship between the action imperative of everyday life and the resonance of collective memories. As such, the time that defines the context can have different duration.

Face-to-face interactions take place in the *short time*. In this here-and-now scale the focus is on the functionality of the repertoires used for making sense. Context, in this scale, consists of a clear description of the interactive situation and of the dialogical inter-animation that is its characteristic.

The *lived-in time* is the expansion of the short time so as to include the determinants stemming from the process of socialization. This is the territory of the *habitus* – the acquired dispositions resulting from the affiliation to specific social groups and the multiple social languages that are acquired in the process of socialization.

However, the lived-in time of group affiliation can be expanded to a wider collective perspective taking into consideration not only the *habitus* but also the more global characteristics of the social context. In this scale, the cumulative web of meanings of our society, *the social imaginary*, comes to the fore bringing us to the frontiers of the history of mentalities.

'Polysemy' is the result of the coming together, in the short time of interaction, of the many voices which echo our social encounters in the lived-in time *and* the cumulative contents of the long time. It is the rule rather than the exception in our dialogical exchanges.

As we move in scale, for example when we focus the shared contents of a segment of society, 'polysemy' is inevitably shadowed by *sharedness* (Rose et al., 1995). When the focus is on sharedness we look for the nuclear contents of representations about specific social objects which circulate in a particular group within society or, on a more macro level, for the world views of a particular socio-historical period.

In other words, sharedness is only one of the many aspects of situated interactions. Focus on sharedness inevitably shadows other aspects, poly-semy among them, because such focus demands a collective approach to social phenomena; an epidemiological (Sperber, 1989) as opposed to a microgenetic approach to the study of the symbolic contents of communi-cation.

In synthesis, when we focus inter-action, seen through the lenses of discursive practices, we find polysemy and contradiction. We come face to face with processuality and with the situated nature of the repertoires used for making sense. We allow for the emergence of the construction of multiple versions of the self. In contrast, as we distance ourselves theor-etically and empirically from the here-and-now time, we highlight abstract constructs such as typification of roles; discursive rules; social languages and social identities.

Choosing to work with the production of meaning at the level of situated dialogical exchanges, research is inevitably carried out at what Duveen and De Rosa (1992) have termed a microgenetic scale, requiring:

- the identification of the voices that are present in the dialogue and the social languages in which they speak;
- an understanding of the process of dialogical inter-animation which takes place at face-to-face interactions: the manner in which utterances come into contact in dialogical interchanges, setting a chain of speech communication.

Researching Meaning in the Health Arena

This approach, integrating the cultural-historical and the local-situated levels in understanding meaning, is here illustrated with a research example in the area of AIDS. The Bela Vista Project is a study of the incidence of infection by HIV in a cohort of men who have sex with men. It is a study financed by the United Nations Program on AIDS (UNAIDS) and by the National Program on STD/AIDS of the Brazilian Ministry of Health.[7]

In this study the volunteers are followed for a three-year period, return-ing to the research unit every six months. At each visit to the unit they undergo a series of procedures: clinical evaluation; collection of blood samples for serology for HIV, hepatitis B and C, and syphilis; a socio-behavioural interview and counselling for prevention of infection by HIV. Various activities are also offered as part of cohort maintenance, such as fortnightly film discussions and workshops.

Recruitment started in August 1994 and consists of 662 volunteers. Many of these volunteers have already returned for the six-month follow-up visit, thus enabling initial analysis to be made of changes regarding safer-sex practices. Comparative data from successive visits on sexual practices and number of partners suggest that, although this is a highly motivated and well-informed group, a high number of risky practices are still carried out. This result has been quite disturbing for the research team who have queried the effectiveness of the counselling techniques presently in use and have asked for in-depth studies in order to better understand how the notion of risk was being construed.

In order to further understanding of the social construction of risk by the volunteers of this cohort, we developed 'risk workshops' aimed at exploring the meaning of risk and its implications for risk management in the AIDS scenario.

Prior to the development of these workshops, research was carried out on the available repertoires concerning risk through an extensive bibliographical review and word-association exercises. The bibliographical review brought to light the multiple meanings of risk historically bound to different domains: gambling, nautical insurance, economics and epidemiological surveillance. This historical exploration revealed an important difference: while in gambling, nautical insurance and economics, risk is imbued with the dual sense of gain and loss, its migration into epidemiology led to an impoverishment of meaning. Risk in this latter domain was divested of its potential positivity, becoming fundamentally associated with probability of morbidity and mortality.

The word-association exercises, based on the eliciting of associations and a hierarchical sorting in search of the central nucleus of representations of risk (Abric, 1994), revealed once again, the intrinsic ambivalence of the term. Risk associations emerged as both positive (challenge, adventure, growth, advancement) and negative (danger, threat, loss).

These explorations into the social imaginary and into the diverse social languages available for talking about risk constituted the necessary antecedents of the 'risk workshops'. In these workshops three exercises were used:

- free associations with the word risk introduced as preliminary sensitization to the objectives of the workshop;
- memories of past experiences of risk situations, aimed at identifying acquired dispositions regarding risk in the socialization process;
- memories of recent situations when participants felt 'at risk' of HIV infection.

For the second and third exercises we distributed slips of paper on which the participants wrote the experiences of risk that they could remember – one experience per slip of paper. Each slip was then placed in one of three different piles on the floor: one for risk situations which were independent of their will; a second for those situations which were consequences of their actions but where there was no awareness of the risk implied; and a third for situations where there was consciousness of the risk involved.

In the second and third exercise, after having been sorted into different piles, the slips were returned to the authors and participants volunteered to read aloud one situation of his choice. It was difficult to limit discussion to this task because each narrative generated new memories of similar events in other participants and the sharing of experiences produced a climate of solidarity which, in one specific case, was turned into a seduction game.

The workshops were tape-recorded with the agreement of the participants. The analyses of these recordings suggest that the risk of 'coming out' as a homosexual was a central element in the construction of 'being at risk'. Furthermore, the various narratives generated an appropriate scenario for a group construction of the meaning of being a homosexual through dialogical inter-animation. This dialogical co-construction is illustrated in the following passage derived from a two-hour workshop.

The chain of speech communication of which these excerpts are part followed the revelation of the contents of a slip of paper concerning memories of past experiences of risk (therefore not necessarily related to AIDS) that participant number one had allocated to the second pile on the floor (situations that were the result of an action of the subject but in which there was no awareness of the risk involved). It is important to note that, on reading it aloud, this young man reconsidered the experience of risk by saying:

> I don't think in fact that it was a risky thing because I was protected. However much it might have been a shock for them [his parents], I knew I was not going to be turned out of the house, be stoned by them, or such like.

The central theme of the sequence chosen for discussion here was the 'revelation' of homosexuality, which was collectively constructed in the dialogues by bringing forth the voices of the family, the 'non-homosexual others', and those who in this workshop situation positioned themselves as homosexuals. The voices of the *family* and of the *non-homosexual others* emerged as the guardians of sexual morality. For example:

> *Number 3:* Now, myself . . . my family that is traditional Italian. I'll arrive and say 'hey folks I am gay'. They will (*inaudible*) or call for Al Capone (*general laughter*). No, seriously, because when I was a child, if you said you were a homosexual you'd get beaten up.
>
> *Number 4:* In reality [the homosexual] is one only thing: a transmitter of AIDS. This is what we are considered by our families, by my family, by anyone's family.

In contrast, the voices of the *participants* bring to the dialogical situation the multiplicity of the ways in which one can be positioned as a homosexual and that can be synthesized in the polarity between discretion and visibility. For example:

> *Number 4 (to Number 1):* Look, there is a great deal of difference here. Everyone can see it. In your position, anybody seeing you anywhere, will he say you are a homosexual?

Number 2: No!
Number 4 (speaking softly): But for us . . . must we say something?
Number 2: No! *(everyone laughs)*

And later . . .

> I'd like to be as discreet as him [referring to Number 1], because wherever I go, wherever I am, wherever I pass I am seen. It is not that I go out with a flag shouting that I am gay, no. However much I might want, especially on the day when I say 'No! today the man in me will materialize. I'll walk sort of with open legs to say I am a man'; this day is the day that I'm most flirted with. It's terrible. So for him [referring to Number 1, the initiator of the narrative of revelation] it's easier. For us it is different.

At each turn of the dialogue, a chain of speech communication was created which claimed inclusion in society but recognized the power of exclusion through prejudice. For example:

> But, you know what happens today, I mean, it has always been like this, everyone sees homosexuals as bed. Just that. Sees the guy with another guy in bed. Nothing else. Doesn't want to know if he works, if he has responsibilities, if he pays income tax. (Number 1)

This is a narrative built by all; the theme is complemented or contested by the other participants so that the dialogue carries on:

> That's it. (many voices)
> They think that we are, I am sorry, that homosexuals are only objects of desire. That they are only good for bed; from bed to bed; from one bed to another . . . (Number 4)

The long time of history makes itself felt through the many images of what masculinity is: walking with open legs; participating in sports – images that are crystallized in the lived-in time of the socialization processes, in which, in this particular exchange, the family plays a central role. In contrast, in the here-and-now time, privileged *locus* of dialogical inter-animation, it is not only the process of making sense of the sexual option which is at stake. This is also the space for affection, be it from the point of view of sharing experiences and jointly constructing a version of what is a homosexual, or from the point of view of developing amorous relationships. Thus, throughout this particular workshop we saw the development of a seduction game between two participants punctuated, initially, by dialogicity, then by seduction gestures (like letting loose one's hair in a seductive manner) and finally by an explicit bringing together of lived experiences in order to demonstrate the inevitability of a common destiny.

Concluding Remarks

The example chosen, although focused on the collective construction of sexual identities, has obvious consequences for preventive work in the AIDS scenario. The potential contributions stem from the attempt to address the multiple meaning possibilities of risk that are derived from acquired dispositions in the context of past experiences in the socialization process and from actual encounters with risk situations.

Understanding acquired dispositions, within the frame of reference delineated in this text, goes beyond concrete life histories. It is anchored also in a deconstruction type of analysis in search for the multiplicity of repertoires that have been cumulatively produced for talking about and dealing with a variety of risk situations: from gambling through to insurance policies, from money investments through to extreme sports.

These meaning possibilities are set in motion whenever social encounters call forth positioning on risk issues such as in the negotiation for the use of condoms, for entering or not entering dangerous situations (such as drunken driving) or exposure of one's sexual orientation.

Integrative research, therefore, necessarily has three consequences with wide theoretical and methodological implications:

1   By focusing on dialogicity, meaning is situated at the interface between instituted social practices and historically constituted discourses, with the implication that a certain degree of historical sensibility is needed.
2   By emphasizing the role of communicative processes, meaning becomes permeated by questions of identity, making the dichotomy between reason and emotion obsolete.
3   By favouring the microgenetic scale of analysis, the concomitance of narratives is highlighted. As in the example here presented, the same conversation can bring forth a multiplicity of competing theories about a social object. To navigate through these narratives implies opening our understanding to the processes of argumentation that uncover the multiple positioning of the self in whose favour the arguments are structured.

Notes

1. From the Greek reference to the simultaneity of many sounds or voices.
2. The confrontation of these forces is best articulated in Bakhtin's notion of 'heteroglossia':

> At any given time, in any given place, there will be a set of conditions – social, historical, meteorological, physiological – that will insure that a word uttered in that place and at that time will have a meaning different than it would have under any other condition; all utterances are heteroglot in that they are functions of a matrix of forces practically impossible to recoup, and therefore impossible to resolve. Heteroglossia is as close a conceptualization as is possible of that locus where centripetal and centrifugal forces collide; as such, it is that which a systematic linguist must always suppress. (Holquist, 1994: 428)

3. The page numbers of the citations from Moscovici and Foucault refer to the Brazilian translations of their work.

4. From the Greek: a word with multiple meanings.

5. The page numbers of the citations from Moscovici and Foucault refer to the Brazilian translations of their work.

6. Conceived as institutionalized language systems, the notion of discourse bears resemblance to the Foucauldian concept of discursive formations (Foucault, 1969). It differs, however, from the manner in which the term is employed by Potter and Wetherell (1987: 7), covering 'all forms of spoken interaction, formal and informal, and written texts of all kinds'.

7. The Bela Vista Project is part of a multicentre research programme that is being carried out in São Paulo, Minas Gerais and Rio de Janeiro. The Bela Vista Project is linked to the São Paulo State Vaccine Committee and has the institutional support of the São Paulo State Health Department (through the Institute of Health and the Centre for Reference and Training in DST/AIDS) and the Municipal Health Department, and the logistical support of the Adolfo Lutz Institute for all laboratory tests. The study has two Principal Investigators: Dr José da Rocha Carvalheiro for the epidemiological aspects and myself for the socio-behavioural component.

References

Abric, J.C. (1994) *Pratiques Sociales et Représentations*. Paris: Presses Universitaires de France.

Austin, J.L. (1962) *How to Do Things with Words*. Oxford: Clarendon Press.

Bakhtin, M.M. (1994) The problem of speech genres. In C. Emerson and M. Holquist (eds), *M.M. Bakhtin: Speech Genres and Other Late Essays*. Austin, TX: University of Texas Press, pp. 60–101.

Beck, U. and Beck-Gernsheim, E. (eds) (1995) *The Normal Chaos of Love*. Cambridge: Polity Press.

Bourdieu, P. (1994) Structures, *habitus* and practices. In *The Polity Reader in Social Theory*. Cambridge: Polity Press, pp. 95–110.

Castoriadis, C. (1987) *The Imaginary Institution of Society*. London: Polity Press.

Davies, B. and Harré, R. (1990) Positioning – the discursive production of selves. *Journal for the Theory of Social Behaviour*, 20 (1): 44–63.

Duveen, G. and De Rosa, A.S. (1992) Social representations and the genesis of social knowledge. *Ongoing Productions on Social Representations*, 1 (2–3): 94–108.

Emerson, C. and Holquist, M. (eds) (1994) *M.M. Bakhtin – Speech Genres and Other Late Essays*. Austin, TX: University of Texas Press.

Foucault, M. (1969) *L'Archéologie du savoir*. Paris: Gallimard.

Geerz, C. (1973) *The Interpretation of Cultures*. New York: Basic Books.

Holquist, M. (1994) *The Dialogical Imagination*. Austin, TX: University of Texas Press.

Ibañez, T.G. (1991) Henri, Serge . . . and the next generation. *Newsletter of the Social Psychology Section, British Psychological Society*, 24: 5–17.

Knorr-Cetina, K.D. (1981) *The Manufacture of Knowledge: An Essay on the Constructivist and Contextual Nature of Science*. Oxford: Pergamon.

Latour, B. and Woolgar, S. (1986) *Laboratory Life: The Construction of Scientific Facts*. Princeton, NJ: Princeton University Press.

Moscovici, S. (1961) *La Psychanalise – son image et son public*. Paris: Presses Universitaires de France.

Potter, J. and Wetherell, M. (1987) *Discourse and Social Psychology: Beyond Attitudes and Behaviour*. London: Sage.

Rose, D., Effraim, D., Gervais, M.C., Joffe, H., Jovchelovitch, S. and Morin, N. (1995) Questioning consensus in social representation theory. *Papers on Social Representation*, 4 (2): 150–155.

Searle, J.R. (1969) *Speech Acts*. Cambridge: Cambridge University Press.

Sperber, D. (1989) L'étude anthropologique des représentations – problèmes et perspectives. In D. Jodelet (ed.), *Les Représentations Sociales*. Paris: Presses Universitaires de France.

Spink, M.J.P. (1994a) Permanência e diversidade nas representações sociais da hipertensão arterial. *Temas em Psicologia*, 2: 199–212.

Spink, M.J.P. (1994b) Desvendando as teorias implícitas: uma metodologia de análise das representações sociais. In P. Guareschi and S. Jovchelovitch (eds), *Textos em Representações Sociais*. Petrópolis, Rio de Janeiro: Vozes.

Wertsch, J.V. (1993) *Voices of the Mind*. Cambridge, MA: Harvard University Press.

7

Feminist Approaches to Qualitative Health Research

Jane M. Ussher

Feminist researchers have been investigating the lives of women since the beginning of this century. Health has always been an issue of central concern in this sphere. In the so called 'second wave' of feminism, which can be dated to the early 1970s and beyond, debates about issues such as contraception, abortion, sexuality and madness dominated the feminist agenda, with well-organized political campaigns and academic critiques leading to both social change and the development of women-centred professional practices. Since the early 1980s, there has been a greater focus on research, with increasing sophistication in the development of feminist theory, epistemology and methodology. In the field of health psychology, this covers a broad spectrum, including research on pregnancy and childbirth, motherhood, premenstrual syndrome, post-natal depression, the menopause, reproductive technologies, abortion, eating disorders, infertility, gynaecological examinations, mental health, AIDS, sexuality and sexual health, lesbian identity and health, breast cancer, cosmetic surgery, the impact of sexual violence and childhood sexual abuse, ethnicity and health, cancer, coronary heart disease, substance abuse and life-span issues, including adolescence, adulthood, and later life (for example, see Boyle, 1997; Chesler, 1995; Malson, 1997; Nicolson, 1998; Nicolson and Ussher, 1992; Squire, 1995; Stanton and Gallant, 1995; Ussher, 1989, 1991; Walker, 1997).

The vast majority of this research is qualitative. However, it would be a mistake to categorize all of the qualitative research which is conducted on women's health[1] as 'feminist'. Much of it is not. Feminist research is distinguishable by its theoretical or epistemological standpoint, rather than by its methods. It will overlap with many of the other approaches to health psychology outlined in this book in both theory and method, yet at the same time will differ from non-feminist approaches in a number of key areas. The aim of this chapter is to illustrate what it is that distinguishes a feminist approach to qualitative health research. In order to do this, in the first half of the chapter I will outline the general over-riding principles of feminist research, and then in the second half, taking the phenomenon of premenstrual syndrome (PMS) as an example, outline the differences between feminist and non-feminist approaches, in order to illustrate the practical implications of this particular theoretical and epistemological standpoint.

Defining Feminist Research

Distilling the essence of a feminist approach to health psychology is not as straightforward a task as it might first appear. Rather than there being one consistent feminist orthodoxy, there are many different 'feminisms', each with different priorities and practices, resulting in a range of feminist epistemological and methodological standpoints.[2] These could broadly be distinguished as feminist empiricist, post-modernist, critical realist and standpoint approaches. However, what these different approaches share is a common agreement about the centrality of the critical analysis of gender relationships in research and theory; the focus on the detrimental impact of patriarchal power and control in both academic theory and professional practice; an appreciation of the moral and political dimensions of research; the view that women are worthy of study in their own right; and the recognition of the need for social change to improve the lives of women. The goals of feminist research could be described as the establishment of collaborative and non-exploitative relationships in research, to place the researcher in the field of study so as to avoid objectification, and to conduct research which is transformative (Creswell, 1998; Wilkinson, 1996). One of the reasons why qualitative methodologies are commonly (but not solely) used by feminist researchers, is because there is an emphasis within feminist theory on giving voice to the subjective views of women, and valuing them in their own right. This is because a central aim of all feminist research is the ending of the invisibility and distortion of female experience, in ways which serve to abolish gender inequalities and discrimination against women (Lather, 1991).

Theory and Critique in Feminist Research

Feminist research is inherently critical. Its starting point is the assumption that mainstream or traditional approaches to the study of women's lives (and thus women's health) are infused with androcentric biases. It is argued that they exclude or distort the experiences of women; that they use male norms to define women as deviant (or not); that differences between men and women are invariably construed as inferiorities on the part of women; that they ignore or deny the impact of social and cultural factors in the aetiology of problems; that they fail to see power relations as central to social life; and that 'woman' is viewed as a unitary category, meaning that differences between women – issues such as ethnicity, sexuality, disability and social class – as well as the complexity of gendered experience, are not acknowledged. In the field of health, medicine, psychology, psychotherapy and the allied disciplines, as both bodies of research and professional disciplines, have been accused of creating theories and therapeutic interventions which potentially damage the health of women through locating problems within the individual, implicitly pathologizing femininity, and ignoring the socially constructed nature of health and illness. The phallocentric or patriarchal nature of health research and health care has been criticized, with researchers and health professionals accused of maintaining and reinforcing gendered power structures which negate the interests and needs of women. For example, the medicalization and subsequent pathologization of female reproduction has been criticized (Ehrenreich and English, 1978; Martin, 1987; Nicolson, 1998), as has the categorization and treatment of women with mental health problems (Chesler, 1995; Ussher, 1991) or with cancer (Meyerowitz and Hart, 1995). Many feminist researchers and clinicians have developed alternative methods of assessing and intervening with women's problems as a result (for example Burstow, 1992; Butler and Wintram, 1991; Worell and Remer, 1992).

Early feminist efforts in the sphere of health were focused mainly on critique – exposing the inherent gender biases as an attempt to redress the balance in both psychology and other health-related disciplines. However, one of the ways in which feminist critics differ from many others loosely defined as post-modernist, is that as well as reconstructing and criticizing existing theory, epistemology, methodology, and professional practice, alternative solutions are posed to forward our understanding of women's lives and women's health, as will be outlined below. In order to provide a concrete example which will allow illustration of the different models of feminist research, I now turn to an area of research where there has been a considerable amount of development of theory and methodology, that of PMS. I will start with a brief discussion of the current state of knowledge in this field, and then go on to look at the various feminist alternatives to mainstream approaches.

Premenstrual Syndrome

Premenstrual Syndrome (PMS) has been a subject of debate for mental health professionals since its first description as 'premenstrual tension' in the 1930s, and latterly its inclusion as 'late luteal dysphoric phase disorder' (LLPD) in the DSM-IV. PMS includes a range of up to 150 different symptoms, including irritability, depression, tiredness, lack of concentration, hostility, aches and pains, diarrhoea and constipation, and it is estimated that between 10 and 40 per cent of women experience serious disruption to their lives premenstrually because of PMS (Mortola, 1992).

A range of aetiological theories and treatments has been proposed to explain the multiple-symptom complex of PMS, with most research focusing on biomedical explanations. However, a number of recent reviews of the literature come to the same conclusion: there is no simple biological substrate for PMS, or simple relationship between hormones and PMS symptoms; and while many medical treatments are effective in symptom reduction, no one treatment has been shown to be consistently more effective than placebo (Bancroft, 1993; O'Brien, 1993). The inconsistencies and contradictions between the biological theories and therapies, the inability of researchers to identify clearly an hormonal substrate, and the high placebo response, have lent strength to the view that psychosocial factors are implicated in the aetiology of PMS. These include stress or life events, marital dissatisfaction, negative attribution of cyclical changes in physiological activation, and individual differences in personality or cognitions associated with menstruation (see Asso, 1988; Bancroft, 1993 for reviews). This has led to the suggestion that psychological interventions may be appropriate, either in addition to or instead of biological treatments (Bancroft, 1993), and there have now been a number of published studies demonstrating the efficacy of psychological approaches such as cognitive or behavioural therapies for PMS (Kirkby, 1994).

However, no one explanation is adequate to explain the multiple-symptom complex of PMS, and no one treatment has been demonstrated to be consistently effective for all women sufferers (O'Brien, 1993). It has been argued that current research on PMS is entrenched in a bipolar split between those who advocate uni-dimensional biomedical theories and treatments, and those who advocate uni-dimensional psychosocial theories (Ussher, 1992, 1997a; Walker, 1995). This has led to what might be termed a crisis or impasse in PMS research: manifested by a fragmentation of theory and practice, a splitting of the research camps, and a distinct absence of progression in both theory and methodology (Ussher, 1992; 1996).

While the field of PMS research is undoubtedly fragmented, and the existing biomedical and psychosocial theories and treatments may appear to have little in common, or even to stand in opposition to each other, what is often overlooked is the fact that researchers in both fields share the same epistemological assumptions and, as a consequence, adopt the same methodology and methods in investigating PMS. It could be argued, because PMS researchers have adopted the realist/positivistic epistemology which has dominated science since the seventeenth century, that little attention has hitherto been paid to what has become a taken-for-granted fact. Yet arguably it is the particular nature of the positivist/realist standpoint that has resulted in the impasse in this field.

This positivist approach has resulted in a concentration on quantitative methodologies, and the focus on achieving statistically significant results in experiments or questionnaire studies, within a hypothetico-deductive framework, which looks for simple causational or correlational relationships between biomedical or psychosocial variables and reporting of premenstrual symptomatology. It has also led to a limitation in the research questions which can be addressed, and to a narrow understanding of the phenomena of PMS. PMS research positioned within such a vein – whether it is biomedical or psychosocial – negates any discussion of PMS as a gendered illness, and limits our understanding of why certain women report PMS, and others don't, as many of the factors which are said to predict reporting of PMS, such as levels of hormones or psychosocial variables, are shared by both symptomatic and non-symptomatic women. It also negates any analysis of the wider social and discursive factors associated with PMS reporting, and the function of the dominant social and medical representations of PMS as a biological 'illness' that can act as a source of attribution for a wide range of female distress, dysfunction, and deviance (Ussher, 1989, 1996).

What is left out of the mainstream agenda is central to feminist critiques of PMS: the acknowledgement that PMS is a socially constructed category which continues the historical connection between femininity and reproduction, between the womb and female subjectivity; the recognition that 'symptoms' of PMS, such as anger or discontent, are frequently those which are at odds with stereotypes of appropriate femininity; the recognition that by including PMS in the DSM-IV a significant proportion of women are implicitly defined as suffering from a psychiatric condition for one quarter of their reproductive lives; the fact that 'PMS' is not a valid syndrome, as there is a low level of concordance between symptoms, and no core set of symptoms which occur for all women who are diagnosed as sufferers; the view that PMS is used as a means of dismissing legitimate anger or discontent experienced by women as being due to raging hormones, thus negating any analysis of the social context of women's lives, or the factors which may lead to the development of psychological symptomatology (see Ussher, 1989).

These opposing theoretical positions may appear to be irreconcilable. However, arguably they are not. Feminist researchers present us with a way out of this impasse. The first solution is through the introduction of material-discursive models for theory and research, where biological, psychosocial and discursive factors can be addressed within a framework that does not privilege one or the other (Ussher, 1997a; Yardley, 1997). This results in a movement away from the existing dichotomy of medical and psychological approaches, and consequently addresses the difficulty of the splitting of research camps, as it is acknowledged that PMS results from a complex relationship between psychosocial and biomedical factors, which interact in the context of the dominant discursive construction of female reproduction as negative, and potentially disabling (Ussher, 1989). This model also acknowledges that PMS is a gendered illness; that the interpretation of symptoms as 'PMS' has to be seen in the context of the current production and reproduction of medical knowledge in relation to female psychology and biology (Rodin, 1992), as well as dominant discourses about femininity (Ussher, 1997b).

The second solution is a widening of the research agenda to include more qualitative methods and data analysis, which will potentially generate a new impetus to a research field which is notoriously atheoretical (Asso, 1988; Parlee, 1991; Ussher, 1992), through providing a rich contextualized account of women's subjective experience of PMS. The existing literature has neglected considerations of women's subjective experience of PMS, or its relationship to female subjectivity, as it is predominantly based on experimental or quasi-experimental research designs. Qualitative research in this field may also add impetus to a long overdue epistemological critique, which will move PMS research away from an entirely hypothetico-deductive vein, thus broadening the type of research questions which can be addressed, and consequently broadening the understanding of PMS which can be achieved. The form this research will take can encompass the whole range of qualitative techniques, from observations, narratives, stories, interviews, and focus group discussions; the 'data' may be produced by researchers, participants, or by agreement between the two; it may be derived from archives. However, while feminist researchers may agree about the socially constructed nature of PMS and about the importance of exploring women's subjective experiences in this arena, they differ in the theoretical and epistemological standpoints which they adopt in their research, as will be illustrated below.

Feminist Empiricism: Counting Women In

Feminist empiricism starts from the assumption that women's experiences have been made invisible within psychology, and that the aim of feminist research is to focus on women. This could be described as 'counting women in', both as researchers, and as participants in the research. Part of this approach is to acknowledge that theory can be grounded in women's experience and that it is appropriate to use one's self as source for the development of theory or research. In this vein, emphasis is placed on the importance of women as scientists; the notion that women researchers may bring a different perspective to the research process, which will be valuable to furthering understanding of the experiences of women. It is assumed that this perspective will be less partial or distorted than that which has gone before under the guise of 'objective' science. While feminist empiricists often use quantitative methods, qualitative research was advocated early on in this endeavour as a flexible means of attending to the complexity and the context of women's lives. However, the epistemological stance of this strand of feminist research is still broadly empiricist (see Henwood 1996 for a discussion of these different strands), with an emphasis on the discovery of valid representations, and the use of content analysis, or protocol analysis as a means of interpreting qualitative texts. There will also be attendance to reliability and replicability in the design of research studies, leading to structured or semi-structured interviews, attendance to consistency in the interview setting, and often attempts to recruit representative samples. The hypotheses of the research do not change as the research progresses. Kidder and Fine (1997) have called this work qualitative research with a *small* q, as it is not part of a radical tradition, in contrast to *big* Q research which is unstructured, inductive, and grounded in the participants' experiences.

In the field of menstruation and PMS, feminist empiricist research has in the main been quantitative, driven by the intention to overturn existing misinformation about female reproduction. For example, there is a vast body of work examining the effects of menstruation on women's performance, demonstrating that there is little or no effect (Sommer, 1992). Equally, feminist empiricists have adopted questionnaire methods to demonstrate that women differentially attribute symptomatology to the menstrual cycle or to life events, depending on the stage of the cycle they are currently at (Koeske, 1983), or to demonstrate that women do not report increases in negative moods premenstrually on prospective questionnaires, while they will on retrospective questionnaires. This research has then been used to challenge many of the reductionist assumptions about the supposed negative effects of menstruation, and to demonstrate that women are not necessarily debilitated by reproduction (Ussher, 1989, 1992).

What marks this strand of work out as 'feminist' is not necessarily the way in which the research is conducted, but the theoretical or ideological assumptions underlying the whole research enterprise, and the use to which the resulting data are put. The methods may follow traditional empiricist standards, but the findings are used in a critical way to explore the androcentric basis of existing assumptions about these areas of women's experience, and in many instances to challenge existing health practices.

Other strands of feminist research take a more critical starting point, questioning the epistemological assumptions of mainstream research, and, as a result, propose alternative strategies for examining PMS, or other aspects of women's health.

Epistemology and Ontology: Reframing the Gaze of the Researcher

Feminist Post-modernist Approaches

Along with many post-structuralist or post-modern critics,[3] a central tenet of this strand of feminist research has been a critique of the epistemological and ontological assumptions of mainstream psychological research, and the development of alternative standpoints for researching the lives of women. Positivism and realism, the epistemological standpoints underlying medicine, psychology and other mainstream health research, and the methodologies which result from this position, have come under particular scrutiny. What is rejected is the notion of universals or metatheory, and the emphasis on rationality, reason and technology. The elements of positivism which are criticized are the emphasis on methodological naturalism, the demand for homogeneous methods and approaches in both the social and natural sciences, with the latter providing the model for the former; the belief that knowledge is only possible as the result of observation, and the only things that can be observed are those which are accessible to the senses; the emphasis on causality in terms of antecedent conditions and general laws governing phenomena; the view that facts and theories can be separated from values, with only the former being the legitimate focus of scientific interest; and the view that the researcher is objective and value-free. The fundamental premise of a realist perspective, that objects have real existence independent of any perceiver, or of any cultural knowledge or practice, is also rejected.

The alternative view which is put forward is that knowledge must be understood in relation to the historical and cultural context in which it is situated; that knowledge is sustained by social practices; and that knowledge and social action go together (Burr, 1995). Subjectivity, behaviour, and the very definition and meaning of what is 'health' and what is 'illness' are seen to be at least partially (if not solely) constructed within social practices and rules, language, relationships, and roles; they are always shaped by culture and history. Science is part of this constructive process, and, as a consequence, research or clinical intervention in the field of health can never be seen as objective or neutral; it is a social practice which partly shapes and constructs knowledge. This does not mean that research is pointless, but merely that reflexivity in theory and practice is an essential part of the research enterprise. In qualitative interviews, attention will be paid to the way in which meaning is actively constructed within the research context, as a result of the interplay between the researcher and the participant. Equally, the way in which meaning is constructed by the researcher at the level of analysis of texts will be openly discussed. This form of qualitative inquiry would fit with Kidder and Fine's (1997) notion of *big Q* research, discussed above.

Feminist post-modernists would argue that judgements about truth and falsity are always socially constructed, and thus as women (or feminist) researchers we cannot claim less distortion or partiality than male (or non-feminist) researchers. What we need to do is be aware of our own particular gaze as researchers, of the influence of our own subjectivity on the research process, and of the moral, political and cultural concerns which shape both ourselves as researchers, the research process, and the lives of the women (or men) we investigate. However, there is also a questioning of the tendency to view women's experience as a pure onto-logical state which precedes social and interpretive processes (Henwood, 1996: 39), so this is always a critical reflexive process, where we are not attempting to uncover 'truth'.

These critiques have been influential in 'dethroning' experts in many arenas, and in challenging the underlying assumptions of science and scientific practice in relation to health. But this feminist post-modernist perspective has also been used as the epistemological basis of much research and clinical practice where the gaze of the researcher is on the 'social' rather than on the individual, and where methodological naturalism is explicitly rejected. One example within the field of PMS is that of a study carried out by Rittenhouse (1991), where the emergence of PMS as a 'social problem' was examined, using qualitative content analytic techniques.

Medical, popular and feminist literature on PMS from the 1930s to the 1980s was deconstructed. Rittenhouse argued that the surge of interest in PMS in the 1980s was, in part, shaped by interactions between popular, medical and feminist responses to two well-publicized British court trials in which women charged with manslaughter used PMS as a defence. She concluded that the increasing emphasis on a reductionist analysis of PMS within medical and mass media accounts, where PMS is considered to be an hormonal disorder which affects large numbers of women, was a reaction to feminist challenges to the notion of PMS. This was used to expose the ideological underpinnings of expert knowledge about PMS. In a similar vein, Laws (1991) interviewed men about their knowledge and perceptions of menstruation and PMS, concluding that PMS is a social category that pathologizes women by placing a biological or medical label on their rebellion or discontent, and thereby dismisses it, a process which implicitly acts to empower men. Lovering (1995) adopted this standpoint to examine the meaning of menarche and menstruation for young girls and boys. Using a Foucauldian (1979) reading of the texts, Lovering identified discourses of shame and embarrassment, and of the 'otherness' of the female body, in the girls' and boys' discussions. These were located in the historical and cultural context which positions menstruation as taboo and a sign of sickness or dirt (Ussher, 1989).

In a separate study, Swann interviewed women attending a PMS clinic, and identified a number of discourses within which women positioned their experience of premenstrual symptomatology: a discourse of biology and embodiment, a discourse of femininity, a dualist discourse, and a discourse of blame and attribution. Within each of these there were con-tradictory and often oppositional descriptions of PMS and of the assumed causes of symptoms (Swann and Ussher, 1995). Framed within a positivist perspective, this would suggest 'unreliable' data. Framed within a post-modern feminist perspective, these contradictions are to be expected, as it is argued that meaning is multiple, fragmented, fluid, and often contra-dictory (Potter and Wetherell, 1987). The basic premise of this epistemo-logical position is that there is no one 'true' story about PMS (or any other phenomenon for that matter). This particular study also illustrated the way in which the women negotiate their status as PMS sufferers within the context of their negotiation of their identity as women. For it was argued that the four discourses outlined fit into a more global discourse of femininity – of what it is to be a 'reproductive woman' (see Ussher, 1996). As was noted above, this issue of negotiation of meaning and explorations of the relationship between PMS and the construction of female identity have thus far been neglected in PMS research.

Feminist Critical Realism

Critical realism is one example of an approach which is used to attempt to reconcile both the biomedical and psychosocial aspects of experience, as well as acknowledge the cultural and historical context in which individual women and men are positioned, and in which meaning about experience is created. It is increasingly being adopted by feminists in both PMS research, and in a wider sphere (Doherty, 1994; Ussher, 1996). Critical realism (Bhaskar, 1989) affirms the existence of reality, both physical and environmental, as a legitimate field of inquiry, but at the same time recognizes that its representations are characterized and mediated by culture, language, and political interests rooted in factors such as race, gender or social class (Pilgrim and Rogers, 1997). Thus the role of hormones, the endocrine system, or physiological arousal, as well as the influence of social stressors, age, or economic factors, can be acknowledged and studied as 'real' in analyses of the aetiology of PMS. The existence of 'real' premenstrual symptoms would also be acknowledged, whether they be psychological or physical, as would the existence of material factors which might precipitate symptoms. However, these symptoms or material factors are not conceptualized as independent entities which exist separately from the historical or cultural context in which the woman lives. They are always positioned within discourse, within culture. 'PMS' is therefore always a product of the symbiotic relationship between material and discursive factors; one level of analysis cannot be considered without the other.

The anti-empiricism and apparent relativism of much of social constructionist and post-structuralist theory is rejected by those positioned within a critical realist epistemology (Pilgrim and Rogers, 1997). But the positivist/realist position that 'reality' can be observed or measured through systematic scientific methods that are objective or value-free is rejected. Critical realism does not limit methodological inquiry to the hypothetico-deductive methods used by positivist/realist researchers, or the qualitative methodologies used by discursive researchers. A variety of *sceptical* approaches is suggested (Bhaskar, 1989), meaning that multiple methodologies can potentially be used, either simultaneously, or in succession. Thus the whole spectrum of methods from experimentation, to questionnaires, qualitative interviews, or participant observation might be used, if they were appropriate to the research question being asked. This approach implicitly accepts as legitimate all the questions that the researchers might set out to answer, rather than limiting the research questions because of epistemological or methodological constraints. So we could ask, 'do women's hormones vary throughout the menstrual cycle?' or 'how do women explain "PMS"?', using the appropriate methods to answer the question, without seeing one question as more legitimate than the other, or one type of methodology as providing more objective answers. The results of individual studies could then be seen as pieces within a complex jigsaw, that has to be fitted together to make sense of the phenomenon 'PMS'. As much research will continue to be conducted within a uni-dimensional vein, due to the constraints of the research enterprise, it will inevitably be at the level of interpretation of research results that this interdisciplinary analysis will take place. This has considerable implications for the status of accounts about PMS. No one level of analysis can any longer claim to be the 'true' account of PMS. Each has to be seen in relation to the other.

The findings of the existing research on PMS could be reinterpreted within a feminist critical realist frame; we could legitimately incorporate the results of experimental research on causation, questionnaire studies, and the discursive accounts of women, into one framework. However, in doing so we would have to reject many of the epistemological assumptions underlying individual studies, and the status given to many existing accounts. For example, critical realism explicitly rejects what have been described as the 'predictive pretensions' of natural science, because in examining both human behaviour and the social sphere we are dealing with open not closed systems, and therefore can only explain and describe, not predict. It is argued that the complexity and fluidity of human agency, and the influence of continuously shifting cultural and historical contexts, excludes any possibility of accurate prediction in the social sciences (Pilgrim and Rogers, 1997). Arguably, this critique can be extended to biomedical research, since biomedical phenomena cannot be considered outside the discursive and social context in which they occur, as was argued above. This suggests that we should abandon all attempts to predict accurately single factors which precipitate onset of symptomatology, or effectiveness of one treatment over all others, within PMS research – an enterprise which has in any case thus far been fruitless. Instead, we should be aiming to describe, explain and understand the symptomatology women experience, what it means to women, the factors which may be implicated in both the timing and degree of symptoms, and the ways in which women cope with perceived difficulty.

The combination of the move away from meta-theory or generalizable laws, and the abandonment of prediction, does not mean that we cannot or should not develop effective interventions for women who seek help with PMS. What it does suggest is that treatment trials for PMS must be conceptualized and interpreted differently. We may still want to examine systematically the effectiveness of a particular treatment option in treating premenstrual symptoms; we may still want to compare treatments. Within a critical realist framework we can utilize whatever methodologies are appropriate to address these research questions. However, we cannot make causal assumptions about the aetiology of PMS on the basis of treatment effectiveness. Equally, if we find that a treatment is effective for a significant proportion of women, we cannot assume that this is *the* cure for PMS, as is often implied in the current research literature (or, conversely, if only a minority of women are helped, we should not reject this as a treatment for all women). As premenstrual symptomatology is a fluid and multifaceted phenomenon with many possible aetiological routes, we should expect to find myriad means of prevention or intervention.

Rather than looking for one treatment which helps the majority of women with PMS and then advocating its ubiquitous use, we should be looking to describe, in detail, which women are helped by which treatments, and then to explain why this is so. This suggests that qualitative techniques will be an essential part of any research study, in order to provide the most complete picture of treatment effectiveness. It also confirms the increasingly common clinical observation that individual symptom-based approaches are most appropriate for helping women with PMS, and that a range of treatments should be available in clinical practice (Chihil, 1990; O'Brien, 1993; Ussher, 1992), tailored to the individual woman, within her particular social context. While clinicians may specialize in one type of treatment because of their own professional training and arena of expertise, there needs to be an acceptance of multidisciplinary approaches, where biological, psychosocial, and discursive factors are acknowledged and integrated into interventions offered to individual women who seek help. What the woman herself wants is an essential part of this decision-making process.

The final and perhaps most radical premise behind a critical realist approach is the acceptance of the legitimacy of lay knowledge, which is invariably viewed as having equal, although not superior, status to expert knowledge (Bhaskar, 1989; Pilgrim and Rogers, 1997). This is central to the feminist agenda, allowing for the voice and views of women who have PMS to be a legitimate part of the research process; it explicitly welcomes an acknowledgement of subjectivity, hitherto marginalized or ignored in PMS research. For example, the way in which women construct their understanding of PMS in relation to both medical and media accounts of female reproduction and 'normal' femininity can be seen as a fruitful avenue of research, shedding light on the perception of symptoms, the course of PMS, and mechanisms of coping adopted by individual women. Critical realism explicitly provides acceptance of the fact that lay knowledge may occasionally be superior to that of the experts (Pilgrim and Rogers, 1997). This does not mean an unquestioning acceptance of lay knowledge as 'truth', for both lay and expert knowledge is open to scrutiny and deconstruction. What it *does* mean is that expert knowledge is not automatically accepted as superior or true.

Feminist Standpoint Theory

A more widely adopted feminist approach, which is arguably a sub-type of critical realism, is feminist standpoint theory (recently renamed 'standpoint theory' by its originator, Sandra Harding). Feminist standpoint theory follows many of the assumptions outlined above: the assumption that knowledge is grounded in social reality; the emphasis on the importance of lay knowledge; the rejection of methodological naturalism, the emphasis on observation and prediction, and the separation of facts from values; the emphasis on reflexivity; and the framing of 'the body' within a social constructionist perspective, while recognizing material aspects of bodily experience (Harding, 1993; Smith, 1987). Where feminist standpoint theory differs from other critical realist approaches is in the specific emphasis on gender at both a material and a discursive level. For its adherents argue that positivist/realist epistemologies have provided distorted accounts of women's experience, partly because science itself is gendered (Keller, 1985). It is argued that a less distorted view can emerge by attempting to view the world 'through our participants' eyes' (Harding, 1991, 1993), thereby valorizing the accounts of women. It is also argued that the distinctive features of women's social situations, in a gender-stratified society, may be directly utilized as theoretical and research resources (Harding, 1993). The assumption here is that if we include into the research process those who have thus far been excluded, less partial knowledge will be produced.

Feminist standpoint epistemology also emphasizes the role of research as an impetus for social change, and encourages the use of the research process for empowerment, through a focus on women's agency and by providing new accounts of women's experience. Thus research can be used both to challenge the status quo, and to provide the material to bring about change (Harding, 1987, 1993). Because this standpoint presumes the individual to be agentic (see, for example, Henriques et al., 1984), women are positioned as instrumental in the process of political and personal change. So feminist standpoint theory is concerned with an emphasis upon research *for* rather than *on* women, moving away from traditional science-based accounts of women's experience, and generating new theoretical accounts through which to bring about social change (Harding, 1993).

In the arena of PMS, feminist standpoint epistemology could specifically harness feminist critiques of PMS, and yet still provide a framework for 'do-able' research in this field, within a material-discursive perspective. It is an approach that has been used to examine women's depression (Jack, 1991; Lewis, 1995; Stoppard, 1997) where similar debates have taken place for decades (Ussher, 1991). A feminist standpoint approach was used by Swann (1996) in a multi-methodological analysis of PMS, which combined both experimental and questionnaire studies with the qualitative analysis of women's discursive experiences of PMS discussed above. In clinical intervention, feminist standpoint theory would follow the principles of a critical-realist approach in the design and conduct of treatment, but would include a specific focus on gender issues as central to the agenda, as is common in feminist therapy.

Conclusion

In this chapter I have outlined the major assumptions shared by feminist researchers, and then described the main strands of feminist theory and epistemology which currently dominate the field: feminist empiricism, post-modernism, critical realism and standpoint theory. Using PMS as an example, I have illustrated how these strands of feminist research would differ in the development of theory, or research design, in the field of women's health. What is implicit in this analysis is the fact that feminist researchers share much with non-feminist researchers both epistemologically and methodologically; they also share many theoretical concerns. However, what distinguishes feminist research is the focus on gender, the attention to issues of gendered power, the view that women are worthy of study in their own right, and the agreement that research must be used to improve the lives (and health) of women. Above all else, feminist researchers are sensitive to the context of women's lives; sensitive to the influence of the world outside of academe or the laboratory. An awareness of the way in which this social and cultural context shapes our experience of health and illness, and the way in which research can feed back to change this social context, is central to a feminist agenda. Thus feminist research can never be purely an academic or intellectual exercise. It brings with it an obligation or duty to attempt to impact in a transformative way on women's experience of health or illness, and to challenge the existing prejudices and practices in health psychology (or the allied disciplines) which have marginalized the interests and needs of women for so long.

Notes

1. Feminist research can be applied to the analysis of the health of men; it isn't necessarily on the health of women. However, in this context I will focus on research on women's health, as this forms most feminist research in this area.

2. In a critical analysis of the epistemological assumptions of science and social science, Sandra Harding (1987) has defined epistemology as a theory of knowledge which sets out who may legitimately be deemed a 'knower', what requirements information or beliefs must meet in order to be legitimated as 'knowledge', and what kinds of 'facts' may be known. Epistemology therefore determines both methodology – the 'theory and analysis of how research does or should proceed' (Harding, 1987: 3) – and research methods – the techniques deemed legitimate or appropriate for gathering evidence or information.

3. While feminists and post-modernists share many assumptions, they are overlapping groups, rather than inseparable groups; many feminists are not post-modernists, and vice versa.

References

Asso, D. (1988) Physiology and psychology of the normal menstrual cycle. In M. Brush and E. Goudsmit (eds), *Functional Disorders of the Menstrual Cycle.* Chichester: John Wiley, pp. 15–36.

Bancroft, J. (1993) The premenstrual syndrome – a reappraisal of the concept and the evidence. *Psychological Medicine, Monograph Supplement* 24. Cambridge: Cambridge University Press.

Bhaskar, R. (1989) *Reclaiming Reality: A Critical Introduction to Contemporary Philosophy.* London: Verso.

Boyle, M. (1997) *Abortion: Psychology, Gender, Power and the Law.* London: Routledge.

Burr, V. (1995) *An Introduction to Social Constructionism.* London: Routledge.

Burstow, B. (1992) *Radical Feminist Therapy.* London: Sage.

Butler, S. and Wintram, C. (1991) *Feminist Group Work.* London: Sage.

Chesler, P. (1995) *Women and Madness* (3rd edn). New York: Four Walls Eight Windows.

Chihil, H.J. (1990) Premenstrual syndrome: an update for the clinician. *Obstetrics and Gynaecology Clinics of North America*, 17: 457–479.

Creswell, S. (1998) *Qualitative Enquiry and Research Design*. London: Sage.

Doherty, C. (1994) Subjectivity, reflexivity and the analysis of discourse. Paper presented at the British Psychological Society London Conference, December 1994.

Ehrenreich, B. and English, D. (1978) *For Her Own Good: 150 Years of Experts' Advice to Women*. New York: Anchor Doubleday.

Foucault, M. (1979) *The History of Sexuality*, part 1. London: Penguin.

Harding, S. (ed.) (1987) *Feminism and Methodology*. Indianapolis: Indiana University Press.

Harding, S. (1991) *Whose Science? Whose Knowledge? Thinking from Women's Lives*. Milton Keynes: Open University Press.

Harding, S. (1993) Rethinking standpoint epistemology: 'What is strong objectivity?' In L. Alcoff and E. Potter (eds), *Feminist Epistemologies*. London: Routledge, pp. 49–82.

Henriques, J., Hollway, W., Urwin, C., Venn, C. and Walkerdine, V. (1984) *Changing the Subject: Psychology, Social Resolution and Subjectivity*. London: Methuen.

Henwood, K. (1996) Qualitative enquiry: perspectives, methods and psychology. In J.T.E. Richardson (ed.), *Handbook of Qualitative Research Methods for Psychology and the Social Sciences*. Leicester: British Psychological Society, pp. 25–40.

Jack, D.C. (1991) *Silencing the Self: Women and Depression*. Cambridge, MA: Harvard University Press.

Keller, E.F. (1985) *Reflections on Gender and Science*. London: Yale University Press.

Kidder, L.H. and Fine, M. (1997) Qualitative enquiry in psychology: a radical tradition. In D. Fox and I. Prilleltensky (eds), *Critical Psychology: An Introduction*. London: Sage, pp. 34–50.

Kirkby, R.J. (1994) Changes in premenstrual symptoms and irrational thinking following cognitive-behavioural coping skills training. *Journal of Consulting and Clinical Psychology*, 62: 1026–1032.

Koeske, R. (1983) Sociocultural factors in the premenstrual syndrome: review, critiques and future directions. Paper presented at the premenstrual syndrome workshop, National Institute of Mental Health, Rockville, MD, 14–15 April.

Lather, P. (1991) *Getting Smart: Feminist Research and Pedagogy with/in the Postmodern*. New York: Routledge.

Laws, S. (1991) *Issues of Blood: The Politics of Menstruation*. London: Macmillan.

Lewis, S. (1995) A search for meaning: making sense of depression. *Journal of Mental Health*, 4: 369–382.

Lovering, K. (1995) *Menstruation: Discourses of Menarche, Girls and Society*. Unpublished PhD thesis, University of London.

Malson, H. (1997) *The Thin Women: Feminism, Post-structuralism and the Social Psychology of Anorexia Nervosa*. London: Routledge.

Martin, E. (1987) *The Woman in the Body: A Cultural Analysis of Reproduction*. Milton Keynes: Open University Press.

Meyerowitz, B.E. and Hart, S. (1995) Women and cancer: have assumptions about women limited our research agenda? In A. Stanton and S.J. Gallant (eds), *The Psychology of Women's Health. Progresses and Challenges in Research Application*. Washington, DC: American Psychological Association, pp. 51–84.

Mortola, J. (1992) Assessment and management of premenstrual syndrome. *Current Opinion in Obstetrics and Gynaecology*, 4: 877–885.

Nicolson, P. (1998) *Post-natal Depression: Psychology, Science and the Transition to Motherhood*. London: Routledge.

Nicolson, P. and Ussher, J.M. (1992) *The Psychology of Women's Health and Health Care*. London: Macmillan.

O'Brien, P.M.S. (1993) Helping women with premenstrual syndrome. *British Medical Journal*, 307: 1474–1478.

Parlee, M. (1991) The social construction of PMS: a case study of scientific discourse as cultural contestation. Paper presented to the conference 'The Good Body: Asceticism in Contemporary Culture', Institute for the Medical Humanities, Texan University, Galveston, 12–13 April.

Pilgrim, D. and Rogers, A. (1997) Mental health, critical realism and lay knowledge. In J.M. Ussher (ed.), *Body Talk: The Material and Discursive Regulation of Sexuality, Madness and Reproduction*. London: Routledge, pp. 67–82.

Potter, J. and Wetherell, M. (1987) *Discourse and Social Psychology: Beyond Attitudes and Behaviour*. London: Sage.

Rittenhouse, C.A. (1991) The emergence of PMS as a social problem. *Social Problems*, 38: 412–425.

Rodin, M. (1992) The social construction of premenstrual syndrome. *Social Science and Medicine*, 35: 49–56.

Smith, D. (1987) *The Everyday World as Problematic: A Feminist Sociology*. Toronto: University of Toronto Press.

Sommer, B. (1992) Menstruation and performance. In J.T.E. Richardson (ed.), *Cognition and the Menstrual Cycle*. London: Lawrence Erlbaum, pp. 39–66.

Squire, C. (1995) *Women and AIDS*. London: Sage.

Stanton, A. and Gallant, S.J. (1995) *The Psychology of Women's Health. Progresses and Challenges in Research Application*. Washington, DC: American Psychological Association.

Stoppard, J. (1997) Women's bodies, women's lives and depression: toward a reconciliation of materialist and discursive accounts. In J.M. Ussher (ed.), *Body Talk: The Material and Discursive Regulation of Sexuality, Madness and Reproduction*. London: Routledge, pp. 43–61.

Swann, C. (1996) *Psychology and Self-reported PMS: An Evaluation of Different Research Strategies*. Unpublished PhD thesis, University of London.

Swann, C. and Ussher, J.M. (1995) A discourse analytic approach to women's experience of premenstrual syndrome. *Journal of Mental Health*, 4: 359–367.

Ussher, J.M. (1989) *The Psychology of the Female Body*. London: Routledge.

Ussher, J.M. (1991) *Women's Madness: Misogyny or Mental Illness?* Hemel Hempstead: Harvester Wheatsheaf.

Ussher, J.M. (1992) The demise of dissent and the rise of cognition in menstrual cycle research. In J.T.E. Richardson (ed.), *Cognition and the Menstrual Cycle*. New York: Lawrence Erlbaum, pp. 132–173.

Ussher, J.M. (1996) Premenstrual syndrome: reconciling disciplinary divides through the adoption of a material-discursive epistemological standpoint. *Annual Review of Sex Research*, VII: 218–251.

Ussher, J.M. (ed.) (1997a) *Body Talk: The Material and Discursive Regulation of Sexuality, Madness and Reproduction*. London: Routledge.

Ussher, J.M. (1997b) *Fantasies of Femininity: Reframing the Boundaries of Sex*. London: Penguin.

Walker, A. (1995) Theory and methodology in premenstrual syndrome research. *Social Science and Medicine*, 41: 793–800.

Walker, A. (1997) *The Menstrual Cycle*. Routledge: London.

Wilkinson, S. (1996) Feminist social psychologies: a decade of development. In S. Wilkinson (ed.), *Feminist Social Psychologies. International Perspectives*. Buckingham: Open University Press, pp. 1–20.

Worell, J. and Remer, P. (1992) *Feminist Perspectives in Therapy. An Empowerment Model for Women*. Chichester: Wiley.

Yardley, L. (ed.) (1997) *Material Discourses of Health and Illness*. London: Routledge.

Part II

Conversing about Health and Illness

8

Interviewing the Ill and the Healthy

Paradigm or process?

Cynthia M. Mathieson

Interviewing is rather like a marriage: everyone knows what it is, an awful lot of people do it, yet behind each closed front door there is a world of secrets.

Ann Oakley, 'Interviewing Women'

Part of the allure of qualitative inquiry into health is its power to contextualize. What it means to be healthy or ill must always be interpreted against a socio-cultural background. At the same time, health and illness are intensely personal, affecting individual bodies and intimate spaces. For health psychologists who seek to study such experiences, the interview is a very powerful tool. Yet there is a world of difference between interviewing the ill and the healthy. The ill experience physical and bodily disruption; they are at the centre of an unfolding illness trajectory that shapes their experience. Ill persons must come to grips with dramatic psychosocial changes and institutional events for which they may be unprepared. Interviewing the ill is always a reminder that the most important event in which the ill person is involved is that of negotiating this illness trajectory.

Interviews make accessible a space for ill persons to describe and validate their experiences. Storied frameworks are bound to emerge in such space. This chapter will not attempt to engage in discussion about the precise characteristics of narrative and stories. However, we usually recognize a story when we hear one, regardless of the conditions under which it appears. A brief example serves to illustrate this. In interviews with cancer patients, we once asked 'Do you feel you have received adequate information from health care professionals?' This was part of one woman's response:

So I got the second round of chemo[therapy], and I was halfway through that when I was really getting beaten into the ground, and I said, 'Look, I was told a half year ago that this was not the route to go with cervical cancer. Now why are we doing this?' and so that's when he admitted, 'We don't know how to treat you' and . . . I told him, 'Please don't ever do that to me again. I don't mind not knowing something, but I don't like you knowing something, and me not knowing something. . . .' So he spent three quarters of an hour with me, and you know what he says? 'There should be more conversations like this.' I said '*You* have to instigate this.' We are all dealing with a very dramatic situation here, and you're telling me there should be more conversations like this? Why didn't you pull me aside two months ago and say, 'Here are your choices' . . . but I was left with the idea that there was absolutely no other solution, and there might not be, but at least advise me . . . so I can't say as to whether I've been greatly informed since then. (Also quoted in Mathieson and Stam, 1995: 298)

What the above is *not* is an answer to a question. Her response is a story through which the interview question is given a personal context. This is a story about the difficulties of negotiating the physician–patient relationship and about the power of information in that relationship. This story sits in a larger narrative, evident throughout the entire interview, about this patient's efforts at gaining her own voice with the medical profession over her many years of living with illness.

Qualitative approaches preserve the richness of the ill person's narrative. Those studied should be able to recognize themselves in the research (Schatzman and Strauss, 1973). Neither off-the-cuff conversations nor practised presentations, research interviews are instances of 'joint action' (Shotter, 1993), a by-product of situated speech. Interviews with the ill reflect that period of time when the individual's stories take on a special meaning: 'In the end, they are more than just stories but the vehicle for making sense of, not an illness, but a life' (Mathieson and Stam, 1995: 284). Whatever specific shape researchers choose for their interviews with the ill and whatever questions are asked, the case can be made that the best research interviews with the ill acknowledge at a fundamental level the ongoing illness narrative. This is a narrative about renegotiating one's identity as an ill person.

This chapter will discuss the form, content and context of the face-to-face interview, with a special emphasis on the semi-structured format, especially suited to exploratory studies of a descriptive nature. It is a major qualitative research method for health psychologists who wish to study the nature of change that characterizes the transition from health to illness: the initial impact of diagnosis; the stressors of treatment; changed relationships with family, friends and employers; new and old relationships with health-care providers. All of these changes form part of the story that will emerge during the transition and that are always ongoing to some extent in the case of illness. The implicit reference point in this chapter is that of chronic illness, whose very nature calls into question how we define disease, health and illness (see Gerson and Strauss, 1975). In addition, our discussion situates the interviewer as an active participant in co-constructing the stories that will emerge in the interview.

The Inter-view

The interview holds an important place in the behavioural and social sciences, disciplines devoted to the study of human behaviour. Four decades ago, Kahn and Cannell (1957: 16) supplied an academic definition of the interview, calling it 'a specialized pattern of verbal interaction – initiated for a specific purpose, and focused on some specific content area'. These authors, along with many social scientists to follow, were interested in the interview as a method, which is why the second part of their definition is so important. Here they suggest that the interview will produce 'consequent elimination of extraneous material . . . a pattern of interaction in which the role relationship of interviewer and respondent is highly specialized, its specific characteristics depending somewhat on the purpose and character of the interview'. This definition captures the prescriptive flavour of interviewing that still holds sway today in the positivist paradigm. In this paradigm, research interviewing seems to be a series of methodological problems that have to be solved. The interview questions should be standardized in order, in wording, and in choices for responses. These factors are important in controlling for nuisance variables such as subjects' response biases. Inaccuracies in subjects' self-reports can also be interpreted as a problem. Interviewers should be unbiased and non-directive but at the same time must gain the respondents' trust. They should ensure that each question has a response. In other words, interviewers should have control of their interviews.

Critiques of this view are not news. First, as Oakley (1993) points out, social scientists' assumptions about the standard interviewing paradigm 'reflect their embeddedness in a particular research protocol', a predominantly masculine model of the 'science of the interview' designed to minimize the interviewing context. Oakley goes on to argue that this model necessarily places interviewees in a subordinate position, in effect protecting an interviewer's status as an information collector who has little responsibility to balance the inequality between participants and researchers. As Oakley points out, 'what is good for interviewers is not necessarily good for interviewees' (1993: 228). Second, as Mishler (1986: 27) argues, the conventional approach is based on a set of assumptions that do not acknowledge the essential feature of interviewing – that it is organized social discourse:

> By adopting an approach that is behavioral and antilinguistic, relies on the stimulus–response model, and decontextualizes the meaning of responses, researchers have attempted to avoid rather than confront directly the interrelated problems of context, discourse, and meaning. Put somewhat differently, standard practice provides a set of blinders that excludes this set of problems from a researcher's field of vision.

The process of interviewing invites both the participant and interviewer to enter into discourse. In this case, it is a discourse about what it means to be ill and healthy in our culture.

Form

The Structure of Interviews

The interview might best be framed as a qualitative endeavour insofar as it reflects what is important to qualitative inquiry in general, regardless of the individual approach used. Kuckleman-Cobb and Nelson-Hagemaster (1987) summarize the important components as: attention to social context; emphasis on the view of the participants; a primarily inductive approach; data-collection techniques that include interviewing, observation and documents; data-gathering tools subject to ongoing revision; an emphasis on description; emergent as opposed to *a priori* hypotheses; and discursive/ narrative analyses. It follows that a few additional open-ended questions do not transform a quantitative study. Theoretical framework is paramount.

Interviews in quantitative research are generally aligned with survey instruments, fixed choice questions, random sampling, and large samples. In contrast, in qualitative work, data collection is more or less open-ended. Interview questions are assumed to be flexible, responses are individualized, and the emphasis placed on depth of information – and subsequent analytic techniques – supports small samples. According to Patton (1990), open-ended approaches include informal conversational interviews, general interview guides or schedules, and standardized open-ended interviews. Spontaneous questioning comprises the natural flow of informal conversational interviews (Chenitz and Swanson, 1986). In a more structured situation, a general interview guide may be used to present a set of ideas or issues to participants, without stringent *a priori* wording or order of questions. Here the interviewer is required to tailor the questions as the interview progresses. Intensive interviewing with the aid of an interview guide can also prove extremely effective in capturing the participant's perspective (Lofland, 1974). McCracken (1990) talks about 'the long interview,' designed intentionally to allow the participant to tell his/her own story, with a subsequent exploration of substantial parts of the interview. Finally, standardized open-ended interviews take the participant through a series of questions in a certain order. What is therefore open-ended under these circumstances is the expectation for the participant to respond to the questions in his/her own words. This last approach may be appropriate when several interviewers are involved and the researcher wants to reduce the risk of variations in responses due to the interviewers' inconsistencies in the posing of questions (Patton, 1990).

Considering the above, it is useful to understand that research interviews can be classified according to some degree of structure. Researchers make a distinction between structured and unstructured interviews on the basis of purpose and on type of questioning (Chenitz and Swanson, 1986; Lincoln and Guba, 1985). That is, the structured interview is used when the interviewer has the knowledge to frame the questions necessary to find out the information of interest. The classic structured format employs an interview schedule with a prescribed order and wording of questions from which the interviewer is not expected to vary. Unstructured interviewing lends itself to relying on participants to identify and explain what is important. Here we locate the intensive or in-depth interview, which has limited preconceptions about either content or form (Walker, 1985). What is relevant and meaningful to respondents should emerge within the interview. Responses continually inform the evolving conversation.

The structured format in general has not been attractive to many qualitative researchers because it harks back to the question–answer volley that characterizes the quantitative paradigm and because it usually exercises at least some control over the response format. On the other hand, it is also sometimes difficult for researchers, especially novice ones, to imagine themselves going to an interview without some structure in place. A common answer to this dilemma is the semi-structured interview, which is a hybrid in that it is organized around a specific area of interest, may employ an interview guide/schedule, but still permits the flexibility needed to obtain depth of information (Polit and Hungler, 1987). The researcher tries to achieve this balance with a list of general areas or topics to be covered; in some cases, there may be questions that act as a pre-liminary guide (Taylor and Bogdan, 1984).

The structure of an interview is intricately related to the purpose of the interview and the interviewer's theoretical stance. Whatever structure is employed, adherence to a research 'protocol' by itself is not a guarantee that the resulting information will be valid. In fact, one could argue that concerns about following protocols have diverted researchers' energies to troubleshooting mechanical problems when they should be evaluating the trustworthiness of their information. Researchers necessarily have some research ideas or questions in their minds when they begin their inquiry. With experience in the area comes the ability to discern patterns in inter-view data, which should in turn inform the evolution of the interview and development of theory. Hence, the process of interviewing is one in which interviewers are constantly using their knowledge to make choices about what to ask, how to ask it, and what to explore further. Making these choices imposes structure.

Repeat Interviews

Depending on the purposes of the study, a logical way to achieve depth of information is to consider repeat interviews. While one-time interviews may be appropriate when the topic can be explored in one contact or when access is difficult, repeated interviews usually result in closer rapport and may be useful when change over time is of interest. Repeat interviewing is an important consideration if one bears in mind the illness trajectory. *When an ill person is interviewed* does make a difference. Chronic illnesses pose evolving questions and present ongoing psychosocial stressors that are accentuated under specific circumstances. For example, interviewing the ill who have been newly diagnosed with a life-threatening illness demands an awareness on the part of the interviewer that there may be an 'existential crisis' underway (Weisman, Worden and Sobel, 1980). In illnesses that have acute phases as well as periods of remission, the impact of the chronicity of the illness might be missed entirely in a single interview. Describing the nature of change has to be intimately bound with an understanding of the trajectory.

Oral Histories

Oral histories utilize unstructured, in-depth interviews in which participants are encouraged to share their life stories and significant milestones. In effect, the participant takes on the role of narrator or autobiographer, the researcher the role of biographer. The collected story also forms possible archival material. Gluck and Patai (1991) make two important points about oral histories. First, they make a distinction between oral narratives and oral histories. The former includes life histories, topical interviews, and testimonies. The latter refers to the entire activity of recording, transcribing, editing, and disseminating results. Second, they advance the case that oral histories are especially important for uncovering women's voices and those of marginalized, disempowered groups.

What can be learned from the oral history perspective is fundamental to interviewing the ill. 'Realizing the possibilities of the oral history interview demands a shift in methodology from information gathering, where the focus is on the right questions, to interaction, where the focus is on process, on the dynamic unfolding of the subject's viewpoint' (Anderson and Jack, 1991: 23). Here we can situate the idea of 'joint action' referred to earlier, but more than this, oral histories are perfect vehicles for ill persons to accomplish their 'biographical work'. In studies examining illness from the framework of identity reconstruction (Corbin and Strauss, 1987; Mathieson and Stam, 1995), it is suggested that the major task facing the ill is one of eventually incorporating the meaning of the illness into one's biography. If personal identity is the result of a cohesive life story, then the articulation of the ill person's autobiography has a dual function. First, there is an acknowledgement that the illness has disrupted an older, pre-illness narrative. Second, by ascribing meaning to the events of illness, the ill person is preparing to incorporate the illness experience into the life story. Accounts of illness, whether fragmented or whole, represent a continuous set of attempts to evaluate the meaning of the experience.

Group Interviews

Group interviews deserve a brief mention, having gained in popularity for investigating questions in health research. They are especially useful when a researcher wishes to explore a phenomenon of interest and can appropriately do so through the questioning of several individuals at once. Aside from an efficiency factor, there may be times when group interviews are preferable to individual interviews. These are situations when (a) there are naturally occurring or homogeneous groups; (b) one wishes to explore attitudes, experiences, or cultural practices; c) participants might be reluctant to speak on their own. Group interviewing methods include activities such as focus groups, brainstorming, and field interviews (see Fontana and Frey, 1994). Methods vary from structured to unstructured. In the focus group methodology (Krueger, 1988; Morgan, 1988), the interviewer is usually directive, providing a series of questions to be discussed by a group of invitees. Kitzinger (1994) points out that while focus groups capitalize on the interactions of participants, the data they produce can be cumbersome. In general, focus group methodology has proved popular in health research examining knowledge, attitudes, and behaviours (for examples see Basch, 1987; Duke et al., 1994; Hughes and Drummond, 1993). In our own research, we have employed focus groups when we are not sure where to start in choosing the major questions that might shape a semi-structured interview at the next level of study.

Content

Exposing the 'Methods' Section

There is sometimes a lack of direct explanation about the nuts and bolts of interviewing in qualitative research with the ill. This seems especially true for research using semi-structured interview techniques. Published research articles may neglect to address how questions were generated, what type of statements/questions/prompts were used, and so forth. This may reflect the assumption that researchers working from a particular framework have no need to explicate their methods since a common discourse is assumed. As a result, even in some of the most interesting research about illness, readers are left to work backwards from analyses to deduce the interview content. Readers searching for mentoring about how to actually go about translating their research question(s) into method usually face a serious challenge. A single reference to the structure of the interview and the illness of the participants is not self-explanatory in this regard.

Researchers need to create accounts of their methods that can stand independently; this makes good methodological sense. One would expect to find some explanation in published work to enable the reader to recognize, and then utilize, the details of the interview approach. For example, there are obvious differences in the level of usable information provided to the reader among the following descriptions of 'methods' found in three studies with the chronically ill:

Example a: The data reported here were gathered by semi-structured interviews with a series of thirty patients being referred . . . to an outpatient rheumatology clinic. . . . The aim was to concentrate on those with emerging illness at the earliest possible point, to explore the problems of recognition and changes in life situation and relationships occasioned by the development of the illness. (Bury, 1982: 167)

Example b: A semi-structured interview was used to obtain descriptions of long-term management of MS [multiple sclerosis]. The interviews lasted approximately one to three hours and were recorded for later transcription. This method allowed for interviewer probes as respondents introduced information valuable to an understanding of the chronic illness experience. (Brooks and Matson, 1987: 80)

Example c: Our discussions with women were guided by an interview schedule constructed in consultation with two health care providers, and a woman with diabetes. Questions covered various aspects of women's lives, such as beliefs about illness, the effect of illness on social relationships, perceptions of relationships with health professionals, help seeking patterns, and daily management of diabetes . . . the discussions were flexible enough to allow women to speak of their experience of living with a chronic illness, and to discuss the areas that were paramount in their lives. . . . Sequential interviews were done over a two-year period to give us a longitudinal perspective on what it was like to live with a chronic illness, and how this illness changed over time. (Anderson, Blue and Lau, 1991: 103)

In the first two examples, we do not know what statements, questions or probes are used. Only the last example provides some sense of direction for researchers hoping to learn about the source and categories of questions actually used. The last excerpt hints at critical background work that led to decisions about how to conduct this study, what to ask, etc. This contrasts with many studies, however, where the inductive work that initiates and feeds into the final method is usually hidden from view. This is especially true in the case of false starts, which are tacitly recognized by qualitative researchers conducting preliminary work, rarely described, but nevertheless set the stage for the researcher in seeing patterns in interview material.

What are Questions and Answers?

Kirby and McKenna (1989) suggest that the basis of all interviews is the question. What follows when we transform a research problem into a series of questions? The way questions are worded, their order, participants' understanding of the questions themselves, and why the question is being asked, are of course important. Yet responses to questions are not samples of decontextualized behaviours, nor are the meanings of questions and answers static or transparent. As Mishler (1986: 7) reminds us, 'Questioning and answering are ways of speaking that are grounded in and depend on culturally shared and often tacit assumptions about how to express and understand beliefs, experiences, feelings, and intentions.' Interviews are specific types of speech situations where the native speakers recognize the requirements of the situation. This point is emphasized in Baker's (1984) research interviews with adolescents, where she concluded that standardized questions and prompts derive their meaning from commonly available cultural interpretations about people's behaviour, and that when answers were similar, it had more to do with the participants' skills in accessing this shared knowledge base than with categories of individual behaviours. What a question-and-answer format accomplishes, then, is an invitation for the ill to co-construct with the interviewer their stories of being ill. Stated in another way, being interviewed when one is ill is a culturally acceptable way to tell one's illness story.

Generating an Interview Guide: an Example

Still, the above does not help to clarify how one goes about designing an actual interview guide. For purposes of discussion, the semi-structured format utilizing an interview guide will be highlighted here as an example. Table 8.1 presents an interview guide from an earlier published study (Mathieson and Stam, 1995: 291). To some extent, this study initially emerged from our informal observations about the amount of 'self' talk that occupied cancer patients' dialogues with health-care providers. This category of talk seemed closely tied with the constant, but different, changes patients were experiencing at all points in their illness trajectory. Patients seemed to be saying that they felt like different people as a result of their diagnosis. How were we to study this? And what exactly was the research question? We started by collecting information, stories in fact, from patients and their families, in unstructured, in-depth interviews about these changes. A certain natural flow emerged in the interviews, chronologically ordered and otherwise, that helped us in the long run to make decisions about placement of questions. We also had the occasion to listen to what patients were saying during therapy sessions. We searched the literature widely, both inside and outside psychosocial oncology, to find an umbrella construct with which to approach a research question. Once we settled on the concept of 'identity' as a possible construct, we asked ourselves if we could frame, or reframe, patients' accounts as stories about identity and threats to identity. This was, more or less, our research problem.

A first draft interview guide was generated, used in several interviews, and then revised to accommodate participants' advice about our questions. We sought out 'key informants' (Patton, 1990; Taylor and Bogdan, 1984) to whom to speak; included were two long-term cancer survivors who were in a position to utilize their cumulative knowledge to help us inform our thinking. In brief, we conducted purposive sampling (Glaser and Strauss, 1967) to maximize our preliminary feedback. These early interviews were all highly interactive. Participants were encouraged to give us as much direction as possible about what they thought we were asking, what we should be asking, and how to ask it. We continued to revise the interview guide with our first volunteers for the study. In this sense, then, the interview guide was 'pre-tested'.

The questions are specifically focused in that they ask about particular issues. Their derivations, however, represent a constant interplay among theoretical formulations, available literature, participants' feedback, and what seemed to work – or make sense – as far as ordering our questions. We paid close attention to how participants responded to our questions in the pre-test phase. Did particular ways of framing questions have the effect

Table 8.1   *A Sample of a Semi-structured Interview*

1. Please think back to the 6 months preceding your diagnosis. How would you describe those months?
2. Describe to me what you recall thinking at the time of the initial diagnosis.
3. I would like you to summarize the course of your disease for me thus far. For example, can you tell me about your treatment? How would you describe your 'normal week'? Describe to me what will happen in terms of your next course of treatment.
4. Do you think you have received/are receiving adequate information from health care professionals?
5. What things are different about your life now than before you had cancer?
6. How have people responded to your cancer? What have they said, or done, which was helpful, or not helpful? (a) spouse, (b) family, (c) close friends, (d) other friends, (e) co-workers, (f) health care professionals, and/or (g) anyone else? Did any of these things change the way you thought about yourself or about having cancer?
7. What is different about yourself since your diagnosis? In other words, is the way you see yourself now different from the way you saw yourself in the past?
8. What is different about your body since your diagnosis?
9. Since your diagnosis, has your relationship changed with your (a) partner, (b) family/ children, and/or (c) friends?
10. What do you think caused your cancer?
11. What does the term the 'future' mean to you right now? What are your feelings about your life expectancy?
12. Do you feel your cancer is/can be cured?
13. Is there anything else that I have failed to ask you in this interview which is important for me to know?
14. Looking over your whole cancer experience, what is the most significant change in your life that has taken place as a result of the diagnosis?

Source: Mathieson and Stam, 1995: 291

of opening up versus closing down the discussion? Field notes, our own handwritten notes on interpretations of what we were hearing and of our personal biases, were invaluable for reflection on the revision of individual questions and on the process as a whole.

Since this interview guide was initially published, we are aware that it has been adapted for interviewing with other cancer patients, men with AIDS, women with HIV positive status, and brain-injured patients. Even if one were not interested in studying identity, we believe the categories of questions are useful in capturing the types of stories that are integral to the illness experience, and are therefore appropriate examples of questions about illness that might be placed in an interview guide when one is pursuing exploratory or descriptive analyses. All the final questions met a basic criterion of making sense to participants; the storied frameworks they evoked in the responses give credence to this assumption.

We always start with some background question(s), or what Spradley (1979) calls 'grand tour' questions. Opening with biographical questions (for example, 'Please tell me a bit about yourself . . .') also enables the interviewer to move into collecting more specific demographic information if warranted. Question 2 has its origin in the literature about the 'existential crisis' of diagnosis (Weisman, Worden and Sobel, 1980), although 2 and 3 together emerged from our in-depth interviews as well. The third question also cues for questions about changes coming up later in the interview. The source of question 4 reflects the research about patient–physician communication. We heard here quite elaborate stories – complaints, in fact – about participants' negative experiences with their health-care providers. This is not surprising, if one considers that in the very act of interviewing, we have created an acceptable way for patients to validate experiences that they would not normally bring forward to their physicians. These are experiences that characterize one of the stressors of being in the patient role. Rather than creating the expectation of a yes/no answer, this question evoked what we might call prototype stories about health care interactions.

Questions 5–9 and 14 address the issue of change as a result of illness. Questions 6 and 9 in particular reflect key articles in the social support literature but also recurring themes in our initial observations and first run interviews. If question 10 had not already been addressed elsewhere, we asked it for purposes of consistency. Questions 11 and 12 are 'future' questions. We took our theoretical impetus for these questions from *Women's Ways of Knowing* (Belenky et al., 1986). In some ways, though, future questions proved to be our most important queries, as they framed the participants' discourse about the old healthy self versus the new ill self. Finally, closing question(s) are critical. Questions 13 and 14 ask the participants to tag overtly for the listener what is most important. In this particular study, in response to question 13, we rarely heard anyone say we had missed anything. We did, however, hear participants repeatedly use this question as an opportunity to highlight what was most important for them in the course of the interview; in other words, we had the sense that they were underscoring the main theme of their story.

This interview guide may be misleading in that it appears to lend itself to an invariant administration. This was not the case either in intent or in actuality. Probes/prompts were introduced and pursued freely, and these probes differed from one interview to another. Often participants anticipated forthcoming questions inadvertently and introduced them on their own. With a few participants we even stepped aside, interview guide and all, and just asked individuals to share their stories.

To summarize, we used an inductive, iterative process to generate our interview guide over several stages of development, always guided by a conceptual framework. We matched our hunches about 'self' talk with the extant literature and observations of cancer patients' informal discussions. Then we revised our questions until no additional information emerged to support further changes, a process roughly parallel to saturation in grounded theory (Glaser and Strauss, 1967). Even after we settled on the semi-structured guide, we used it only as a guide.

Context

One of the well-discussed motivations for qualitative inquiry with the ill is the tendency of quantitative studies to strip the context from interpretation and analysis of interview material. We can think about context on two levels. One is the context in which the ill actually experience what illness means. A second understanding of context can help us to address the role of the interviewer. Working from the interview-as-survey perspective, Benney and Hughes (1956: 141) explain:

> . . . the interview is designed to minimise the local concrete, immediate circumstances of the particular encounter – including the respective personalities of the participants – and to emphasize only those aspects that can be kept general enough to be counted . . . recorded in such a fashion that elements of communication in common can easily be isolated from more idiosyncratic qualities.

By now, the issue of neutralizing the interviewer's role in the interview has been recognized and criticized. Oakley (1993) provides such a critique by evaluating her own experiences in interviewing women. Her argument is generally framed against the standard textbook paradigm of the research interview as mechanical data collection in which interviewers are reduced to question-asking. In her own work, Oakley pinpoints two areas of difficulties in adhering to the notion of interviewing as a research protocol: her participants asked many questions of her, and repeated interviewing 'established a rationale of personal involvement' that was unavoidable. These are problematic areas if one believes that interviewers need to maintain distance in order to get good data.

If the ill engage in interviews partially or entirely, intentionally or unintentionally, to tell their stories, then the goal of detachment is misguided, if not inappropriate. In fact, probably one of the most universal experiences my colleagues and I have shared about conducting interviews is the way unplanned levels of engagement between the interviewer and participants are hidden from view in analyses and final reports. This includes everything from spontaneous questioning of the interviewer, to asking for advice, to participants who virtually interview the interviewer. There are also social situations that emerge as adjuncts to the interviewing context, such as invitations to coffee, tea or dinner. In quantitative paradigms, these events are extremely problematic. They interfere with comparisons across interviews, suggest that interviewers do not have proper control of their interviews, and force the researcher to sidestep context. On the other hand, in the qualitative process, they are part of the texture of the interview, appearing in field notes at least and contributing important clues as to the meaning of the interview for the participant.

What is Rapport?

An implicit factor of a successful interview is that of good rapport between the participant and interviewer, but this is a surprisingly ill-defined concept, given its centrality to social science research. Although everyone agrees that rapport is essential, situations that accentuate rapport, such as repeated interviews, have also been seen as problematic methodologically. The familiar paradigm is that of interviewing as a one-time event (Laslett and Rapoport, 1975).

Interviewers' understanding of who they are in the interview context preempts the notion of rapport. Paget's work (1982) is instructive here. Although her research focuses on in-depth interviewing only, a case is made for reflexiveness on the part of the interviewer that is continually activated during the interview. Paget's conceptual stance is that of presuming neither objectivity nor neutrality, but rather personal engagement in her participants' activities and that of her own research project.

Discovery and interpretation are critical to the interview context. As Kvale (1988) explains, the participant discovers new patterns and relationships while talking. The interviewer interprets and reflects back what is heard, summarizing and condensing information. In other words, the interview is truly being 'co-authored'. Anderson and Jack (1991) think of this context as the researcher/interviewer 'shedding agendas' and 'listening for meaning'. The interviewer is transformed into a listener by understanding, indeed by believing, that she is an active participant in the process and that without her presence the space would not be created for these particular illness stories to be told at this particular time. For Jack, this means not appropriating what is said to pre-existing ideas, but listening carefully to what is missing or not said, and intentionally probing the language and the meaning of the narrator's stories. Anderson's caveat, based on her own experiences interviewing women, is important: 'the scholar's search for generalizations undermined the interviewer's need to attend to an individual's experience. Ideally, the process of analysis should be suspended or at least subordinated to the process of listening' (Anderson and Jack, 1991: 15). Taken together, the ideas presented above signal a shift from thinking about the interview context in terms of interviewer–participant roles to those of narrator–listener. For the listener, this is a stance of engagement versus distance.

Recording the Interview

Issues about instrumentation, sampling and analysis are beyond the scope of this chapter. The reader is referred to Miles and Huberman (1994) for a full discussion of these topics. However, a few words should be said about recording the interview. Permission to audiotape interviews is always part of our informed consent procedure. One obvious reason is that the tapes and subsequent transcriptions into text comprise the to-be-analysed data. Even in more structured interviews where participants might be requested to fill in a paper-and-pencil checklist of some sort in part of the interview, we keep the tape running throughout the entire interview. This has proved most informative for learning how participants interpret questions, given the reflective nature of talking to oneself during such tasks. Equally important is our ability to offer participants a copy of what they have said in the interview, either for their personal purposes or for helping us as researchers to obtain direct feedback from participants. Participants have told us that these tapes are a record of their stories, further confirming the interviewers' contribution in co-constructing the final product. Making a copy of the tape available acknowledges that we are not in the business of collecting information which then becomes our sole property.

The Process of Interviewing

Interviewing is a process of story-building. It goes without saying that the same principles that guide interviewing the ill also guide interviewing the healthy. Fundamentally, the process needs two people, a narrator and a listener. The structures we as interviewers superimpose upon the interchange and the questions we choose to ask are methods, to be sure. More than that, however, they are reference points for interpreting meanings and, as such, are only as good as our understanding of why we speak in storied frameworks in the first place. As Plummer (1995) suggests, story-building is a process of incorporating events around instances of disclosure, then reinterpreting the events of one's life according to currently available discourse. This is precisely what the ill must do. Hence, interviews with the ill are not devoid of medical talk, which is but one type of discourse available to them. On the other hand, it is the qualitative interview that has the power to place this medical discourse in its proper context.

Reshaping our fundamental expectations for interviews, especially in regard to talking to the ill, is a challenge for health psychologists. It is the qualitative researchers who are in a position to sustain this dialogue. What is provocative – and critical – to qualitative health researchers may be precisely the 'extraneous material' of the interview. In discourse, nothing is extraneous; responses are never just answers to questions. In every interview about health or illness, there is a narrative underway. What ultimately drives this narrative is the universal need to find meaning. As health psychologists, we have a responsibility to train ourselves to hear this narrative. As qualitative researchers, we have the theory, methodology and analytic techniques to accomplish this. Accounts from ill persons are not all that different from the fundamental stories all of us generate, whether healthy or ill, to identify who we are. Stories told in interviews have the power to reveal the meaning of what it is to be ill in our society and the opportunity to claim, or reclaim, the sense of agency that underlies good health.

References

Anderson, K. and Jack, D.C. (1991) Learning to listen: interview techniques and analyses. In S. Berger Gluck and D. Patai (eds), *Women's Words: The Feminist Practice of Oral History*. New York: Routledge, pp. 11–26.

Anderson, J.M., Blue, C. and Lau, A. (1991) Women' perspectives on chronic illness: ethnicity, ideology and restructuring of life. *Social Science and Medicine*, 33: 101–113.

Baker, C.D. (1984) The search for adultness: Membership work in adolescent–adult talk. *Human Studies*, 7: 301–323.

Basch, C. (1987) Focus group interview: an under-utilised research technique for improving theory and practice in health education. *Health Education Quarterly*, 14: 411–418.

Belenky, M.F., Clinchy, M., Goldberger, N. and Tarule, J.M. (1986) *Women's Ways of Knowing*. New York: Basic Books.

Benney, M. and Hughes E.C. (1956) Of sociology and the interview. *American Journal of Sociology*, 62: 137–142.

Brooks, N.A. and Matson, R.R. (1987) Managing multiple sclerosis. *Research in the Sociology of Health Care*, 6: 73–106.

Bury, M. (1982) Chronic illness as biographical disruption. *Sociology of Health and Illness*, 4: 167–182.

Chenitz, C.W. and Swanson, J. M. (eds) (1986) *From Practice to Grounded Theory: Qualitative Research in Nursing*. Menlo Park, CA: Addison-Wesley.

Corbin, J. and Strauss, A.L. (1987) Accompaniments of chronic illness: changes in body, self, biography and biographical time. In J.A. Roth and P. Conrad (eds), *Research in the Sociology of Health Care*, vol. 6. *The Experience and Management of Chronic Illness*. Greenwich, CT: JAI Press, pp. 249–281.

Duke, S.S., Gordon-Sosby, K., Reynolds, K.D. and Gram, I.T. (1994) A study of breast cancer detection practices and beliefs in black women attending public health clinics. *Health Education Research*, 9: 331–342.

Fontana, A. and Frey, J.H. (1994) Interviewing: the art of science. In N.K. Denzin and Y.S. Guba (eds), *Handbook of Qualitative Research*. London: Sage, pp. 361–376.

Gerson, E. and Strauss, A. (1975) Time for living. *Social Policy*, 6: 12–18.

Glaser, B.G. and Strauss, A.L. (1967) *The Discovery of Grounded Theory: Strategies for Qualitative Research*. Chicago: Aldine Press.

Gluck, S. Berger and Patai, D. (eds) (1991) *Women's Words: The Feminist Practice of Oral History*. New York: Routledge.

Hughes, D. and Drummond, K. (1993) Using focus groups to facilitate culturally anchored research. *American Journal of Community Psychology*, 21: 775–806.

Kahn, R. and Cannell, C.F. (1957) *The Dynamics of Interviewing: Theory, Technique, and Cases*. New York: Wiley.

Kirby, S. and McKenna, K. (1989) *Experience, Research, Social Change: Methods from the Margins*. Toronto: Garamond Press.

Kitzinger, J. (1994) The methodology of focus groups: the importance of interactions between research participants. *Sociology of Health and Illness*, 16: 103–127.

Krueger, R. (1988) *Focus Groups: A Practical Guide for Applied Research*. London: Sage.

Kuckleman-Cobb, A. and Nelson-Hagemaster, J. (1987) Ten criteria for evaluating qualitative research proposals. *Journal of Nursing Education*, 26: 138–143.

Kvale, S. (1988) The 1000-page question. *Phenomenology and Pedagogy*, 6: 90–106.

Laslett, B. and Rapoport, R. (1975) Collaborative interviewing and interactive research. *Journal of Marriage and the Family*, 37: 968–977.

Lincoln, Y. and Guba, E. (1985) *Naturalistic Inquiry*. Beverly Hills, CA: Sage.

Lofland, J. (1974) *Analysing Social Settings: A Guide to Qualitative Observation and Analysis*. Belmont: Wadsworth Publishing Co., Inc.

McCracken, G. (1990) *The Long Interview*. Newbury Park, CA: Sage.

Mathieson, C. and Stam, H.J. (1995) Renegotiating identity: cancer narratives. *Sociology of Health and Illness*, 17: 283–306.

Miles, M.B. and Huberman, A.M. (1994) *An Expanded Sourcebook: Qualitative Data Analysis* (2nd edn). Thousand Oaks, CA: Sage.

Mishler, E.G. (1986) *Research Interviewing: Context and Narrative*. Cambridge, MA: Harvard University Press.

Morgan, D. (1988) *Focus Groups as Qualitative Research*. Newbury Park, CA: Sage.

Oakley, A. (1993) Interviewing women: a contradiction in terms? In A. Oakley, *Essays on Women, Medicine and Health*. Edinburgh: Edinburgh University Press, pp. 220–242.

Paget, M. (1982) Your son's cured now; you may take him home. *Culture, Medicine and Psychiatry*, 6: 237–259.

Patton, M.Q. (1990) *Qualitative Evaluation and Research Methods* (2nd edn). Newbury Park, CA: Sage.

Plummer, K. (1995) *Telling Sexual Stories: Power, Change and Social Worlds*. London: Routledge.

Polit, D. and Hungler, B. (1987) *Nursing Research: Strategies for a Natural Sociology* (3rd edn). Philadelphia, PA: J.B. Lippincott.

Schatzman, L. and Strauss, A. (1973) *Field Research*. Englewood Cliffs, NJ: Prentice-Hall.

Shotter, J. (1993) *Cultural Politics of Everyday Life*. Buckingham: Open University Press.

Spradley, J.P. (1979) *The Ethnographic Interview*. New York: Holt, Rinehart and Winston.

Taylor, S.J. and Bogdan, R. (1984) *Introduction to Qualitative Research Methods: The Search for Meanings*. New York: John Wiley and Sons.

Walker, R. (1985) *Applied Qualitative Research*. Aldershot, UK: Gower.

Weisman, A.D., Worden, J.W. and Sobel, H.J. (1980) *Psychosocial Screening and Intervention with Cancer Patients. Research Report, Project Omega*, Department of Psychiatry, Harvard Medical School.

9

Talking to Children about Health and Illness

Christine Eiser and Sarah Twamley

In modern western society, children's health is very much taken for granted. Improved nutrition and housing, vaccination and antibiotics have drastically reduced the incidence of illness among children – so much so that children rarely experience serious illness. However, children still do develop a variety of less serious health problems. They will also encounter some children with serious illnesses. In this changing situation what do children think of health and illness? It is possible to point to a very substantial literature concerned with adult views of health and illness and ask why we should consider the question separately for children (Petrie and Weinman, 1997). Differences between the types of illness that affect children and adults, differences in cognitive and emotional response to illness, and the greater involvement of the family all necessitate a distinctive approach. The aim of this chapter is to consider some of the methodological issues involved in conducting different types of qualitative research with children and to discuss some areas of application for qualitative methods in health psychology research.

Studying Children and Illness

Children's Concepts of Illness

The first attempts to describe how children think about health and illness were based on methods developed by Piaget to investigate the understanding of physical concepts such as space or time (Bibace and Walsh, 1980; Perrin and Gerrity, 1981). These authors used semi-structured interviews to determine children's understanding of common and less common illnesses, their causes, and rationale for treatment and prognosis. These interviews produced qualitative accounts from the children. The data were, however, subject to formal content analyses, based on a theoretical framework which emphasized children's naivety. It is this framework which has been criticized from many directions.

The Piagetian approach to children's concepts of illness focuses on what children do not know or understand, and draws on a stage model of cognitive development. This model suggests that children go through different stages of conceptualizing health, very much paralleling the schema described by Piaget to account for their understanding of physical concepts such as space or time. In the pre-operational stage (4–7 years) children are unable to differentiate between illnesses and cannot separate cause from effect. At the concrete operational stage (7–11 years) children are more likely to understand illness in terms of contagion or contamination. With the benefits of formal schooling, children in the formal operational stage (from 11 years old) adopt a more biological approach; they understand the causes of illness in terms of breakdown of specific body parts. Empirical work has generally supported this schema, though the practical difficulties of coding children's responses should not be underestimated. More recent workers in the cognitive tradition have offered alternative conceptualizations. For example, Carey (1985) suggested that young children accept a human approach to illness (illness is a result of failing to follow parental advice or not eating when told to). Again this is followed by a biological bias around 11 years of age.

Increasingly it has been shown that many of the underestimates of children's understanding of illness were due to methodological problems in the studies reported. Criticisms have been made regarding the way in which information was elicited from children; the repetitive nature of question-asking and the asymmetrical power relationships between the child and the adult interviewer (Siegel, 1988). Criticisms have also come from other disciplines, notably sociology and nursing, which object to the artificial experimental situations favoured by many psychologists.

Further, allying the socially and culturally immersed concepts of health and illness with the more abstract physical concepts such as space can be problematic (although initially providing a spurious methodological respectability). Research in the Piagetian tradition, focusing on what children do not know, often misses out on what children actually do understand. More recent work involving healthy (Eiser, Eiser and Lang, 1990) and sick children (Bearison and Pacifici, 1989) suggests that they are able to report detailed and accurate accounts of illness events. Research should be *for* rather than *on* children, looking at children as active participants within their own cultural world rather than as incompetent or at best immature adults.

From a social constructionist perspective there is a need to connect the children's expressed beliefs with the immediate and broader social context. Prout (1986) argues that previous work in this area has ignored the routine, everyday framework of childhood illness. In his own ethnographic study, Prout (1986) studied children's claims about sickness at school and at home, and how these are shaped by context and interaction with others. Similarly, Mayall (1993) emphasized the differing perceptions of children as active individuals, not as objects of socialization or as developmentally 'incomplete' beings. She described how children understand and negotiate their status in different settings, and the implications this has for their health-care responsibilities. She argues that the 'distinctive social and emotional context of the home and school are critical for the structuring of children's health care and experience' (Mayall, 1993: 464).

Children's Reaction to Illness

As in other areas of psychology, the traditional and often preferred approach to investigating the impact of illness on children has been to employ standardized assessment instruments. Thus, we may choose between measures of function (for example, Walker and Greene, 1991) or depression (for example, Birleson, 1978). There are also disease-specific scales to measure, for example, the child's perception of quality of life in asthma (Juniper et al., 1996) or cancer (Varni et al., 1998). These tests are very attractive to use; they are usually relatively quick, easy to score, and yield a number, thereby allowing us to compare one child with another. The method offers adequate reliability and apparent precision. This 'scientific' approach is much favoured by journal editors and reviewers.

Despite the apparent scientific rigour, we might question whether this method really provides comprehensive information about the child's thinking. Although the question is asked in a standard way, children may not interpret it so. Considerable research suggests that this might be the case. For example, attempts have been made to distinguish between healthy children and those with a chronic condition on a number of outcome measures, usually on the assumption that sick children will evidence poorer function or well-being. However, evidence suggests otherwise. For example, when children with cancer were compared with healthy children in terms of depression, there was no difference (Greenberg, Kazak and Meadows, 1989). More difficult to interpret is the fact that, on occasions, children with cancer report less depression than healthy children (Canning, Canning and Boyce, 1992). One explanation that is often given for this finding is that sick children interpret the assessment task differently. In particular, they may readjust their expectations about what they want, or are able to do. Thus, children with serious illness would seem to interpret 'standard' questionnaires differently from healthy children.

Qualitative Methods

The above criticisms emphasize the need for a qualitative approach when studying children's understanding of health and illness. There are rarely standardized measuring instruments available for use with children, so the conventional questionnaire approach is not an option. Further, sick children deserve and demand sensitive methods of data-gathering; impersonal, closed-ended questionnaires are unlikely to provide this. Methods must be chosen to reduce the prospect that participation in research will upset the child, and this is more likely to be achieved where sensitive methodologies are chosen, which allow children ample opportunity to express their views rather than restrict them to a narrow range of answers that reflect the adult's view.

In nearly all circumstances the best source of knowledge about what a child thinks and feels is most likely to be gained directly from the child. Talking to children is, however, challenging: children have a limited (and different) vocabulary compared with adults. They may not be capable of abstracting their feelings sufficiently to talk about them. Children often approach adult conversation warily, searching for the 'correct' response (Siegel, 1988). As a result, parents have often been consulted as substitute experts on their child's view. Parents, however, are often inaccurate reporters, their answers too often reflecting their own concerns and anxieties. Although accurate when identifying behavioural or 'acting-out' problems, they may often miss feelings of anxiety or sadness in the child. Sometimes this may be the result of a situation in which the child deliberately avoids a topic which clearly provokes an anxious response. At other times, the child may exaggerate symptoms as a means of getting attention from the parent. Equally, parents are not in a position to know about the difficulties a child may experience at school or with friends.

Interviewing Children

Many of the requirements for conducting a good interview with adults apply equally when working with children. It is important to establish rapport, to reassure them that there are no right or wrong answers, and to make provision for adequate support after the interview if there is any chance it may lead to distress. What exactly does it mean to establish rapport with a child, and how easy is it to achieve? It is essential to try to establish an equality between interviewer and child, a relationship that may be especially difficult to achieve given the established power differential between children and adults (Ginsberg, 1997). Second, children need some explanation for the event. This can require sensitive explanation and careful planning. Children are likely to be suspicious about explanations that 'today we are going to play some special games together' and will look for motives more in keeping with normal adult activities!

The interview, in theory, has considerable merit over questionnaires as a source of child-centred data. However, the interview can be difficult to conduct and analyse. Ross and Ross (1984) argued some time ago that it is important to create an appropriate setting for the work. They suggested that children respond well to interviewers who emphasize why it is important that this particular child is interviewed. Children respond well to being told that they are the 'experts' and that the researcher has much to learn from them. It is important that children do not see the interview situation as a test. Identifying and promoting children's viewpoints entails shifting the conventional balance of power, so that children feel more in control of the situation. This can be difficult to achieve; children are not socialized to be assertive in a world of unfamiliar adults.

Alderson (1993) also suggested that it is important to focus on eliciting children's experiences rather than their opinions. Interviews should be conversational in style, using a topic guide (Fielding and Conroy, 1992). Interviews that arise naturally and informally are seen as most appropriate. For children with a short attention span, a number of sessions is likely to be necessary. As is often argued in qualitative work, it is important to return to the participant to verify the interpretation. This may be especially important when working with children, as it may be difficult for the interviewer to interpret responses as easily as when working with adults.

Working with sick or impaired children necessitates methodological flexibility and a fair degree of ingenuity. Researchers may often have to deal with situations where children are very young; for example, the mean age on diagnosis of leukaemia is 4 years of age (Boring et al., 1994). Very ill children may not have the energy or physical ability to complete written measures or talk much. Dealing with children who do not reply can be embarrassing for everyone but also creates a dilemma for the interviewer. Is the child not responding because this is a very distressing topic that should be allowed to drop, or does the child consider the question so trivial as not to merit an answer? There are few guidelines about how far to push the non-responsive child, and decisions have to be based on experience and clinical judgement.

Drawings

Talking may present problems where children do not have the vocabulary to articulate complex concepts or feelings. In this situation, having children represent their thoughts in drawing can often be helpful. Using drawings as part of research has also been found helpful with special needs students, younger children and children where the language of instruction is not their first language (Pridmore and Bendelow, 1995). As drawing is something that is often part of the school routine, this is a very non-threatening approach. In conjunction with an interview the drawing can serve to facilitate communication between child and researcher, perhaps especially where children are being asked to talk about their feelings. An inevitable difficulty with interpretation of more symbolic material can be partially resolved by asking children to explain their drawing themselves. These comments should also be recorded and analysed. Drawings have been widely used in health education to trigger discussion and seek solutions to health issues.

One method that has been used with children is the 'draw and write' technique. Charlton (1980) used this method to explore children's beliefs about cancer. Children were asked to use 'draw and write' in order to explore 'what cancer means to me'. Themes arising from the children's drawings were then used to inform the development of a later survey. Drawings also have potential when working with children from different cultures. They have been used, for example, to examine beliefs about health and illness in primary school children in Botswana (Pridmore and Bendelow, 1995). Children were asked to draw and write about what makes them healthy, what makes them unhealthy and what people die from. The study showed that children in Botswana perceived death to be caused by disease and 'spirit people'. Interestingly, the children's perceptions of what made them healthy all fell into one category – food.

Play

Play has proved a good medium for work with sick children, especially in preparing them for complex medical procedures. Olvera-Ezzell et al. (1994) used structured play to examine Mexican-American children's under-standing of the relationship between health behaviour and health status. Children were encouraged to role-play being a parent to the experimenter. The experimenter would then lead the child through various everyday situations and elicit the child's opinion, for example asking, 'Mummy can I eat this carrot off the floor?' and then 'Why?' or 'Why not?' Questions regarding illness contamination were assessed with the help of a toy puppet. The explanations were then coded according to the rationale used by the child, for example:

Magical ('Don't play outside after dark because of the monsters.')
Punishment ('The police will take you to jail if you don't wear your seat belt.')
Appearance ('Your hair will turn white.')
Sickness ('Don't eat too much or you will be sick.')

Although this was not strictly a qualitative study it is illustrative of the rich data that play can provide, and shows that play methods would certainly be adaptable to a qualitative approach.

Focus Groups

An alternative method of working with children is the use of focus groups. A method that originated within market research, it essentially involves a group interview/discussion focusing on a particular topic, led by the researcher using a semi-structured interview guide. The exchange is usually transcribed and may also be videotaped to allow behavioural observation. This method is particularly useful where time and resources are at a premium. Allowing children to explore topics in their own words with their peers enables the researcher to observe group interaction, how children discuss issues between themselves, and may provide a picture of how consensus can be reached. Conversational exchanges between chil-dren may be less intimidating for the children and be less restrained than the interview situation. This can also encourage children to be active participants, thereby overcoming potential problems where children play a passive role in interviews searching for the 'right answer'. The disadvantage of this method is that inevitably some children may contribute less within a group situation, so that follow-up individual interviews may be useful.

Ross (1995) used focus groups to examine schoolchildren's food choice. With approximately seven children in each group, discussion lasted half an hour. The discussions were conducted using a topic guide looking at issues such as food preferences, good/bad foods, etc. Topics were addressed according to the children's flow of thought but introduced by the researcher if not raised spontaneously. The study showed that the children spoke consistently about foods in terms of like and dislike, for example, 'It's no point eating it if I don't like it' (ibid.: 316).

Case Studies

Using case studies is an important way to focus attention on specific clinical issues that cannot be sufficiently explicated within a larger-scale quantitative study. Case studies have been criticized on the grounds of limited generalizability and conflicting explanations of findings. Data from case studies – which by their nature allow a far more in-depth examination – are often a fruitful source of hypotheses for future research. They can also have an educational value in calling attention to unusual diagnostic/treatment problems and illustrating new treatment methods.

Case studies are particularly effective if the information is tightly focused on a salient concept or issue (Wells, 1987). The challenge and advantage of the case report is that different types of information are involved (history, interview and observational material) but authors must be careful to integrate all this information. Case reports are often recommended as a useful way to integrate clinical observations and methods with research data (Drotar et al., 1995).

Uses of Qualitative Data

As a Unique Contribution to Work with Children

Improvements in medical care and more sophisticated medicines have resulted in increased survival for children with conditions such as cancer or cystic fibrosis. Qualitative research can make a unique contribution in this area by challenging some of the established beliefs about what children think about illness and what they should know. It also enables the development of a more sophisticated understanding of the connection between the children's health beliefs and their family and/or medical context. Further, adult health and illness beliefs do not emerge fully formed. Rather, they evolve gradually during childhood in interaction with parents, siblings and others. Qualitative research is necessary to map out this development, to consider the relationship between the way children view the world and themselves.

As a Precursor to the Development of More Formal Assessment Measures

Researchers have also used qualitative methods to collect data to develop more formal measures. For example, Eiser et al. (1995) argued that attempts to describe the impact of cancer on a child's quality of life were invariably based on reports made by mothers. These measures, therefore, were a reflection of mothers' worries and concerns just as much as those of the child. Preliminary interviews were conducted with children with cancer, adopting an essentially narrative approach. The interviews were transcribed and coded. As a result, a number of themes were identified which appeared to reflect the areas of greatest concern to the children.

In subsequent work, these themes were represented in a formal instrument to assess the impact of illness from the child's perspective: the Perceived Illness Experience Scale (PIE). Such an approach appears to have considerable face validity; the content of the scales is based on children's own reports about the impact of cancer on their lives. At the same time, development of a formal measure means that it is possible to compare children and thus determine whether or not some are coping better than others, or identify any in need of special care and support. Focus groups may also be used as precursors to quantitative methods: a focus group which raises relevant issues and attitudes is often recommended as the base for a subsequent questionnaire.

As a Basis for Interventions

Qualitative work can also be an integral part of clinical interventions. The information derived from it can be used to fine-tune the character of the intervention. In this sense it becomes a form of action research. Examples of the different types of intervention are given in the next section.

Qualitative Research as Basis for Health Care

Giving Information about Life-threatening Conditions

In the past, it was considered inappropriate that serious illness should be discussed with a child. It was feared that this would cause unnecessary distress, and reduce the extent to which the child complied with treatment. The decision whether or not to tell a child that he or she has a life-threatening condition remains extremely complex and has been subject to much discussion. There is now much more of an ethos among pediatricians to inform children about the nature of their disease and proposed treatment. Proponents of this 'open' approach suggest that children who are informed are more adherent to treatment, less likely to be difficult patients and better adjusted because of their greater trust in doctors and parents to tell them honestly about what is involved.

These suggestions have been taken to imply that children benefit from information about their illness. Although this certainly applies to some, others may well prefer not to know (Eiser et al., 1997). Some children reported that they did not need to know about the illness because they trusted doctors to know what to do, or trusted their parents to do what is best (for example, 'I knew mum and dad would not put me through this without a reason'; 'I don't see the point in asking questions when doctors know so much better what they are doing'). They were also more likely to report that they would have worried if they had known more. Qualitative work can throw some light on how children think in these situations. Decisions about informing children can then be based on relevant data, rather than adult assumptions about what is appropriate.

Consent to Treatment

Increasingly children are being asked to take part in complex decision-making situations, such as are involved in consenting to participate in clinical trials or in choosing between alternative treatment options (Postlethwaite et al., 1995). The question arises as to how to present the advantages and disadvantages of treatments to children in such a way that they are made aware of the known facts and can decide for themselves how far they want to participate in further treatment. Alderson (1993) has done much to emphasize that children are more able to make decisions and participate in complex decision-making than has been assumed in the past.

Further work needs to be conducted on how children make real-life medical decisions – previous work has often been based on healthy children making hypothetical decisions (Weithorn and Campbell, 1982). Care needs to be taken especially where these decisions appear to be equivalent with regard to short-term implications but may have differential implications for future health and well-being.

Pain

As a result of widespread misconceptions, it has been suggested that children feel pain less intensely than adults. Controlling as far as possible for the type and intensity of pain likely to be experienced, it seems that children are often given less pain medication than adults. Beyer et al. (1983) found that after open-heart surgery, 24 per cent of children were not given any pain-relieving medication at all. While understandable concerns about over-medicating children inevitably play a role here, it is also clear that certain assumptions are being made about children's pain tolerance. It is important therefore to understand how children feel pain in order to provide effective interventions and pain management.

Pain is a highly subjective experience and can only really be assessed using self-report data. Pain is difficult to quantify, even in adults. Inherently subjective, self-report is nevertheless considered 'the most reliable indicator or the most valid evidence of pain' (Beyer and Creer, 1986). However, it has often been assumed that children are less able, or even unable, to locate and identify pain with any reliability. In the past, therefore, parents' reports of children's pain (particularly mothers') were most often used. Examination of the evidence, however, shows that parents' reports are quite often inaccurate and too easily influenced by the parents' own anxiety.

As early as 18 months of age, children have some concept of pain. Using story-telling and play tasks research has shown that children are able to locate the pain and suggest pain-relieving strategies such as hugs or medicine. By 3 years, children naturally use distractive strategies to cope with pain (McGrath and McAlpine, 1993). Such research shows that children are able to talk about their pain experience if the methodology is right. Children need child-oriented measures which recognize their personal vocabulary (Woodgate and Kristjanson, 1996). It must be recognized that eliciting information about their pain experience can be complicated by the behaviour of their parents. If care-givers seem to be distressed or anxious themselves this may aggravate the child's distress (Blount, Landolf-Fritsche and Powers, 1991).

Ross and Ross (1984) found that interviews that used open-ended questions asking the child to generate pain-management strategies were far more effective than questionnaires that supplied options. When children were interviewed after filling in a checklist of pain descriptors, 40 per cent admitted that they chose words because they thought they were 'correct' or that they selected all the words to signify the magnitude of their pain. Such findings offer convincing support for a qualitative approach.

Woodgate and Kristjanson (1996) studied young hospitalized children, using qualitative observational and interviewing techniques. Researchers conducted informal and formal interviews with children at different stages of hospitalization. This enabled the researchers to talk to the children immediately after injections were administered and to observe the pain-relieving strategies they used in practice. Although the researchers used the 'faces' scale (Wong and Baker, 1988), they found the children generally selected extremes on the scale, and interview data were far more revealing. For example, from talking to the children it was possible to identify the meaning of pain and show that this was inextricably linked to overall well-being. Rather than isolating painful areas as adults might, children described their pain using more general terms such as 'I am not better.'

Adherence

Adherence is a major problem in paediatric medicine. Rates of non-adherence range from 20 to 80 per cent (Litt and Cuskey, 1980) for both acute and chronic diseases. Examples of adherence behaviours include taking medication, keeping appointments, and taking prescribed exercise. In many cases, children are encouraged to be responsible for much of their own care: those with cystic fibrosis, for example, are expected to take their daily medication and eat appropriately; children with diabetes are expected to administer their own insulin. Non-adherence increases with the greater complexity and disruptiveness of treatment. In many cases non-adherence is not surprising; treatments may have unpleasant side-effects such as weight gain, or expose the child to ridicule for being 'different'. Studies have also found that within the family situation poor communication and bad parent–child relationships have an adverse effect on adherence. In this context non-adherence may be a form of rebellion.

Qualitative research has been used to understand the reasons for non-adherence from the child's point of view, from a perspective that is non-judgemental. One example of such work is a phenomenological study that looked at the impact of treatment on children with spina bifida. Mulderij (1996) wanted to highlight the perspective of children themselves on their disability and treatment rather than adopt the 'medical account' looking at the treatment and educational implications. Using open-ended interviews and participant observation, the study highlighted the conflicts of interest between children and health professionals. Mulderij showed how the child's day revolved around appointments with different 'experts' such as the physiotherapist and the speech therapist. So many interventions meant that little time was left over for being a child: everything from sitting, walking and eating was an exercise in learning to do things the 'right way', for example 'Always that crap about what's good for you' (1996: 319). Often what was necessary and helpful for the child in the long term was contrary to adult expectations, for example 'I want to crawl but I'm made to walk' (ibid.). Studies like these provide insight into the motives behind non-adherence and may help to develop intervention programmes that take the child's perspective into consideration.

Health Promotion

Ross (1995) used focus groups and qualitative observational techniques to examine the social and cultural context of food choice among school-children. Her study indicated that food choice was not determined by health attributes of food but values of preference and convenience, and that consequently health promotion initiatives might more fruitfully be directed toward the providers of children's meals. Mayall (1993) also used focus groups as well as drawings, observation and interviews to study the division of labour in health care between children, parents and teachers. Her findings suggest that children see the home as the principal site for health care and learning about health. Health issues were conceived as complex moral issues embedded within the family context. Mayall (1993) suggested that school health education programmes are unlikely to be successful since they are situated within an environment which children do not recognize as the primary site for learning about health and where they have less control over their everyday activities. At home the child is encouraged to initiate health-related activities such as washing, going to the toilet and fetching drinks, whereas at school these activities are more controlled by rules and customs.

All parents know how difficult it can be to encourage children to participate in recommended health-promotion activities. Parents report difficulties requiring toddlers to wear seat-belts, and parents of older children have difficulties in encouraging the use of bicycle safety helmets. Would parents have greater success if they understood better the reasons for the child's refusal? Peterson, Saldana and Schaeffer (1997) categorized children's excuses for not wearing a helmet as follows:

> Appearance, for example, 'The helmet will wreck my hair.'
> Comfort, for example, 'It must be 100 degrees outside. The helmet gets so hot and my head gets sweaty, I just can't stand it!'
> Supervision, for example, 'I don't need it when I ride with grandma because we ride really slow and she can look after me.'
> Distance of ride, for example, 'I'm only going one block.'
> Peer influence, for example, 'None of the other kids wear them. I'll feel like a nerd.'

Mothers were presented with scenarios based on these accounts and asked how they would respond. Mothers tended to rely on discussion with their children to encourage helmet use, and this was virtually independent of age or gender. Peterson, Saldana and Schaeffer (1997) suggested that mothers are in need of guidance over how to enforce this kind of discipline, as they appeared to have few successful strategies against which to counter their children's arguments. The hope is that increasing understanding of the reasons used by children will enable mothers to develop more targeted counter-arguments.

Conclusion

There has been much justified criticism of the traditional quantitative approach. However, a purely qualitative approach can also have limitations. Qualitative work necessarily involves small samples which cannot be considered representative in statistical terms and can raise questions about the generalizability of the findings. Conrad (1990: 1258) suggests that qualitative researchers need to review generalizability in this context and to look at 'generalizability of concepts rather than in terms of sample (or data *per se*)'. In this way it is the resulting theory that is evaluated for its applicability to other samples and situations. In adopting qualitative methods, it is important to adhere to the basic principles of good research. Although qualitative work may be based on a small and often select sample of children, standard research requirements demand specification of the sample and details of the interview.

Further, the use of both qualitative and quantitative approaches concurrently has been recommended (LaGreca and Lemanek, 1996). 'Triangulation' refers to an approach whereby more than one method is applied to the same research issue to widen the perspective and strengthen the findings of a study (Krahn, Hohn and Kime, 1995). Such a combination of methods would be particularly useful when working with children.

Quantitative and qualitative research methods can be complementary. While quantitative work provides us with focused and highly generalizable information, qualitative work is particularly useful for new or sensitive areas where little may be known, or where the aim is to obtain understanding of more subjective and cultural aspects of illness. Ultimately, 'each type of approach while distinctly different in orientation, focus and application is able to contribute to the understanding of health problems and in the development of solutions. The strengths of one approach do not diminish the other. Qualitative and quantitative techniques are complementary and both are powerful tools in their own right' (Roche, 1991: 136).

There are many contexts in which we need to be able to communicate effectively with children about health and illness. In many circumstances, the child's physical and psychological well-being may be dependent on good communication. Given the importance of the context, we should not allow ourselves to be bound by either quantitative or qualitative methods but recognize the potential contribution of each.

Acknowlededgments

Christine Eiser is funded by the Cancer Research Campaign (CP1019/1010) U.K.

References

Alderson, P. (1993) *Children's Consent to Surgery*. Buckingham: Open University Press.

Bearison, A.C. and Pacifici, C. (1989) Psychological studies of children who have cancer. *Journal of Applied Developmental Psychology*, 5: 263–280.

Beyer, J.E. and Creer, T.L. (1986) Knowledge of pediatric pain: the state of the art. *Children's Health Care*, 13: 150–159.

Beyer, J.E., DeGood, D., Ashley, L. and Russell, G. (1983) Patterns of postoperative use with adults and children following cardiac surgery. *Pain*, 17: 17–81.

Bibace, R. and Walsh, M.E. (1980) Development of children's concepts of illness. *Pediatrics*, 66: 912–917.

Birleson, P. (1978) The validity of depressive disorder in childhood and the development of a self-rating scale: a research report. *Journal of Child Psychology and Psychiatry*, 22: 73–88.

Blount, R.L., Landolf-Fritsche, B. and Powers, S.W. (1991) Differences between high and low coping children and between parent and staff behaviors during painful medical procedures. *Journal of Pediatric Psychology*, 16: 795–809.

Boring, C.C., Squires, T.S., Tong, T. and Montgomery, S. (1994) Cancer statistics. *CA: Pediatrics*, 69: 305–327.

Canning, E.H., Canning, R.D. and Boyce W.T. (1992) Depressive symptoms and adaptive style in children with cancer. *Journal of the American Academy of Child and Adolescent Psychiatry*, 31: 1120–1124.

Carey, S. (1985) *Conceptual Change in Childhood*. Cambridge, MA: MIT Press.

Charlton, A. (1980) 'A penny for your thoughts': pupils' concepts of cancer expressed in pictures. *Journal of the Institute of Health Education*, 17: 51–56.

Conrad, P. (1990) Qualitative research on chronic illness: a commentary on method and conceptual development. *Social Science and Medicine*, 30: 1257–1263.

Drotar, D., LaGreca, A.M., Lemanek, K. and Kazak, A. (1995) Case reports in pediatric psychology: uses and guidelines for authors and reviewers. *Journal of Pediatric Psychology*, 20: 549–565.

Eiser, C., Eiser, J.R. and Lang, J. (1990) How adolescents compare AIDS with other diseases: implications for prevention. *Journal of Pediatric Psychology*, 15: 97–103.

Eiser, C., Havermans, T., Craft, A. and Kernahan, J. (1995) The development of a measure to assess the Perceived Illness Experience (PIE) following treatment for cancer. *Archives of Disease in Childhood*, 72: 302–307.

Eiser, C., Cool, P., Grimer, R.J., Carter S.R., Cotter, I.M., Ellis, A.J. and Kopel, S. (1997) Quality of life in children treated for a malignant primary bone tumour around the knee. *Sarcoma*, 1: 39–46.

Fielding, N.G. and Conroy, S. (1992) Interviewing child victims: police and social work investigations of child sexual abuse. *Sociology*, 26: 103–124.

Ginsberg, H.P. (1997) *Entering the Child's Mind*. Cambridge: Cambridge University Press.

Greenberg, H.S., Kazak, A.E. and Meadows, A.T. (1989) Psychological functioning in 8–10 year old cancer survivors and their parents. *Journal of Pediatrics*, 114: 488–493.

Juniper, E.F., Guyatt, D.H., Feeny, D.H., Ferrie, P.J., Griffith, L.E. and Townsend, M. (1996) Measuring quality of life in children with asthma. *Quality of Life Research*, 5: 35–46.

Krahn, G.L., Hohn, M.F. and Kime, C. (1995) Incorporating qualitative approaches into clinical child psychology research. *Journal of Clinical Child Psychology*, 24: 204–213.

LaGreca, A. and Lemanek, K.L. (1996) Editorial: Assessment as a process in pediatric psychology. *Journal of Pediatric Psychology*, 21: 137–151.

Litt, I.F. and Cuskey, W.R. (1980) Compliance with medical regimens during adolescence. *Pediatric Clinics of North America*, 27: 3–15.

McGrath, P.J. and McAlpine, L.M. (1993) Psychological perspectives on pediatric pain. *Journal of Pediatrics*, 122: S2–S8.

Mayall, B. (1993) Keeping healthy at home and school: 'It's my body, so it's my job'. *Sociology of Health and Illness*, 15: 464–487.

Mulderij, K.J. (1996) Research into the lifeworld of physically disabled children. *Child: Care, Health and Development*, 22: 311–322.

Olvera-Ezzell, N., Power, T.G., Cousins, J.H., Guerra, A.M. and Trujillo, M. (1994) The development of health knowledge in low-income Mexican-American children. *Child Development*, 65: 416–427.

Perrin, E.C. and Gerrity, P.S. (1981) 'There's a demon in your belly': children's understanding of illness. *Pediatrics*, 67: 841–849.

Peterson, L., Saldana, L. and Schaeffer, C. (1997) Maternal intervention strategies in enforcing children's bicycle helmet use. *Journal of Health Psychology*, 2: 225–230.

Petrie, K.J. and Weinman, J.A. (eds) (1997) *Perceptions of Health and Illness*. Chur: Harwood Academic Press.

Postlethwaite, R.J., Reynolds, J.M., Wood, A.J., Evans, J.H.C., Lewis, M.A. and Eminson, D.M. (1995) Recruiting patients to clinical trials: lessons from studies of growth hormone treatment in renal failure. *Archives of Disease in Childhood*, 73: 30–35.

Pridmore, P. and Bendelow, G. (1995) Images of health: exploring the beliefs of children using the 'draw and write' technique. *Health Education Journal*, 54: 473–488.

Prout, A. (1986). 'Wet children' and 'Little Actresses': going sick in primary school. *Sociology of Health and Illness*, 8: 111–136.

Roche, A.M. (1991) Making better use of qualitative research: illustrations from medical education research. *Health Education Journal*, 50: 131–137.

Ross, D.M. and Ross, S.A. (1984) The importance of type of question, psychological climate and subject set in interviewing children about pain. *Pain*, 19: 71–79.

Ross, S. (1995) 'Do I really have to eat that?' A qualitative study of schoolchildren's food choices and preferences. *Health Education Journal*, 55: 312–321.

Siegel, M. (1988) Children's knowledge of contagion and contamination as causes of illness. *Child Development*, 59: 1353–1359.

Varni, J.W., Katz, E.R., Seid, M., Quiggins, D.J.L. and Friedman-Bender, A. (1998) The Pediatric Cancer Quality of Life Inventory-32 (PCQL-32). Reliability and validity. *Cancer*, 82: 1174–1183.

Walker, L. and Greene, J.W. (1991) The functional disability inventory: measuring a neglected dimension of health status. *Journal of Pediatric Psychology*, 16: 39–58.

Weithorn, L.A. and Campbell, S.B. (1982) The competency of children and adolescents to make informed treatment decisions. *Child Development*, 53: 1589–1598.

Wells, K. (1987) Scientific issues in the conduct of case studies. *Journal of Child Psychology and Psychiatry*, 28: 783–790.

Wong, D.L. and Baker, C.M. (1988) Pain in children: comparison of assessment scales. *Pediatric Nursing*, 14: 9–17.

Woodgate, R. and Kristjanson, L.J. (1996) 'My Hurts': hospitalized young children's perceptions of acute pain. *Qualitative Health Research*, 6: 184–201.

10

Qualitative Research in the Field of Death and Dying

R. Glynn Owens and Sheila Payne

The notions of 'qualitative research' or 'qualitative methodology' have been considered in at least two related but distinct ways in psychology, a distinction which is also apparent in considering psychological research in the field of death and dying. In a simple sense, any research which uses non-numerical data – which is concerned with language, words, meanings, etc. – can be considered to be qualitative. In this sense, qualitative research is defined by exclusion, as being that research which is *not* concerned with quantitative measures; no particular philosophical or theoretical under-pinning is necessarily implied, and such an approach is essentially seen as extending and complementing traditional quantitative research (Good and Watts, 1996).

The term 'qualitative research' has, however, also been used to refer to research which differs in a much more fundamental way from its counter-part, stemming from quite different philosophical assumptions. Especially associated with a social constructivist perspective, qualitative research in this sense is fundamentally concerned with issues of interpretation and meaning considered in context. Such an interpretation may raise important issues regarding the extent to which qualitative research can be conceived of as being concerned with 'the discovery of truth' as opposed to providing an interpretive framework (which may be one of many) within which some topic may be considered. From such a perspective, qualitative research may be seen as having a distinct philosophical and theoretical stance, beyond its purely methodological features, and may often if not always be seen as opposed to, rather than complementary to, traditional approaches (Banister et al., 1994).

In considering aspects of death and dying, there is clearly a role for qualitative research within both of these frameworks. Much of the data of interest to those concerned with death and dying is non-numerical in nature and, of course, much of the experience of dying people is concerned with 'making sense' of their world in a way in which internal coherence may be of greater relevance than any notion of objective 'truth'.

Early Research into Psychological Aspects of Death and Dying

Unlike many topics within health psychology, death (as a subject for research) has from its early days drawn on qualitative methodologies. To some extent this may reflect the fact that the bulk of research has been conducted in relatively recent times, when the over-riding dominance of quantitative perspectives had already begun to be challenged. In part, however, it may also reflect a wider recognition of the difficulties of reducing such a complex topic to a form suitable for traditional research designs. Thus studies conducted before World War II examining children's views and understanding of death drew heavily on the use of interview procedures (Nagy, 1948; Schilder and Wechsler, 1934), with researchers interpreting the statements made by children in order to obtain a picture of the children's understanding of death, in particular paying attention to developmental sequences and such notions as the irreversibility and inevitability of death, together with (in the Nagy study) notions of the personification of death. Such studies provide clear examples of early work which has continued to be of relevance in the field.

It was, however, in the late 1960s and early 1970s that research into psychological aspects of death and dying really took off in earnest. In part this is probably a consequence of the fact that in those countries where psychological researchers were most active, dying people were for a long time kept in ignorance of their status. As long as it was believed that the people who were dying did not realize how ill they were, questions such as how people coped psychologically in such conditions could be seen as almost meaningless. However, an increasing tendency for medical service workers to be honest with patients, coupled with an increasing provision of hospice services designed explicitly to help those with potentially fatal illnesses, meant that more and more people who were dying were known to be aware of their state, and as a result researchers began to look at the psychological well-being and responses of such individuals.

Of course, much of the work at this time was conducted within a traditional quantitative framework. Workers such as John Hinton reported widely on such matters as the prevalence of depression among dying patients (see, for example, Hinton, 1963). While such work provided valuable information about the experience of dying patients, it was the intensive qualitative work reported by Elisabeth Kubler-Ross which captured the popular imagination and made her a key name in the field of terminal care. Her 1970 book *On Death and Dying* described her experience of two-and-a-half years working with dying patients, prompted originally by an approach by theology students in Chicago and considered primarily from a psychodynamic perspective. An original attempt at an interview of a dying man in the presence of the students grew into a weekly seminar with up to fifty participants. Her approach anticipated much of the later flourishing of qualitative approaches, in particular her attempt to adopt a broadly narrative approach – 'simply telling the stories of my patients . . .'. Her extraction from the qualitative data of recurrent themes led to the development of her famous five-stage model of coping with dying. In this, she described a progressive series of 'stages' – denial/isolation, anger, bargaining, depression and acceptance – through which patients were seen to progress on their journey from diagnosis to death. It is important to note that this model has been subject to considerable criticism; problems include the heavy reliance on retrospective data, the lack of clear evidence that people do indeed move through these stages, and the possibility that concentration on 'stages' might lead to an unduly narrow focus on these aspects to the neglect of the rest of the person's life (Corr, 1993; Kastenbaum, 1986; Metzger, 1979). Despite the problems of the model, it is probably fair to say that it provided considerable inspiration and a focal point for those caring for dying patients. Arguably, part of this resulted from the 'order from chaos' that it provided, professionals in the field finding that they could make sense of many of their experiences by drawing on Kubler-Ross's model (Klass, 1982).

Since the early 1970s, research into psychological aspects of death and dying has flourished, with qualitative research continuing to make a substantial contribution to the literature. While much of this research predates recent enthusiasm for qualitative approaches in other areas of psychology, there are often close parallels with the strategies and philosophies adopted elsewhere. The tremendous growth of interest in this area means that it is no longer possible within the space of a single chapter to give a comprehensive survey of studies in a particular field, and indeed it is not possible even to give examples of all the ways in which qualitative approaches have been used to further knowledge of issues relating to death and dying. The purpose of the present chapter is therefore simply to illustrate some of the ways in which some of the strategies of qualitative research can be used to help our understanding in this area.

Examples of Qualitative Approaches in the Field of Death and Dying

Interview and Similar Studies

The use of interviews by Kubler-Ross in her work has already been alluded to, and of course in many senses the work of Nagy (1948) on children's views of death can also be seen as a close relative of such approaches. In a similar way many other researchers have used various forms of interview while attempting to emphasize in their data-gathering the importance of leaving participants to tell their own stories in order best to obtain a sense of the meaning they give to their experiences. Kubler-Ross herself continued within this broad vein in such studies as her *On Children and Death* (1983), extending her earlier work not just to a younger population but also taking explicit account of such things as sudden death, head injuries, near-death experiences and other issues. Other workers made good use of interview procedures, with some individuals eschewing any approach to analysis, leaving the text simply to speak for itself. Krementz (1991), for example, simply presented verbatim the descriptions of a parent's death given by eighteen children. Such an approach can be seen as minimizing the impact of the investigator on the data. It would perhaps be a mistake, however, to assume that this approach totally eliminates the investigator's values from the findings. While the data are presented verbatim, the investigator none the less plays a major part in deciding which individuals to include in the study, how to start an interview, when to stop, and so on.

The use of interview procedures provides a means whereby individuals can describe fully their experiences while still leaving the researcher the opportunity to give more or less direction as appropriate. This makes the interview a particularly useful tool both for covering a broad topic and for focusing in greater detail on particular issues. Thus, Young and Cullen (1996) made extensive use of interviews both to follow twelve East London individuals through their experience of coping with their illnesses through to death, and to examine their relatives' reactions for a year or more afterwards. With such intense and continued observation they were able to highlight a number of key issues that arose for the people concerned, not least of which was the importance of control and the way in which having a terminal illness whittled away the individual's autonomy.

Interview approaches have also been used to address much more specific issues. Thus, Kelner, Bourgeault and Wahl (1994) used semi-structured interviews to investigate the views of health-care professionals about regulation and legislation in the field of death and dying. Interviews with forty respondents (doctors and nurses) indicated considerable variation in views on the adequacy or feasibility of legal safeguards for professionals whose actions hasten the death of patients, and little agreement on who should prepare such guidelines (although there was considerable agreement that it should not be lawyers).

Case Histories and Patient Series

The case history, of course, has a long and respected tradition within medicine and psychotherapy, a tradition which has been carried over into the field of death and dying. An extension of the case study approach is that of the patient series (Owens, Slade and Fielding, 1995) in which the experiences of several patients – a 'series' – is drawn upon to develop understanding or to illustrate the applicability of theoretical models, therapeutic interventions and the like. Such studies go beyond simple interviews to involve a more intimate relationship between therapist and informant. Such a relationship may accord well with the emerging practice in qualitative research of recognizing the responsibility of the researcher to give to those who are providing information, as well as to take – that is to say, for research to be seen as a collaborative effort between researcher and informant. Such a structuring of the research and therapy process may be particularly apparent within some frameworks such as the social learning approach of Bandura (1969) or the cognitive therapy approach (for example

Young and Beck, 1982). In these approaches the therapeutic relationship is explicitly conceptualized as a joint problem-solving activity in which both therapist and client have equal status (Owens, 1995).

Case history and patient series approaches in the field of death and dying may focus on either specific aspects and topics or broad, all-encompassing issues. Thus, Bosnak (1989) describes in detail his work with an AIDS patient, concentrating almost exclusively on the joint efforts of therapist and patient in interpreting the patient's dreams. By contrast, Klass (1993), using a broadly patient series approach, draws on the experience of over ten years of study of a self-help group in formulating understanding of patterns in the responses of bereaved parents to the loss of a child. Clearly each of these has its own strengths and weaknesses; the detailed investigation of a single aspect of a single individual's experience permits a depth of consideration and understanding which would, at best, be impractical in considering a large number of such individuals with a broader focus. On the other hand, the study of a large number of people over a prolonged period permits the identification of recurring themes and patterns in a way that a narrowly focused study of a single individual could never do.

Participant Observation Studies

While at first glance the notion of a 'participant observation' study in the field of death and dying might seem macabre and improbable, there is nevertheless a substantial tradition of such reports. In some ways the participant observation study can be seen as a logical development of the case history tradition, with the 'case' here also including the role of researcher or co-researcher. Of course, much of the participant observation data have been generated with no intention, originally, of forming part of a broader research literature. Works such as Mary Jones's (1988) account of her husband's death give a 'straight-from-the-hip' account of responses, thoughts and emotions with little in the way of comment. By contrast Freda Naylor's account of the time between her cancer diagnosis and her death is presented in an edited form which intersperses discussion of what has been said and possible implications (Owens and Naylor, 1989). When researchers provide such 'editing', the stark presentation of personal responses can be used to provide illustrations of more general strategies and principles that can be adopted by dying people and their carers. In such a case, however, the direct impact of the personal account is markedly weakened, and inevitably contaminated by prejudices, preconceptions and assumptions brought in 'from outside'.

Perhaps unsurprisingly, a number of the most poignant and moving accounts by professionals in the field have been of their own experiences of bereavement. Awoonor-Renner (1991), for example, describes her actions and reactions on hearing of the news of her son's death in a road traffic accident. While this is again offered directly and without comment, it none the less manages to present a number of issues directly and powerfully. For example, she describes how she was 'allowed' to go alone into the room where her son's body was lying on the condition that she 'didn't do anything silly'. The conflict between her urge to hold her son and the constraints of the implicit message led her to, as she put it, betray her instincts, not even lifting the cloth that covered him. Movingly she talks of how all expressions of love and care were denied, leaving a pain and distress that might never heal.

Similar participant observations from professionals have been reported in other contexts. Heller (1989), for example, describes his experiences as a doctor called to the scene of the major disaster at Hillsborough football ground. He describes his feelings of helplessness and the way in which he and colleagues later sought each other out for mutual support – and the way in which, despite such support, despite professional counselling, he nevertheless continued to experience a feeling of being 'non-specifically upset'.

Clearly the participant observation approach has a number of strengths, not least of which is the potentially high validity associated with eliminating the distinction between researcher and informant. Inevitably, however, there are also weaknesses. In practice, the use of participant observation approaches almost inevitably limits severely the range of experiences on which the research can draw. Even though it is conceivable that a moderately large group of dying individuals might collaborate on researching their experiences, it is still likely that their experiences would fail to sample the range apparent in the broader population. Given that participant observation in this context is almost universally associated with the experiences of a single dying or bereaved individual (a problem it shares with the case history), the scope for generalizing is bound to be limited. This problem is exacerbated since those individuals researching their own deaths are likely to be atypical in a number of (not necessarily obvious) ways. Despite these problems, however, it is clear that participant observation approaches have much to offer, not least in the directness of the experience communicated by the researcher to the reader. Reports of such research often have an emotional impact which is hard, if not impossible, for a less involved researcher to achieve.

Personal Construct Theory Approaches

Recent years have seen an awakened interest in the use of more or less structured procedures in the gathering, analysis and interpretation of qualitative data. Of particular prominence here has been a resurgence of interest in the repertory grid procedure developed by Kelly (1955) in the context of his Personal Construct Psychology. In the basic grid procedure the informant is asked to consider specific and personal exemplars of general concepts or categories relevant to the topic under investigation. Such exemplars are known as elements and may be drawn from social (for example 'A person I really admire') or physical (for example 'A book I really enjoyed') domains. Typically, some twelve to fifteen such elements are nominated by the informant, although in some cases these might be more or less precisely specified by the researcher (for example 'myself as I am now' or 'myself as I would ideally like to be'). Groups of three such elements ('triads'), possibly selected at random from the twelve, are then presented to the informant who is asked to indicate some important way in which two are similar to each other but different from the third (for example 'these two people are friendly, and this one isn't'). This characteristic, and its converse, define what Kelly termed a construct, a bipolar dimension specifying one of many according to which an individual experiences and makes sense of the world (Kelly chose the term 'construing' to denote this process).

A particularly influential variant of the repertory grid technique has been devised by Krieger, Epting and Leitner (1974). In this the elements were specified by the researcher/interviewer and consisted of brief descriptions of death-related situations (and included the single element 'death'). These were then used to elicit constructs from the individual, although in a variation on Kelly's original procedure the selection of triads is constrained to include the 'death' element on each occasion. Neimeyer, Epting and Rigdon (1984) provide a guide to using this procedure, specifying a total of thirty constructs to be elicited.

Following this the researcher/interviewer then asks the informants to consider one by one the constructs that have been elicited and to specify which pole of the construct they associate more with themselves and which they associate more with their death. This procedure has then been used to devise a summary measure of the extent to which the individual perceives death as threatening as reflected in the extent to which the self and death are seen as associated with opposites on the various constructs. Subsequent variations of the Threat Index procedure have included a 'provided' version of the Index in which constructs are specified rather than elicited and which can be self-administered. By contrast Meshot and Leitner (1994), while making use of the 'provided' version, also returned to a traditional grid format in examining the responses of individuals between the ages of 12 and 18 to the death of a parent.

Such uses of the repertory grid technique, however, not only move away from the original conceptual framework of Kelly's (1955) theory, but also, arguably, negate the qualitative strengths of the procedure by reducing the data to a somewhat sterile numerical score. As yet, there appears to have been little research making use of repertory grid techniques in their original guise as a means of clarifying the ways in which individuals construe particular aspects of their world, and the application of the repertory grid remains largely within the context of Threat Index measures. Thus, Ingram and Leitner (1989) used an interpersonal repertory grid as well as the grid-based Threat Index, but the use of the former was primarily as an instrument to obtain threat of death scores which could be correlated with those from the Threat Index. There remains considerable scope for the use of repertory grid procedures in clarifying the experiences of people involved in death and dying, including patients, professionals, other carers, friends and family, as well as providing a useful tool for the investigation of perceptions of death and related issues within healthy populations.

Grounded Theory Approaches

Although, as mentioned earlier, much of the theoretical work in the field of death and dying has evolved from qualitative observations, these have often been developed outside of any systematic research strategy. Grounded theory approaches have evolved as a means of approaching the process of theory development in a way that is (hence the name) firmly 'grounded' in the context to which the theory refers. Perhaps unsurprisingly, such approaches have had particular appeal in areas such as nursing, where recognition of a lack of a coherent theoretical perspective relating to clinical interactions has driven the need for a research perspective which can be seen to be relevant to everyday practice (Chenitz and Swanson, 1986).

Central to the approach is the strategy of developing a conceptual framework in direct interaction with the data collection procedure. This, of course, contrasts markedly with traditional quantitative perspectives which have often been characterized either by the attempt to concoct a theoretical model to account for existing data or by the attempt to gather data to test an existing theoretical model. Grounded theory approaches involve an interactive process whereby an initial gathering of data leads to the development of preliminary concepts which are then refined, tested, extended and so on as a result of further data collection. The result is that data analysis and collection go on simultaneously, rather than in separate stages of a study or project. Questions relating to the social construction of events, and to their meaning are central to the approach.

Grounded theory has been used effectively by Braun and Berg (1994) in developing a framework within which to understand the experiences of mothers bereaved by the loss of a child. Drawing on data derived from long, open-ended interviews with members of a support group, and making use of computerized data analysis software, they were able to draw attention to what they termed the 'prior meaning structure' as the core variable in terms of which the experiences of their ten respondents could be understood. Aspects of this core variable included issues of personal and external control, the mothers' beliefs about the existence of order in the world, the nature of life, and the child's position in the mother's view of life. Prior meaning structures which failed to provide a meaningful context for the child's death might thus be ones in which the child was central to the mother's sense of meaning and purpose, an extension of herself, and in which death was not seen as something that happened to children. Such a prior meaning structure would be hard to reconcile with the experience of the child's death, and would imply that the mother would experience a period of disorientation before any adjustment would occur. Such disorientation could involve feelings of being out of touch with the rest of society and changes in views about life, the future, and personal control. At its most extreme, disorientation could leave the individual feeling there was no longer any purpose in life. Adjustment could be facilitated most by talking about the child and the experience of the loss, and by conveying a feeling that others understood. In this context there would appear to be an obvious value for the kind of self-help and support groups from which the individuals were recruited. It is important to remember, however, that the finding may simply reflect a selection bias. The members who take part in such groups are likely to be those who find them particularly helpful, and the possibility remains that there may be others who do not find the group helpful and therefore effectively exclude themselves from study.

As yet there appear to have been few studies in the field of death and dying which have made substantial use of grounded theory approaches, although recent years have seen some reports appearing such as Candy's (1991) study of student nurses' views of 'Do Not Resuscitate' orders, or Davies et al.'s (1996) study of nurses' experience of caring for dying children. This may, in part, be due to the historical antecedents of the approach falling largely within sociological rather than psychological disciplines. However, with the increasing recognition of the value of multidisciplinary research in death and dying, and the rise of disciplines such as medical sociology and the profession of the research nurse, it seems likely that the use of such approaches will increase.

An especial strength of the grounded theory approach is its ability to permit investigation of process rather than merely outcome. Moreover, the analysis can incorporate multiple perspectives – for example, by comparing the responses of patients and their relatives, or by highlighting differences and similarities between the views of patients and health professionals. This can be demonstrated by an example. Sque and Payne (1996) conducted narrative interviews with twenty-four bereaved people following their agreement to donate the organs of their loved ones. The analysis documented the process of how they became aware of the seriousness of their loved ones' condition, through their ambivalence at attempts at life-prolonging treatment and the realization of death (often before it was officially confirmed by the attending medical staff), to agreeing to organ donation. These experiences were interpreted as a theory of dissonant loss, in which relatives of organ donors face a series of conflicts and seek resolution.

Discursive Approaches

Discursive methods present a new approach in psychology and have been gaining in popularity especially within social and health psychology (Stainton-Rogers, 1996). These approaches tend to emphasize language use and the social functions of discourses in shaping cognitions and behaviours. Currently there is little research which has investigated death and dying using these methods, although Langley-Evans and Payne (1997) have recently examined discourses used in three palliative day-care units. They sought to explore how 'open awareness' – recognition and acknowledgement of their own limited life expectancy – was constructed in the discourses of patients, volunteers and staff. They proposed that the light-hearted and humorous nature of patient 'death talk' served an important psychological function in allowing patients to distance themselves from their own deaths while simultaneously permitting an acknowledgement of their terminal condition.

The Role of Qualitative Research in the Field of Death and Dying

Clearly the examples given above neither give an exhaustive account of the studies which have been conducted using the methodologies specified nor even an exhaustive account of the methods which have been subsumed under the general rubric of 'qualitative research'. It is important to remember that much useful research has been conducted and is currently under way using these and other approaches. It would however take more space than is practical to attempt to be exhaustive, and it is perhaps more appropriate to consider such examples in the context of the broader question of what might be the appropriate role for qualitative methods in this field.

From the outset it should be emphasized that the value of a qualitative approach to research in this area does not imply that other research is inappropriate or invalid. While a number of proponents of a qualitative approach have suggested that other perspectives have severe failings (for example, Banister et al., 1994), few would argue that quantitative approaches should not be used at all, and many would argue that the two can usefully be seen as complementary. Nevertheless it is important to recognize that qualitative approaches do have some distinct strengths and to consider ways in which these might be especially appropriate within the context of studies in death and dying. Such strengths might include the following.

EMPHASIS ON MEANING AND COHERENCE BY CONTRAST WITH THE PURSUIT OF A SUPPOSED OBJECTIVE TRUTH   At an extreme level it might appear almost obvious that any search for the 'truth' about death and dying is at worst a hopeless task and at best subordinate to the importance of understanding the social meaning of such issues. This is perhaps most obvious when one considers studies of dying patients themselves, their experiences, hopes, fears and beliefs. Arguably, the 'truth' of these is of less importance than their role in helping individuals make sense of what is happening in their lives. Qualitative research's explicit emphasis on these dimensions can be seen as rendering it particularly appropriate. The argument need not however be restricted to studies of dying patients; even studies of healthy populations and their understanding of death-related issues can be seen as singularly suitable for a qualitative approach. The studies mentioned at the beginning of the chapter, for example, on children's concepts of death were explicitly concerned with the subjective understanding of the children involved, in a way which would be difficult to pursue if their responses had been forced into some kind of artificial and quantifiable framework.

MINIMISING OF POWER IMBALANCES BETWEEN RESEARCHER AND RESEARCHED A recurring theme within qualitative research has been the impact within psychology of the perceived imbalance between researcher and researched, and the way in which this might lead to distortion of the results, a phenomenon emphasized by the classic studies of obedience by Milgram (1963) and formalized within the concept of 'demand characteristics' by Orne (1962). When dealing with people who are seriously ill or dying, there is perhaps an especial imperative to avoid any potential for abuse or exploitation. To the person who is dying, every minute may be precious, too precious to spend participating in research of indifferent value to themselves or others. Moreover, the person who is dying is typically already in a relatively powerless position; actions and procedures which are central to their survival may be in the hands of relatively powerful others – physicians, nurses, family members and so on. Under such circumstances it is important that a research strategy be pursued as far as possible in the form of a collaborative enterprise with the individuals concerned, and with a real commitment to conducting the research in such a way as to be of benefit to the participants, not just the researcher.

USE OF LANGUAGE   Probably even the most determined critics of qualitative research would, if pressed, be forced to concede that traditional psychological research has tended to neglect people's utterances as material for study, while qualitative methods have embraced these wholeheartedly. When studying topics related to death and dying it almost goes without saying that each person's experience is likely to be highly individual, and that the opportunity to express their views, feelings and perceptions will be necessary to any sharing of these with a researcher. A number of writers have emphasized the importance of listening to patients in terminal care, and that the commonly voiced complaint of 'not knowing what to say' is probably less important than knowing how to listen; indeed good listening has been emphasized as being beneficial in itself (Buckman, 1988). Seen in this light, research which involves dying patients having the opportunity to be heard, in their own words, has the potential not only to help our understanding of the experience in general but also to be of benefit to the participants themselves.

EXPLICIT REFLEXIVITY   It almost goes without saying that the emotional strain of conducting research with dying people is likely to be considerably higher than that involved in running experimental laboratory studies of reinforcement schedules in pigeons, or perceptual processes in undergraduates. Qualitative perspectives have commonly emphasized the central role of the researcher in the research process, and the inclusion of a 'reflexive account' in reporting qualitative research can be traced back at least as far as Skinner's (1957) *Verbal Behavior*, and probably earlier. Consideration of issues relating to death and dying is likely to lead researchers themselves to consider their own mortality to a greater or lesser degree, a process which is unlikely to take place without some emotional turmoil and need for readjustment. The use of an explicit reflexive account by qualitative researchers provides both an opportunity for the researcher to address these issues directly and for the reader to recognize the extent to which such experiences may have coloured the findings and the conclusions drawn therefrom.

Prospects for the Future – and Some Caveats

It is already possible to detect a marked growth of interest amongst researchers in topics relating to death and dying. Given the existing strong tradition of using qualitative methods in this area, it seems likely that these will continue to play a major part. Even when more traditional quantitative methods are being employed, qualitative methods are likely to be increasingly accepted as having a complementary role. This may involve providing guidance and direction to subsequent quantitative studies. For example, studies of cancer patients and others undergoing Magnetic Resonance Imaging scans (for example Thorp et al., 1990; Mackenzie et al., 1995) have drawn on qualitative data from participant observation, interview, and open-ended questions to direct the quantitative researchers both to appropriate questions and to possible solutions to problems detected. The incorporation of qualitative methods can also be invaluable in helping understand apparently anomalous quantitative data. For example, in studying attitudes to organ donation after death Kent and Owens (1995) found a marked reluctance regarding corneal donation compared to other possibilities such as kidney or heart donation. This reluctance could not be explained by quantitative measures such as ratings of the perceived effectiveness of the procedures, but direct questioning of respondents gave rise to a range of unexpected reasons including a notion that eyes were more central to the individual's sense of identity and even that it was important to keep one's eyes in order to be able to see in the afterlife. Such concepts would be difficult if not impossible to extract using purely quantitative approaches.

Apart from the combination of quantitative and qualitative approaches, different qualitative approaches could be used in combination to understand better the processes and phenomena of interest. Such 'triangulation' procedures (Campbell and Fiske, 1959) may involve the use of data derived from different designs or approaches, or, more recently, have been extended to data derived by different investigators, different theoretical perspectives, and so on. Central to the idea is the recognition that any investigative procedure has its weaknesses, ones which may be complemented by another approach whose weaknesses are different. The notion of triangulation is of considerable importance in discussion of any concept of validation of qualitative research, and in the field of death and dying, as in other fields, it is likely to have a central role.

In this context, it is important to remember that any or all of the research studies alluded to already, like all research, have their failings. Qualitative research, while having particular strengths, can also be seen as being at particular risk of weakness in other areas. Methodological concerns, which all researchers learn in their early days, cannot necessarily be ignored when a different methodology is adopted. Issues such as sampling bias may be of little importance to the investigator who declares an interest only in the meanings and experience of the individuals who participated in the study, but once the investigator claims a relevance to a broader population, questions regarding representativeness cannot be ignored. As was noted earlier, a study which praises the value of self-help groups, having only sampled those who participate in them runs the risk of disenfranchising those who prefer not to be involved in these groups. Qualitative research, in general, has a good track record in recognizing and making explicit such things as the potential influence of the researcher in determining the nature of the data, but it is important to remember that simply recognizing that such an influence is possible or probable may not take us forward in finding out what we need to know in improving the quality of life of those for whom it is nearly at an end.

Despite these problems, however, it is clear that the strengths of qualitative research are such as to ensure its continued central role in the study of psychological aspects of death and dying. Indeed, when considering some of the issues of special importance, it is often hard to imagine any other way of conducting appropriate research in this field. Topics which are perhaps particularly of note in this sense include issues of meaning and spirituality, matters of tremendous concern to those involved, but difficult to research effectively within anything but a qualitative framework. As an example, attempts using a quantitative framework to determine the impact of religious belief on such matters as diagnosis of diseases like cancer, or diagnoses of terminal illness, have typically produced at best only confusing or conflicting results (see for example Hinton, 1975; Hughes, 1987). Such confusion seems likely to stem, in part, from issues relating to the meaning of religious or spiritual beliefs to the individual, an issue much more amenable to qualitative than quantitative analysis.

It may also be argued that the specific ethical problems of research in death and dying are such as to endow qualitative approaches with a particular appeal. A number of writers have highlighted particular ethical concerns in working with groups such as those who are terminally ill, or those who have been bereaved (see for example Parkes, 1994). Qualitative approaches, of course, have often been especially conscientious in addressing the ethics of research studies, with explicit concerns regarding such matters as the ownership of the research, potential power imbalances and the like. In the light of such concerns the use of qualitative approaches can be seen to have a particular appeal, often giving those whose experience is the central topic of the research the feeling of being genuine partners or collaborators in the study.

When, in addition to these issues, it is remembered that qualitative approaches are themselves still in a process of development, with new methodologies continuing to be developed, it can be seen that in increasing our understanding of people's experience in the field of death and dying, the use of qualitative approaches is certainly here to stay, and in all probability will account for an increasing percentage of research in the field. Given the recognition that much of the early work in the field rested heavily on qualitative approaches, it is perhaps especially appropriate that in this area such methods should continue to play a central role.

References

Awoonor-Renner, S. (1991) 'I desperately needed to see my son'. *British Medical Journal*, 302: 356.

Bandura, A. (1969) *Principles of Behavior Modification*. New York: Holt, Rinehart and Winston.

Banister, P., Burman, E., Parker, I., Taylor, M. and Tindall, C. (1994) *Qualitative Methods in Psychology: A Research Guide*. Buckingham: Open University Press.

Bosnak, R. (1989) *Dreaming with an AIDS Patient*. Boston, MA: Shambhala Publications.

Braun, M.J. and Berg, D.H. (1994) Meaning reconstruction in the experience of parental bereavement. *Death Studies*, 18: 105–129.

Buckman, R. (1988) *I Don't Know What to Say*. London: Macmillan.

Campbell, D.T. and Fiske, D.W. (1959) Convergent and discriminant validation by the multitrait–multimethod matrix. *Psychological Bulletin*, 56: 81–105.

Candy, C.E. (1991) 'Not for resuscitation': the student nurse's viewpoint. *Journal of Advanced Nursing*, 16: 138–146.

Chenitz, W.C. and Swanson, J.M. (eds) (1986) *From Practice to Grounded Theory: Qualitative Research in Nursing*. Menlo Park, CA: Addison-Wesley.

Corr, C.A. (1993) Coping with dying; lessons that we should and should not learn from the work of Elisabeth Kubler-Ross. *Death Studies*, 17: 69–83.

Davies, B., Clarke, D., Connaught, S., Cook, K., Mackenzie, B., McCormick, J., O'Loane, M. and Stutzer, C. (1996) Caring for dying children: nurses' experiences. *Pediatric Nursing*, 22: 500–507.

Good, D.A. and Watts, F.N. (1996) Qualitative research. In G. Parry and F. Watts (eds), *Behavioural and Mental Health Research: A Handbook of Skills and Methods*. Basingstoke: Taylor and Francis, pp. 253–276.

Heller, T. (1989) Personal and medical memories from Hillsborough. *British Medical Journal*, 299: 1596–1598.

Hinton, J. (1963) The physical and mental distress of the dying. *Quarterly Journal of Medicine*, 125: 1–21.

Hinton, J. (1975) Influence of previous personality on reactions to having terminal cancer. *Omega*, 6: 95–111.

Hughes, J. (1987) *Cancer and Emotion*. Chichester: John Wiley.

Ingram, B.J. and Leitner, L.M. (1989) Death threat, religiosity and fear of death; a

repertory grid investigation. *International Journal of Personal Construct Psychology,*
2: 199–214.

Jones, M. (1988) *Secret Flowers.* London: The Women's Press.

Kastenbaum, R. (1986) *Death, Society and Human Experience.* Columbus, OH: Charles
E. Merrill.

Kelly, G.A. (1955) *The Psychology of Personal Constructs.* New York: Norton.

Kelner, M.J., Bourgeault, I.L. and Wahl, J.A. (1994) Regulation and legislation of the
dying process: views of health care professionals. *Death Studies,* 18: 167–181.

Kent, B. and Owens, R.G. (1995) Conflicting attitudes to corneal and organ
donation: a study of nurses' attitudes to organ donation. *International Journal of
Nursing Studies,* 32: 484–492.

Klass, D. (1982) Elisabeth Kubler-Ross and the tradition of the private sphere: an
analysis of symbols. *Omega,* 12: 241–261.

Klass D. (1993) Solace and immortality: bereaved parents' continuing bond with
their children. *Death Studies,* 17: 243–368.

Krementz, J. (1991) *How it Feels when a Parent Dies.* London: Gollancz.

Krieger, S.R., Epting, F.R. and Leitner, L.M. (1974) Personal constructs, threat, and
attitudes towards death. *Omega,* 5: 299–310.

Kubler-Ross, E. (1970) *On Death and Dying.* London: Tavistock.

Kubler-Ross, E. (1983) *On Children and Death.* New York: Macmillan.

Langley-Evans, A. and Payne, S. (1997) Light-hearted death talk in a palliative day
care context. *Journal of Advanced Nursing,* 26: 1091–1097.

Mackenzie, R., Sims, C., Owens, R.G. and Dixon, A.K. (1995) Patients' perceptions
of magnetic resonance imaging. *Clinical Radiology,* 50: 137–143.

Meshot, C.M. and Leitner, L.M. (1994) Death threat, parental loss, and interpersonal
style: a personal construct investigation. In R.A. Neimeyer (ed.), *Death Anxiety
Handbook: Research, Instrumentation and Application.* Washington: Taylor and
Francis, pp. 181–191.

Metzger, A.M. (1979) A Q-methodological study of the Kubler-Ross stage theory.
Omega, 10: 291–302.

Milgram, S. (1963) Behavioral study of obedience. *Journal of Abnormal and Social
Psychology,* 67: 371–378.

Nagy, M. (1948) The child's theories concerning death. *Journal of Genetic Psychology,*
73: 3–27.

Neimeyer, R.A., Epting, F.R. and Rigdon, M.A. (1984) A procedure manual for the
Threat Index. In F.R. Epting and R.A. Neimeyer (eds), *Personal Meanings of Death.*
Washington: Hemisphere, pp. 213–234.

Orne, M.T. (1962) On the social psychology of the psychological experiment: with
particular reference to demand characteristics and their implications. *American
Psychologist,* 17: 776–783.

Owens, R.G. (1995) Radical behaviourism and life–death decisions. *Clinical
Psychology Forum,* 80: 12–16.

Owens, R.G. and Naylor, F. (1989) *Living while Dying.* Wellingborough: Thorsons.

Owens, R.G., Slade, P.D. and Fielding, D.M. (1995) Patient series and quasi-
experimental designs. In G. Parry and F. Watts (eds), *Behavioural and Mental
Health Research: A Handbook of Skills and Methods* (2nd edn). London: Taylor and
Francis, pp. 229–251.

Parkes, C.M. (1994) Guidelines for conducting ethical bereavement research. *Death
Studies,* 19: 171–182.

Schilder, P. and Wechsler, D. (1934) 'The attitudes of children toward death'. *Journal
of Genetic Psychology,* 45: 406–451.

Skinner, B.F. (1957) *Verbal Behavior*. New York: Appleton Century Crofts.

Sque, M. and Payne, S. (1996) Dissonant loss: the experiences of donor relatives. *Social Science and Medicine*, 43: 1359–1370.

Stainton Rogers, W. (1996) Critical approaches to health psychology. *Journal of Health Psychology*, 1: 65–77.

Thorp, D., Owens, R.G., Whitehouse, G. and Dewey, M.E. (1990) Subjective experiences of magnetic resonance imaging. *Clinical Radiology*, 41: 276–278.

Young, J. and Beck, A.T. (1982) Cognitive therapy: clinical applications. In A.J. Rush (ed.), *Short-term Psychotherapies for Depression*. London: Guilford, pp. 182–214.

Young, M. and Cullen, L. (1996) *A Good Death*. London: Routledge.

11

Cross-cultural Research in Health Psychology

Illustrations from Australia

Jane Selby

> If you have come to help me, you are wasting your time, but if you have come because your liberation is bound up with mine, let's work together.
>
> Lilla Watson

This chapter examines interpersonal abilities relevant to the management of the methodological themes of power, collaboration, emotional dynamics and clarity in the research process. It contributes to ensuring adequate theorization of research methodology so that emotions and research relationships are neither reduced to anecdotal asides in a research write-up, nor ignored and so assumed as background skills to the scientific methods followed, something Devereux (1967) and Selby (1990) warn us against. The chapter acknowledges those debates in psychology which emphasize reflexivity in qualitative research (for example, Henriques et al., 1997; Hollway, 1989; Boonmongkon, 1993). This is a particularly apt starting point for health psychologists since it is in the health field that cultural and personal values and ways of organizing or defending against life's anxieties can be centrally experienced (see Johnson and Sargent, 1990: throughout). Thus the researcher needs to be aware of his or her own values, the conceptualizing and structuring of work through institutional, funding and career needs, and how these mesh or not with the interests and experienced needs of the culture under scrutiny. But of course, researchers are not omniscient, even about themselves, and during the course of research may have to confront new insights about their own motives and their place in cross-cultural politics.

So much cross-cultural research is between cultures of significantly different material power over each other. If we take the lead from Miller's 1969 American APA Presidential Address, in which psychology is called upon to promote 'human welfare', working cross-culturally in health psychology often takes us into the domain of 'distrust', for example of white researchers in ethnic communities in the US, as discussed in Jemmott and Jones (1993). Working cross-culturally also takes health psychologists into areas outside 'health' as managed by health professionals. For example, we must also consider 'not just the physical well-being of the individual but the social, emotional, and cultural well-being of the whole community. This is a whole-of-life view and it also includes the cyclical concept of life–death–life' (National Aboriginal Health Strategy Working Party, 1989: x). Putting the emphasis on the promotion of human welfare and working across a cultural divide holding tensions, distrust and struggles of empowerment and justice, the research worker nowadays needs clarity on the political and ethical context of his or her work.

These themes are crucial to successful qualitative cross-cultural research. I focus, then, on our relationships with those researched. These are typically neglected in methodological texts. For example, neither Miles and Huberman (1984), in their now classic presentation, nor Yoddumnern-Attig et al. (1993) in their useful contemporary focus on East Asia, address relationships as holding theoretical importance. I advocate structuring a 'reference group' into any research design. Depending on the ethical requirements for a particular piece of research, such a group may have to be set up anyway. As well as its main function of representing the target population for ethical and protocol advice, this group can help the researcher manage methodological requirements linked to (a) the importance of relations of power cross-culturally; (b) the expectations professional researchers can make about collaborators from their target group; (c) insight into the often powerful emotional dynamics between highly motivated people working together; and (d) continual clarification about why and how the researcher is conducting particular research. In this chapter, I address these requirements in detail using examples from projects I have led.

The researcher has to consider what is in the best interests of a cultural group and how to assess these, as well as to negotiate concerns about the locus of control over research methods and findings. Whose problem is it? Is it a problem for the people themselves? Should the government continue to allow corpses to rot in public as is traditional, but a health hazard, in the Western Province of Papua New Guinea? To what extent should alcohol-related violence be relatively tolerated where it would seem part of a 'norm', and so have researchers focus on evaluating casualty units in hospitals rather than alcohol programmes? To what extent should a nutritional programme be pushed where communities cannot see its value (Stacy, 1983)? When are we 'minimizing' problems, colluding in what is accepted as 'normal', and when are we to be led by minority community concerns (Brady, 1991; Marshall, 1990)?

Whether evaluating a health-promotion programme or exploring health-related beliefs or the experiences of hospital patients, the researcher is an interventionist at the heart of cultural and personal change. Intervention occurs in many ways, from galvanizing a local maternal and infant mobile clinic into following the researcher from village to village, when it normally hardly moves around (Selby, 1993b), to deciding that you need to inform the population about relevant upcoming events you have heard about (Boonmongkon, 1993), through to considering that even to 'characterize people in any way is to intervene in their lives' (Johannsen, 1992: 77). These raise ethical, methodological and personal issues for the researcher. In many cases one works with a community member as a colleague, or employs someone as a cultural broker or research assistant. This level of collaboration has its own cautionary points, as tokenism, access to resources and status issues are clarified and properly anticipated. From the start, then, the success of any cross-cultural collaborative venture is totally dependent on the quality of the collaborative relationship.

Principles of empowerment, collaboration and ownership here set a model for research generally, qualitative methods included, forcing a critical eye on motives, relevance and relationships. While these considerations are important to all forms of cross-cultural research, for the health psychologist working in a qualitative way they become crucial. For qualitative research design requires being able to decide *where to look* for processes rather than *what to find* (Finch and Mason, 1990), and to justify an exploratory stance in data collection. Thus why be interested in questioning the marital relationship of a couple when studying the design of housing? How can the couple concerned feel secure that it is in their interests and those of their community to disclose private concerns? In practical terms it is a question of who can look at your files, whether there are any 'private' notes you can make, of when your methodology is independent of your results in terms of ownership; or of whether you keep your data for storage, give it to community groups, write it with a co-worker, or publish and hence hold copyright. There are links here with current debates in psychology and psychoanalysis (Dean et al., 1996) about the ethics of writing up case material for publication so that the vulnerability of clients and their rights are taken into account. There are parallels also in the often complicated contracts with government departments when providing a research consultancy. In all cases, the issues are daunting and even potentially disabling of the researcher, for example censoring by communities, or self-censoring, of information collected because of how it could be used by the popular press. For example, in Australia, Kelly (1992) opted not to write up her psychologically based observations and accounts of indigenous drinking habits. Instead she provided an insightful analysis of the history and politics of the introduction of alcohol to the community, an analysis which could be of more direct use to the people she had studied.

I take illustrations from research projects. I use ideas about the importance of conceptualizing interpersonal power and the language of psychoanalysis as a resource for insights into the emotional dynamics between motivated people.

Three Illustrations

Richard and I Work on an Anti-smoking Intervention and Evaluation

I am not sure he has understood my question. 'What can you do in the classroom to get them interested in health?'

'Well, it was on the train, from Mt Isa, I was looking out, I saw the sky. It was blue and there were some clouds . . .' And he started to tell me, let me know the vastness, let me know the gulf, the abyss between the lives of these children and our preoccupation with stopping them from smoking. Of course he didn't say this but he let me know. He may not himself have known or acknowledged the gulf between what the project demanded and what was possible. Don't these educated whites on big salaries know what they're doing? Best then just to make sure that whatever's happening is not my fault, so truthful talk, talk about the time I was thinking about those kids. This is described in detail, around and around, knowing the truth lies there.

We had spent ages to get this far. Richard had completed a Certificate course on Research Design in Aboriginal Health, for which the only qualification for entry, besides being indigenous or Islander, was being motivated. The Department of Health keenly funded the initiative – indigenous and Islander health is third world health and we all know it. We had produced, after a year, a joint research proposal, and again, eagerly the Department funded us. Richard and I, black and white, male and female, apprentice and boss, we probably didn't understand each other but we were both highly motivated.

The project is elegant. To work with older schoolchildren (13–14 years) on their production of an anti-smoking campaign for the youngies (7–9 years). The school, the community leaders, are keen, hungry for help, tempted to position me as a benefactor, someone who can give them something useful. I resist this role and observe the ensuing struggle. We talk with an important community man, who knows the history, knows the politics, the scandals of whites coming in. He is dignified, aloof, then on sensing no threat he is the little boy-man, sliding into mateship, maybe I know about his very ordinary but violent past.

Then the real struggle begins. This is Richard's province, but the burden's too great. How to write up this stuff, these insights, the histories, the ways of childhood, the health and the pains? Huge pieces of paper are produced with bits of note-it yellows referring to different sorts of ideas and people. A joint paper is written for presentation in the state's capital. Richard goes there and he discovers others like him, the indigenous workers, tokens in the system, expected to be trained like graduates and to proceed with authority, without confusion. His own presentation changes to talk about this, this is important. But then the conference comes and goes and we still have the data, not even data like that upstairs in our building where mosquitoes are counted and examined for viruses.

Now Richard is on to other things. After his experiences with classrooms he is perfect for educational programmes with difficult ones, the ones in the prisons, the boys with a fate. And I am left with the writing up, still not done. The Department of Health holds me to account and they have to wait and wait while Richard and I start to re-negotiate our roles.

This account points to aspects of cross-cultural research crucial to success. Talking about train trips and the sky colouring was not irrelevant to our work, but inevitable. This recognizable indigenous way of approaching discussions, may be linked to insights by Walkerdine (1994), in her analysis of western rationality as crucially involving the 'forgetting' of context. This contrasts with indigenous characterizations of reasoning and discussion in which much detail and context is brought into play, is not 'forgotten' as the furtherance of debate or discussion occurs. Thus too are the characterizations of indigenous community meetings which last long hours, as is proper.

But besides such cross-cultural insights explored incidentally, yet clearly relevant to our understanding of the children's narratives, my own experiences of the process involve an uncomfortable disjunction between my research preoccupations and the narrative of my collaborator. Impatience (let's get on with it?); bewilderment (is this relevant, what is he up to?); pleasure (I'm enjoying the account, the conveying of experience and development of his insights). I get to understand something of the children's perspective which would be impossible through looking at interview transcripts or accounts of classroom activities of exuberance and shyness. I tolerate my mounting worries, and keep faith that my collaborator's actions and speech are important, even while I am confused.

Second, this illustrates how hard it was for him to show me, for me to understand what he did not know/could not do. The writing up, the pulling together as a research outcome, tasks usually expected of Honours graduates. How easy the slippage from knowing his strengths, knowing his centrality to the project and my dependence on him, to expecting these strengths to extend into areas of western expertise. How can the strengths and limitations each brings to the work be safely explored and acknowledged?

Establishing a Sex Offender Programme with a Community Organization

The boy is personable and receptive. A male indigenous mental health worker and I are interviewing Eric, 14, in a detention room around a large table, under which most of my body is hidden, since Eric is understood to have few boundaries to protect himself from responding to women and younger children sexually. As usual, the assessment interview is powerful and deeply moving. What he says and his responses to me paint a clear picture of his violent hatred of and desperate longing for his abusive mother. How such things translate into his extreme danger for those who become vulnerable to him is for future treatment, care and placement, if it can be made available. Meanwhile here he is, and in response to one question he jokes about what girls 'are good for'. He looks anxiously at the male interviewer, and is reassured, since he too laughs at girls' fates and their accessibility for sex. I have to let it go. There are complexities and struggles afoot in coming together to work with these boys, for we are also working on ourselves, our own violence, our own values, our own inter-sex hostilities.

During training at the community organization I work with, we start with familiar hurdles – being able to talk about sexuality in a mixed-sex, and mixed-race group (Aboriginal, Islander and Anglo-Celt), being able to think about the similarities and differences between what you do with a woman who has been leading you on all night, then tries to get out of it later in a house, between this and attacking a child down the road, full of the knowledge of her evil, and between these and a gang in a car, having fun with a reluctant slut. Sniggers, or 'Shoot 'em'. The theory is there, a grounding in feminist research and activism over decades, my experience as a practising and supervising psychologist, and my respect for different values and practices. What do I need to do to help develop and evaluate the programme with my co-workers, with the staff at the detention centre, with the boys and their families or communities? I see no answers, but try to keep stepping back to what remains clear to me. We are a team trying to work in this area, work which will be evaluated for its impact and success. I take the lead in setting precedents for talking and thinking about violence and sexuality. So the structure of the group and its relations slowly take a shape which defines us as professionals together, exploring topics without me as the point of authority.

There are defences here brought into play against feeling vulnerable or anxious together and include transferring, or projecting denied impulses on to someone else or their activities. Thus, for example, the men in the team came to represent, on occasions, violent sexuality which the women say they 'don't understand'. Some sexual offences of the adolescents provoked responses such as 'Shoot 'em', which helped us manage some of our own feared sexual potentials or desires. Such reactions were high-lighted in a timely way when our local newspaper published the names of those paedophiles who had been charged and convicted and who were living locally. The newspaper was enormously supported and encouraged by readers and commentators throughout the country for doing 'the right thing'. The destruction of the families, employment and social lives of those men was simply worth the rush of relieved feelings and excitement on the part of the self-righteous.

What is important to grasp, to gain conceptual purchase on here for the researcher? I illustrate my discomfort and conflict. I had to help contain and to model the capacity to contain the anxieties present in ourselves as individuals or a group. This instead of jumping in with solutions, ideas and rules about what should happen, what was right, and how people should think about cross-sex relations, as though I knew, from my designated position of trainer, consultant, expert. The trap would draw upon the psychological defences against anxiety associated with neediness and seemingly intractable problems, including reparation attempts and delusions of omniscience. The trap would have me collude with this position of authority, as the one who knows, who then becomes part of the cycle of knowledge, authority and eventual disappointment as my knowledge cannot solve the questions, problems and anxieties which my team members bring to the project and to our collaboration.

This saviour mentality is a process familiar to those working cross-culturally. In parts of indigenous Australia it is called 'white cunting', a term which expresses the contempt for whites who present to help, but who fail, a process which can be exploited by either side in a war between the haves and the have-nots. It's easier to have a common enemy, the white who stuffs up, and experience a moment of moral gain, the 'bad' transferred to the white, the disappointment of a somewhat idealized authority failing, another letdown.

Evaluating a Government Child-care Programme in Indigenous Communities

It's hot all the time on the island, and the plane lands with its high-profile whites and Islander women whose organization may already have too much power for some – women with four-wheel drives and budgets of tens of thousands, something's gone wrong with nature. We land and no one greets us as we walk all the way to the community council building. We sit with the local representative of the programme – outside because it's a mess inside from a party last night. We wait, chat – no water, no greetings, except from some of those elders who want us to act, to do something, arrest someone, do something since the allocated money has gone astray. The conspicuously absent man bought a flash car on the mainland and enjoyed fast living. These elders are not amused, ashamed that so many are here to sort out the problem. The senior government official is relaxed; she chats, sits, smokes, pulls out soft drinks from her bag, smiling as though she'd hate to be anywhere else. We have a circle of chairs, and the elders talk, while others come and go, keeping the community informed, looking out for danger from us – what sort of trouble? who will be to blame? will we have to compensate for what the rascal has done? Slowly it's clear that there's to be no fuss, the official has every confidence that the community can sort this out, with help to make sure the paperwork is written up, changes in budget iteming completed, the car sold. The relief is too great for the old man – those are tears I see, shame, relief and tears, but no one is arrested.

Whole sets of difficulties, of discord, within the community, between it and government, between the sexes were 'contained' here. The parties need not have come up, instead they could have spent time on the phone laying down the law to those who would pick up the phone. By visiting, it was made clear to all that some of the most difficult aspects and possibilities within the programme could be addressed directly without fear, and problems looked at without prior assumptions as to what the solution should be. Those individuals in authority were able to contain the complexities without recourse to dominating the process of resolution.

Throughout the time I was evaluating, with the communities affected, this government programme, including my attendance at this island meeting, there were many criticisms of different sorts levelled at the government and at the officers responsible. Rarely was anything perfect, and bringing in resources to dispossessed communities was always going to feed into schisms and tensions already there. But my research showed that the programme was successful, in amongst the documented failures, in developing community focus and planning so as to lay the foundation for healthier and more secure children.

Success, I argued, was a function of at least three identifiable cross-cultural practices. From these we may also draw general methodological points for research. First, the budget supported advisory group meetings lasting over a few days, to which anyone from the thirty to forty communities involved was welcome – usually between one and three from each. This differs from a traditional government 'reference group' which has a fixed personnel through position held or expertise. As requirements for a reference group in research increase and as the benefits of one become clear, membership and function have to be explored. The researcher can seriously consider making it possible for the group to have an 'open' component to it of this sort.

The reference group in this programme used their meetings to decide how the money should be spent. The meetings also provided, among other things, workshops for brainstorming intractable problems, and plenty of time and space for negotiating and setting the agenda by the group. It was next to impossible for everyone to understand and hold in mind the complexities of government funding, especially since the community representatives changed over time. Concurrent anxieties and practical considerations led to the processes being explained again and again, as the training modules were repeated. These repetitions were part of the process, neither redundant nor a waste of time, but centrally related to sharing power and knowledge, and contributing to offsetting anxieties in a containable way – structuring the knowledge.

The second characteristic identified by the evaluation research was the government department's decision to simplify radically the paperwork needed for groups to access money and account for it. The simplification of 'red tape' so that those who were semi-literate or for whom English was a second, third or fourth language could fill in the forms, allowed a much greater potential pool of groups of people to apply for money. These forms were filled in sometimes during the advisory group meetings or after discussion there. This simplification makes explicit that however competent and insightful the representatives are about their own communities, they should not be mistaken for highly educated westernized people, able to organize and plan bureaucratically, as those with years of institutional experience may be able to do. It breaks the linkage between the competencies of indigenous individuals and their ability to work the government systems of protocol. Even though people may be unable to function at a bureaucratic level we may expect of western organizations, this does not mean they are incompetent or unable to plan and establish what they know is needed in their communities. Compare, for example, the expectations placed on Richard, above, a highly talented man without the four to six years of university psychology training usual for a non-indigenous in his position.

The third and most psychological characteristic of the programme, already touched on, was the management style. The officers, mostly indigenous, and in particular the senior resource officer (then non-indigenous), were able to tolerate and withstand pressures to act, solve, intervene and take over during times of uncertainty and conflict. They demonstrated clear insight and understanding of how groups in general are likely to behave, including those group processes which inevitably throw up uncertainty, strong reactions and different viewpoints. These understandings of groups allowed the officers to use the groups to discover practical solutions. Thus instead of acting to solve or systematize procedures of response to complaints or problems, the officers kept faith with the idea that the groups themselves, within a structured, containing environment, could 'play' and so find solutions.

This is highly controversial – if the group/community fails to produce what they said they would, shouldn't the money be given to others, as was suggested of the island discussed? And if the programme means communities fail, then aren't we simply setting them up to fail again, showing the authorities how hopeless these groups are, and reinforcing to the communities their own inadequacies? This is not the place for a general discussion of these questions, but what I refer to is what is going on when the interventionists, including researchers, have decided or are deciding to risk the uncertain outcomes inherent in qualitative data collection and to tolerate a measure of failure. They are aware of different instincts they have but refuse to dominate the process for the comfort of feeling clear and certain about what is happening. The alternatives, total withdrawal of resources or government/white management, would cripple community development, which in turn is crucial to improving individual health. The qualitative researcher finds a very similar position. The inherent flexibility in data-gathering and analysis makes inevitable uncertainty and the need to tolerate associated anxiety. Without a clear framework for addressing such anxiety and uncertainty and their effects on our thinking and quality of information gained, the researcher is shackled and less likely to manage these tensions as productive of insight rather than as glitches or problems of a seamless methodological formula.

It is within these cross-cultural conflicts that we find lessons for research. The value of a reference group is that it can both provide structured play and contain the ensuing anxieties as the group and interpersonal processes of collaboration and data collection get underway.

The Researcher's Perspective

Conducting research is an emotional business. It is too demanding not to take on major personal significance (Selby, 1985). As a central vision of research, this view is in contrast to a vision of research which focuses on those moments of research when you feel like a disinterested scientist, secure in the knowledge that by following particular agreed-upon methods you are a part of discovering the world in an unbiased and objective way. But few from any research tradition now deny that research includes uncertainty, the ability to contain the anxiety this uncertainty produces, and the fact that there is a gap of creativity between data and interpretation, however scientific the work. There is a large literature addressing this. Some philosophical and historical texts on these include Fuller (1993), Matthews (1995) and Megill (1991). This creativity is at the heart of understanding qualitative methods, with the coding categories of textual data developed after rather than before their collection.

In focusing on the precarious and fragile moves to empowerment when working across divides of cultural disadvantage, I have drawn on practices which can work with 'failure' as well as with success, reflecting a flexibility characteristic of qualitative research. The research can shift during its administration, something goes wrong, the aims cannot be met, principal players refuse to work together, an unexpected avenue of investigation invites exploration. How these events are handled and decisions made will partly determine the outcome, the insights and the knowledge that can be shared. There will be a relationship between the intellectual, personal and political playing materials brought by a researcher and the insights then accessible to the researcher for publication. This is often seen as a problem for students of research design (and not only these), for whom it is difficult at first to envisage valid research as anything other than the discovery of a single objective truth about the phenomena under investigation, free of the bias of the researcher. It is important then that researchers have the conceptual tools to help them as much as possible in understanding the genesis of their ideas and insights and the importance they attach to them.

I draw upon two traditions to help present cross-cultural negotiations in health psychology research. One is best illustrated through the debates and procedures now established throughout western organizations for understanding and managing sexual harassment. In particular there is the idea that regardless of any emotional vulnerability of a (typically male) senior harasser and of any personal power held over him by a (typically female) subordinate whom he desires, the onus of responsibility and understanding of the structure of the relationship rests with the senior person. Helen Garner's book *The First Stone* (1995) touches the sore point, in our (western) cultures where sexual desirability, independence of character, misogynistic institutions and those in authority within them intersect for young women at the start of their careers. While these are diverse and conflicting forces, it is the person with material power who has the onus of distinguishing between 'mutually enjoyable workplace flirtation' (ACTU Working

Women's Centre, 1983: 1) and illegal sexual pressure. This is grounded in the fact of how organizational and material power is fundamental but not coterminous with personal power, a theme developed by feminist scholars in their treatment of the relationship between psychoanalysis and Marxism (Selby, 1993a). The analogy with working across culture is not the issue of sexual harassment (although this is possible), but an awareness of the personal dynamics linked to the complexities of power and responsibility and of the experiences of power(lessness) on both sides when representatives of institutions of differing types of authority and influence come together to work together.

From positions then of institutional advantage, the researcher/interventionist has particular ethical and conceptual responsibilities, illustrated by the child-care evaluation described earlier. These responsibilities include the task of containing and making visible the axes of power at work in collaboration, as the researcher is aware of them. This includes awareness and clarification of how power is held on both sides. This requires, at the very least, a (continual) explanation and revealing to the collaborator of the organizational and financial underpinning of the work. In seeing clearly how the supraordinate organization/system works, representatives from the disempowered group are better placed to negotiate their needs. And it is their experienced needs which in contemporary cross-cultural research have to be represented.

The second reference point in helping thought about cross-cultural research work from the researcher's perspective is the literature and therapeutic practices which have developed the concepts of 'containment' and 'play' of which I have already given examples, to explain how what happens in relationships (of any sort) between people comes about. These developments, through the analysis of that microcosm of intense 'play' between therapist and analysand, point to issues of vulnerability as each one becomes vulnerable to the other, to their own internal needs and to the anxieties raised by both. In practice, sharing power as I have described translates into managing quite diverse impetuses, for example in recognizing how you don't know the answers about what to research or how to intervene, while positioned to lead the process. These experiences of uncertainty while in positions of leadership or authority have been explored in other arenas, for example in counselling and psychoanalysis (Coltart, 1992; Miller, 1987; Selby, 1990), supervision (Nahum, 1993), and in management (Sinclair, 1996).

These terms help develop our understandings of the role and management of emotion and conflict in cross-cultural work with traditionally oppressed groups. In turning to 'containment' through the researcher's perspective, I refer to the ability symbolically to hold together disparate aspects of a relationship or personal impulses which provoke vulnerability experienced otherwise as anxiety or as denial of the significance of what is happening. In psychoanalytic practice 'containment' can be represented by quite physical structures – a room where people can feel safe to 'play'. In health psychology research using qualitative methods, the research design and management provides the containing opportunities for collaboration, for 'play' and creativity. The researcher also needs inner containment for the management of the experience of conflicting and powerful needs, of one's self or of others.

This is a very similar concept to the 'holding' described by Winnicott. One illustration he gives of such holding is:

> A child is playing in the garden. An aeroplane flies low overhead. This can be hurtful even to an adult. No explanation is valuable for the child. What is valuable is that you hold the child close to yourself, and the child uses the fact that you are not scared beyond recovery, and is soon off and away, playing again. (Quoted in Davis and Wallbridge, 1983: 108)

If the child/person is provided with 'enough' of such 'holding' experiences Winnicott argues that the individual is preparing to be able to hold *themselves* together during moments of anxiety and threat later on. In this way the possibility of containment is internalized as *self*-containment. Likewise, a researcher must be able to contain, first, their own uncertainties and anxieties if they are to be able to gain insight into what is brought to the research by those studied or by a collaborator. Without being alert to these processes the researcher is limited in how he or she understands the topic under scrutiny and therefore limits in unconscious ways the collaborative relationship. Interestingly, Devereux's (1967) understanding of research in the behavioural sciences is that its methodology is a highly developed response to the anxieties inevitable to encounters with people. Research, in this view, and consistent with critical analyses provided by feminist scholars (for example, Mitchell, 1974; Sayers, 1986; Wilkinson, 1986), then systematically limits what can be experienced and so seen by the researcher.

The other term mentioned, 'play', refers to the central arena offered by psychoanalysis (and other forms of therapy and change management) during which people feel safe to 'freely associate' or explore their emotional or irrational aspects and through them find possibilities for insight and action. Such play invites the possibility of re-assessing and gaining purchase on how powerful previous experiences are evoked within present relationships. For both (or more) involved in this discussion, 'brainstorming' or play provides a method for examining what is brought, sometimes unconsciously, by the participants, to be examined for relevance to the task in hand (see Relke, 1993, for extended discussion of 'counter-transference', the therapist's own 'play').

Living with Uncertain Collaboration

'Cups of tea, Jane, drink endless cups of tea', an experienced cross-cultural worker educated me.

'I just sat there, every week I went to the Community Health Centre and sat there for half a day, a white psychiatrist, just being there,' an inter-state colleague told me.

> What is needed by the 'white' professional worker working from a position of apparent strength and authority as they negotiate cross-racially with the disadvantaged? For successful research I have, so far, emphasized (a) the ability to articulate an awareness of the economic and institutional relations of power; (b) the ability to contain anxiety; and (c) the ability to work with a reference group.

For all three of these abilities the issue becomes one which is less of selling your product, your brilliant research proposal, your intervention for happiness, such that it is then 'owned', but more that in the first instance you know why you are there and are able to articulate this. You may be a government psychiatrist given responsibility for 'Aboriginal and Islander Mental Health', with a budget, or you may hold a belief that your research methods can help provide a voice for those you judge need one or that by taking photographs and writing about them you are providing a potential resource for the community. Your circumstances, plans, relationship to institutions may have to be repeated and explained many times, within the reference group and during fieldwork, making intelligible why you are there. In all cases you may have something very useful to offer, and to write about eventually, but it can only be used if judged or recognized as useful by the group concerned.

I have described situations in which you may find yourself negotiating and developing your role, which takes time. This sort of stance would be familiar to anyone who has done fieldwork as an anthropologist or who has conducted open interviews for research or psychological assessment. It would be familiar to the government officer, above, who can retain and bring together both her official role and duties with a respect for the locus of significant meaning in the group/individual she is there to work with, a group or individuals who start from a position of disempowerment, disadvantage and need.

Working across cultural lines in a context of power struggle and differential means that ordinary human processes will be exacerbated and need to be understood. Successful researchers manage these 'snags' intuitively, but the processes can and should be spelt out. Once they are thought to be understood then the onus is on the researcher to express and allow space for discussion and interpretation of difficulties and anxieties. For example, in response to Richard's talk of his trip from Mt Isa, I might have become impatient and claimed he was wasting time, or point out that the trip was irrelevant to thinking about what to do in the classroom. The difficulties or breakdown between us this might have caused would have had to be addressed by discussing some of how I understood the different meanings of the work in hand.

Although not developed through examples here, we may also be referring to how we position people as having characteristics, intentions and powers because of previous relationships which that person evokes in some way, consciously or otherwise. It is a task for all of us to be able to differentiate between our own reactions to people based on our own backgrounds, and what can be attributable to the person in the present. The more unconscious the responses the more primitive and powerful they are, especially when responding through envious attacks, idealizations and compulsive reparation needs. These terms come from the 'object relation' school of psychoanalysis. They are also central emotions for those working together when there is a differential access to resources and a divide between the 'haves' and 'have-nots'.

The whites are helping the disadvantaged, determined to make good, but overlooking the gratification of assuaged guilt buried deep in a child-hood characterized by a depressive mother. Or here too there is the fury of the indigenous against their 'oppressors', including some researcher who disappoints, 'ripping them off' again. At the same time the indigenous Australians may forget their own parents who could not free themselves of managing despair without alcohol, so neglecting their child, withholding the good things children have a right to.

Reference groups are essential, if not mandatory, for working cross-racially in Australia – few ethics committees would approve work without one (National Health and Medical Research Council, 1991; Aboriginal Primary Health Care Project, 1994). This group can be invaluable in a range of ways, but one for which they are under-used is as a sounding board for debriefing and developing insights into what may be happening between collaborators so as to be able to articulate issues and help find solutions. In general terms this group should represent relevant professions and members of the target population, with a mandate to be in regular contact and to be willing to read and respond to the researcher's work.

Concluding Remarks

I have provided illustrations from which to draw practical and theoretical lessons for qualitative health psychology research. I have focused on research as intervention and as involving relationships with groups and individuals. Theoretically, the analysis here provides language and insight in collaborative relations. Practically I point to the need for a reference group for researchers and to ways of managing cross-cultural relationships and their human/psychological consequences. Nowadays relational and ethical issues are standards by which a piece of research in which the researcher is working with disadvantaged people is evaluated. They are central to the protocol guidelines and philosophy of research. I have illustrated aspects of working relationships and touched on the possibility of tokenism and on the status of collaborators.

The starting point has been to link research processes and cross-cultural work to a discussion of understanding and coping with relationships between those of unequal economic power. Emotional and relationship dynamics should be expected to be relevant and a normal part of ensuing research, especially qualitative research with its flexible, negotiated quality. But precisely because of its flexible process, qualitative research requires rigorous and clear accounting of the process whereby the researcher reaches his/her insights. I have referred to a rich and highly developed scholarship and sets of practices in psychotherapy which can provide insight and language for addressing the relational forms I have illustrated, and which form part of qualitative research methods. In providing ourselves with a model of interpersonal emotions, we are enabled to manage personally and find ways both of discussing and solving apparently intractable personal and political tensions and of demonstrating rhetorically powerful insights in the conclusions of our research.

Understanding the processes of containment and play as well as having the ability to tolerate disparate emotional responses on the part of one's self and others provides a secure basis from which to research and train researchers to work across culture and participate in the fragile and insecure process of developing productive work relationships. There is always some equivalent of drinking lots of tea together, the ritual itself affording play space. They'll find what you have to offer if it is relevant to them.

Acknowledgements

Funding came from the Department of Health, Queensland, for the smoking intervention, from the Department of Families, Youth and Community Care, Queensland, for both the sex-offender programme (administered through Cleveland Youth Detention Centre and Townsville Aboriginal and Torres Strait Islander Mental Health Corporation) and the review of the remote Aboriginal and Torres Strait Islander child-care programme. James Cook University contributed financially as well as administratively. Individuals I refer to in this chapter are either disguised, or are a composite from incidents put together to examine issues. The chapter has been read and discussed with collaborators from each of the projects cited. My thanks to them, to Ben Bradley, Wendy Hollway, Valerie Walkerdine, my editors and to those I have worked with for these projects.

References

Aboriginal Primary Health Care Project (1994) Protocols for consultation with Aboriginal and Torres Strait Islander Communities: Position paper. Cairns: Aboriginal Primary Health Care Project, Unpublished document.
ACTU (Australian Council of Trades Unions) Working Women's Centre (1983) *Working Women's Charter Implementation Manual, no.1: Sexual Harassment.* Melbourne: ACTU.
Boonmongkon, P. (1993) 'Khi Thut' – 'the disease of social loathing': an anthropology of leprosy in rural Northeastern Thailand. In B. Yoddumnern-Attig et al. (eds), *Qualitative Methods for Population and Health Research.* Salaya: Mahidol University, pp. 358–374.

Brady, M. (1991) Making research into Aboriginal substance abuse issues more effective. In A. Duquemin, P. d'Abbs and E. Chalmer (eds), *Making Research into Aboriginal Substance Misuse Issues more Effective. Working Paper, no.4*. Sydney: National Drug and Alcohol Research Centre, University of New South Wales, pp. 8–17.

Coltart, N. (1992) Slouching towards Bethlehem . . . or thinking the unthinkable in psychoanalysis. *Slouching towards Bethlehem . . . and Further Psychoanalytic Explorations*. London: Free Association Books, pp. 1–14.

Davis, M. and Wallbridge, D. (1983) *Boundary and Space: An Introduction to the Work of D.W. Winnicott*. Harmondsworth: Penguin.

Dean, S., Beaufoy, J., Tonge, B. and Rodrigues, S. (1996) Psychotherapy: children's rights and ethics in research. Second national conference on child and adolescent mental health: Who counts? Mental health outcomes for Australia's young. Melbourne: November.

Devereux, G. (1967) *From Anxiety to Method in Behavioral Sciences* (English edition). Paris: Mouton and Co.

Finch, J. and Mason, J. (1990) Decision taking in the fieldwork process. *Studies in Qualitative Methodology*, 2: 51–76.

Fuller, S. (1993) *Philosophy, Rhetoric, and the End of Knowledge: The Coming of Science and Technology Studies*. Madison: University of Wisconsin Press.

Garner, H. (1995) *The First Stone: Some Questions about Sex and Power*. Sydney: Picador.

Henriques, J., Hollway, W., Urwin, C., Venn, C. and Walkerdine, V. (1997) *Changing the Subject: Psychology, Social Regulation and Subjectivity*. London and New York: Methuen.

Hollway, W. (1989) *Subjectivity and Method in Psychology: Gender, Meaning and Science*. London: Sage.

Jemmott, J.B., III, and Jones, J.M. (1993) Social psychology and AIDS among ethnic minorities: risk behaviors and strategies for changing them. In J. Pryor and G. Reeder (eds), *The Social Psychology of HIV Infection*. Hillsdale, NJ: Erlbaum, pp. 183–244.

Johannsen, A.M. (1992) Applied anthropology and post-modern ethnography. *Human Organisation*, 51 (1): 71–80.

Johnson, T.M. and Sargent, C.F. (eds) (1990) *Medical Anthropology: A Handbook of Theory and Method*. Westport, CT: Greenwood Press.

Kelly, K. (1992) *Contextualising the 'Problem' of Aboriginal Alcohol Use*. James Cook University: Honours thesis, Department of Psychology and Sociology.

Marshall, M. (1990) 'Problem deflation' and the ethnographic record: interpretation and introspection in anthropological studies of alcohol. *Journal of Substance Abuse*, 2: 353–367.

Matthews, J.R. (1995) *Quantification and the Quest for Medical Certainty*. Princeton, NJ: Princeton University Press.

Megill, A. (1991) Four senses of objectivity. *Annals of Scholarship*, 8: 301–320.

Miles, M.B. and Huberman, A. (1984) *Qualitative Data Analysis: A Sourcebook of New Methods*. London: Sage.

Miller, G.A. (1969) Psychology as a means of promoting human welfare. *American Psychologist*, 24: 1063–1075.

Miller, M. (1987) Introduction. *The Suppressed Madness of Sane Men: Forty-four Years of Exploring Psychoanalysis*. London: Tavistock, pp. 1–11.

Mitchell, J. (1974) *Psychoanalysis and Feminism*. Harmondsworth: Penguin.

Nahum, T. (1993) Playing within the boundaries of supervision. *Australian Journal of Psychotherapy*, 12: 108–121.

National Aboriginal Health Strategy Working Party (1989) *A National Aboriginal Health Strategy*. Canberra: Report to Ministerial Forum on Aboriginal Health.

National Health and Medical Research Council (1991) *Guidelines on Ethical Matters in Aboriginal and Torres Strait Islander Health Research*. Brisbane: Interim Report.

Relke, D.M.A. (1993) Foremothers who cared: Paula Heimann, Margaret Little and the female tradition in psychoanalysis. *Feminism and Psychology*, 3: 89–109.

Sayers, J. (1986) *Sexual Contradictions: Psychology, Psychoanalysis, and Feminism*. London: Tavistock.

Selby, J.M. (1985) *Feminine Identity and Contradiction: Women Research Students at Cambridge University*. University of Cambridge: PhD Thesis.

Selby, J.M. (1990) Uncertainty in counselling and psychology. *Proceedings of Third National Conference of the Alcohol and Drug Foundation*. Brisbane: Drug and Alcohol Foundation, pp. 102–134.

Selby, J.M. (1993a) Psychoanalysis as a critical theory of gender. In L. Moss, W. Thorngate, B. Caplan and H. Stam (eds), *Recent Trends in Theoretical Psychology*. New York: Springer Verlag, pp. 307–318.

Selby, J.M. (1993b) *Summary Report on November Trip to Western Province Using Seeding Money for Evaluation of the Filariasis Eradication Programme*. Townsville: James Cook University.

Sinclair, A. (1996) *Journey without Maps: Transforming Management Education*. Inaugural Professorial Address. Melbourne: Melbourne Business School.

Stacy, S. (1983) Aboriginal nutrition. In R. Williams (ed.), *The Best of 'The Science Show': (ABC Radio)*. Melbourne: Thomas Nelson, pp 32–37.

Walkerdine, V. (1994) Reasoning in a post-modern age. In J. Edwards (ed.), *Thinking: International Interdisciplinary Perspectives*. Victoria: Hawker Brownlow Education, pp. 116–126.

Watson, L. (1992) Untitled. *Health for women (3)*. January, Brisbane: Department of Health, p. 1.

Wilkinson, S. (1986) *Feminist Social Psychology: Developing Theory and Practice*. Milton Keynes: Open University Press.

Yoddumnern-Attig, B., Attig, G.A., Boonchalaksi, W., Richter, K. and Soon-thorndhada, A. (1993) *Qualitative Methods for Population and Health Research*. Salaya: Mahidol University.

Part III

Transforming Talk into Text

12

Using Grounded Theory in Health Psychology

Practices, Premises and Potential

Kerry Chamberlain

Grounded theory is one of the many and various qualitative research methods available for researchers to choose from. It is a popular method, widely adopted in some disciplines such as nursing, and beginning to be used more frequently in psychology (Henwood and Pidgeon, 1994). It appears to have a particular appeal for researchers who are relatively new to qualitative research, possibly because several texts which describe the method are readily available (for example, Glaser, 1978; Glaser and Strauss, 1967) and perhaps, more importantly, because several texts which document detailed procedures for conducting grounded theory research exist (for example, Chenitz and Swanson, 1986; Strauss and Corbin, 1990). Recently it has been suggested that grounded theory 'runs the risk of becoming fashionable' (Strauss and Corbin, 1994: 277), which Annells suggests means that grounded theory has become 'vulnerable to uncritical acceptance and imprecise application' (1996: 391). In this chapter I want to consider the techniques of grounded theory, the premises underlying it, and draw some conclusions on its potential as a research method for health psychology.

Practices

It is difficult to describe grounded theory succinctly because the various aspects of the method are interconnected and interrelated, and it does not lend itself readily to a linear presentation. As Keddy, Sims and Stern aptly express it: 'doing grounded theory, rather than a tidy process, is as messy as preparing a gourmet meal, where all the parts need to come together at the end' (1996: 450). This should be borne in mind in reading the account below, as should the fact that this presentation will inevitably offer a simplified account of the method.

The essential features of grounded theory are that it is grounded and theoretical. By theoretical is meant that a theory of the phenomenon in question must be developed, and this must be more than a descriptive account. The researcher moves from a descriptive classification of events and facts to an abstract theory of the phenomenon that accounts for relationships and processes. By grounded is meant that a theory must emerge or be developed from the data, and not from predetermined hypotheses or formulations. In other words, the theory presented must be grounded in the data. The researcher begins with data which relate to specific incidents, facts or events and progressively develops more abstract classifications or categories which integrate and explain the data and organize the relationships within them.

It is often stated that grounded theory is an inductive method, but this is an oversimplification of the processes involved. It is inductive in so far as understandings, categories and theory are developed directly from the data, rather than through approaching the data with predefined constructs to investigate and hypotheses to test. However, as analysis proceeds, the researcher actively seeks to develop understandings and hypotheses as to what is going on and how it is ordered. This stage is essential in developing a theory of the phenomenon. These ideas are then tested deductively through further data collection and analysis. Thus, doing grounded theory involves a sequence of inductive and deductive thinking throughout the process. The inductive label is often given to grounded theory because of its emphasis on the principle that all aspects of this process must be grounded in the data.

The Inter-relation of Sampling and Analysis

Grounded theory specifically involves processes which are designed to maintain the 'groundedness' of the approach. Data collection and analysis are deliberately inter-related, and initial data analysis is used to direct further data collection. This is intended to provide the researcher with opportunities for increasing the 'density' and 'saturation' of recurring categories, as well as for following up unexpected findings. Interweaving data collection and analysis in this way is also intended to increase insights and to clarify the parameters of the emerging theory. The approach also argues for initial data collection and preliminary analyses to take place in advance of consulting and incorporating prior research literature. This is intended to ensure that the analysis is based strongly in the data and that pre-existing constructs do not shape the analysis and subsequent theory formation. Of course it is impossible for a researcher to select and develop a question to research without having some understandings of the field, but grounded theory emphasizes that the researcher must be alert to the influence of these and not allow them to contaminate the theory which is developed. Ideas, intuitions and hypotheses need to be checked and confirmed against the data. The theory must be grounded in the data, and the researcher must always attend closely to the data and ensure that all aspects of the theory can be justified in the data. Note that reading and integrating literature is delayed, not omitted, and is regarded as forming an important part of theory development. If existing theoretical constructs are utilized, they must be verified in the data. Researchers are also encouraged to use their knowledge of the field, both professional and personal, to inform, clarify, and substantiate the theory in the later stages of its development. This process is referred to as theoretical sensitivity, but is not usually discussed directly in published grounded theory studies. However, Donovan (1995), in researching the feelings and relationships experienced by men during a partner's pregnancy, documents how she initially deferred the incorporation of prior research but then utilized diverse theoretical and historical literature to situate and interpret her findings, referred her findings back to the participants, discussed the emerging categories with a co-researcher, and reconfirmed findings through resampling data and literature as the theory was developed, in her efforts to achieve theoretical sensitivity.

The Three Phases of Sampling and Analysis

It is helpful to think of grounded theory development as proceeding in three phases. However, these are not independent or necessarily sequential, as the gourmet meal simile serves to remind us. Each phase involves a different sampling procedure and has an associated style of analysis to meet different analytic goals. Data collection is guided by theoretical sampling, or sampling on the basis of theoretically relevant constructs rather than for population representativeness. The specific sampling procedures at each phase have a different focus designed to serve the goals of analysis. Sampling may involve data collection from any or all of persons, sites or documents, and should not be thought of as obtained solely through interviews with respondents, even though these constitute the most common source of data.

   In the first phase, the researcher uses any relevant sampling process, preferably purposive or systematic, but perhaps fortuitous, to obtain data which are relevant to the research question. This is called open sampling and is accompanied by the first phase of analysis, open coding, so called because data are 'broken open' to identify categories. In the second phase, the researcher uses relational or variational sampling, either purposive or systematic, to locate more data which can confirm and elaborate categories, identify relationships between them, or suggest limits to their applicability. The analysis process associated with this is labelled axial coding, and results in categories being refined, developed and related to one another. Of course, this phase may also result in the identification of new categories, and require further relational sampling. The third phase utilizes discriminate sampling, which involves deliberate and directed selection of further data from persons, sites or documents to confirm and verify the 'core category' and the theory as a whole, and to ensure that the theoretical account is saturated. The analysis process here is called selective coding, where the core category, or central category that ties all other categories in the theory together, is identified and related to other categories.

Sampling and Saturation

Sampling in grounded theory, therefore, is associated with explicit sampling for information to refine and develop theory, rather than containing notions of representativeness or randomness. This is why grounded theory refers generically to its sampling procedures as theoretical sampling. Sampling is guided by the need to develop a comprehensive grounded theory from the data, and the different stages of sampling are intended to facilitate that process. Sampling also serves another important function. As categories are developed from the data, the question arises as to how important or central each of these are for the phenomenon under investigation. As understanding develops and categories become more abstracted, some categories will take a more prominent role in the theory being formulated and evaluated. Sampling, particularly discriminate sampling, is used to ensure that these categories are correctly located in the theory and that the theory is saturated and comprehensive.

Saturation is an essential component of a grounded theory. Saturation of the theory is considered to have occurred when no new categories are found which relate to the central issue or process being researched, and the theory can account for all the data that have been obtained. To check this, it is recommended that the researcher examine negative instances or cases that do not fit the theory and attempt to incorporate all variation. Saturation will often be met part way through the analysis and can be confirmed as further data are sampled and analysed. Data collection can cease when there are no gaps in the theory and all categories can be linked meaningfully together to provide a comprehensive explanation of the phenomenon.

Coding and the Constant Comparative Method

Data analysis in grounded theory involves coding, through which the data are given meaning and interpretation. In initial coding, raw data are examined and reduced by identifying concepts or categories and their properties. In later stages of the analysis, coding is directed at identifying more generic and abstract categories which are developed and integrated into the theory. Glaser (1978) presents a large set of theoretical codes which can be drawn on to question the data and promote theoretical links between categories. A practical discussion and some detailed illustrations of coding practices using health psychology examples are provided by Charmaz (1995), demonstrating how line-by-line open coding is used to identify initial concepts in the data (such as predicting rejection, avoiding stigma, keeping others unaware) which are amalgamated into more general categories (such as avoiding disclosure) in later axial coding (or focused coding as Charmaz prefers to call it). Making comparisons is an important technique for both identifying and developing categories, and the constant comparative method is a hallmark of grounded theory studies. This involves comparing incidents, informants or categories systematically for similarities and differences between them. This is intended to promote the identification of the properties of categories (for example, when does this category not apply?) and also of the links and relationships between categories. Note that these processes, coding and the use of the constant comparative method, do not proceed independently, but are intertwined with other analytic processes such as questioning, memo writing and hypothesis formulation.

Theory Development

It is evident that the stages of sampling and analysis discussed above involve progressively more abstraction from the data to theory as the analysis develops. Theory development is aided by the processes of questioning and hypothesizing. As coding progresses, questions are continually asked of the data. In the early stages of the study, the researcher might ask: What is this event characteristic of? Whom does it apply to? Where does it occur? Why is it happening? As categories are developed, the focus of questions will change, and the researcher might ask: What does this incident reveal? What does it mean? How does it relate to other incidents? Does it apply to all informants? Is it specific to one type of setting? Questioning, like categories themselves, becomes more abstract as the analysis proceeds. At the same time, the researcher is developing hypotheses about the properties of categories and the relationships between them. Through collecting and examining other data, and particularly through consideration of negative instances, these hypotheses can be tested and revised, and the theory elaborated. Categories may be split apart or amalgamated, or moved in terms of their level of abstraction and relationship with other categories. However, at every point the theory must be grounded by being located back into the data.

Two important strategies which are used to assist theory development are writing memos and drawing diagrams. These are not specific to grounded theory, but have been widely associated with the method and are considered highly valuable techniques for theory development within grounded theory. Memos are simply notes of ideas, interpretations, and hypotheses written up throughout the analysis process. Their use obliges the analyst to engage with the data and its interpretation, providing a strategy for examining the emerging categories critically for their properties and inter-relationships, and for developing the overall theory. Again, Charmaz (1995) provides a useful illustration of memo writing in practice. Diagrams are used similarly, to assist in identifying relationships between categories, and to clarify the core category of the theory and its relation to other categories. Diagrams are visual representations of the analysis which provide an overview of it. They can be used throughout the analysis to help clarify present understandings and identify where the theory needs further development.

Core Categories

In the development of a theory, there is an attempt to identify the predominant or superordinate category that ties all other categories together and unifies the theory. This is called the core category (Glaser, 1978), and its centrality is based on its ability to account for wide variation in the phenomenon under study, and to link all categories identified in the analysis logically together. Many grounded theory studies seek to clarify process, and the core category identified will often be a central process underlying the phenomenon. In this instance it is referred to as the basic social process or the basic social psychological process. Often the core category will be a basic social process, although this need not be the case. Grounded theory studies are often easily identifiable because they will suggest one overarching process that accounts for the major effect of a phenomenon. For example, Keller (1991) identifies seeking normalcy as the core category explaining the aftermath of coronary artery bypass surgery and Siegl and Morse (1994) identify tolerating reality as the basic social process for parents of HIV positive sons. An analysis may identify more than one core category (see Barclay, Donovan and Genovese, 1996), but Glaser (1978) suggests that grounded theory reports should present only one core category and it is rare to find a grounded theory account which goes beyond this.

Theory can be developed at different levels of abstraction, varying from the descriptive to the substantive and beyond to higher-order formal theories, and grounded theory studies reflect this variation in practice. Although grounded theory exponents (for example, Glaser and Strauss, 1967) argue strongly that a grounded theory should be abstract and more than a description, Charmaz concludes that most grounded theory studies have 'aimed to develop rich conceptual analyses of lived experience and social worlds instead of intending to create substantive or formal theory' (1995: 48). However, some attempts to develop higher-order theories using grounded theory methodology can be found, such as the work of Morse and Johnson (1991) on illness experience and of Olshansky (1996) on infertility.

Evaluation of Theory

How do you decide if you have a good grounded theory? Strauss and Corbin (1990) provide four criteria for assessing this. First, the theory should fit well with the phenomenon being researched. They argue that this will occur if the theory has been derived carefully from a diversity of data and represents the everyday reality of the phenomena faithfully. Second, the theory should provide understanding, in the sense of being comprehensible both to the persons studied and to others involved in the area. Third, the theory should provide generality. They argue that this will be achieved provided the data are comprehensive, the interpretation is conceptual and extensive, and the theory includes adequate variation and is abstract enough to be applicable to a wide variety of contexts in the area. Finally, a good grounded theory should provide control, both in the sense of clarifying the conditions under which the theory is applicable and in providing a basis for action in the area. As is obvious from these criteria, a good theory will be derived from good practice in developing it. Leininger (1994) outlines a set of six criteria for evaluating qualitative research in general which includes and extends these ideas, involving considerations of recurrent patterning, meaning-in-context, and saturation, along with the credibility, confirmability and transferability of findings.

Obviously not all studies which label themselves as grounded theory adequately meet these criteria, and Becker (1993) and Wilson and Hutchinson (1996) present discussions of common problems experienced in grounded theory research. The most common problems are with studies that fail to go beyond a purely descriptive level to generate theory or, conversely, with studies that fail to ground the theory adequately in the data.

Debate about Practice

In describing grounded theory above, I have inevitably simplified the practices to some degree, and have also tended to imply that there is a defined way to do grounded theory. Certainly one can readily obtain this impression from some of the more detailed and prescriptive accounts of the technique such as that offered by Strauss and Corbin (1990) or some chapters in Chenitz and Swanson (1986). However, we should be aware that grounded theory, like all other research methods, is a site of discussion about underlying assumptions (for example, Annells, 1996) and debate about what constitutes 'proper' practice (for example, Glaser, 1992). Charmaz (1995), for instance, provides a detailed account of the practice of grounded theory, but she challenges the notions that theory emerges from the data and can be independent of researchers' presuppositions, arguing that any theory is a result of the interaction between researcher and research participants and that theory is constructed in this process.

Perhaps one of the most obvious divisions in grounded theory approach has resulted from a substantial debate between the two founders of the method, Barney Glaser and Anselm Strauss. Glaser (1992) reacted strongly to the version of grounded theory propounded by Strauss and Corbin (1990), arguing, amongst other things, that it forced results rather than letting them emerge, that it asked directing rather than neutral questions, and that analysis was based on preconceived ideas rather than being open to emergent categories. Glaser suggested that Strauss and Corbin had lost the essentials of the grounded theory method, and claimed that what they described 'is surely not grounded theory' (1992: 62). This is clearly an overstated claim, as can be seen from a recent comprehensive and considered discussion of the differences between the two positions (Melia, 1996). Stern (1994) suggested that it may be appropriate to consider that there are two varieties of grounded theory, Straussian and Glaserian.

Other methodological challenges to grounded theory practice such as the development of dimensional analysis (Schatzman, 1991) have also appeared. Partly in reaction to the prescriptive practices that have been presented for some aspects of grounded theory, and partly because he felt that techniques for theory discovery were not sufficiently developed, Schatzman developed a general framework for analysis which is intended to keep the researcher focused on the data rather than the techniques of analysis. Although remaining close to grounded theory principles and methods, dimensional analysis does offer some different procedures. Perhaps one of the most important moves away from grounded theory is that dimensional analysis does not attempt to identify the basic social process, but instead to locate a central perspective from which the data can be interpreted and presented. Dimensional analysis procedures are intended to give every dimension a chance to be considered for the role of central perspective, and the researcher is supposed to follow natural analytic processes to arrive at the best interpretation. Brief accounts of dimensional analysis are given by Robrecht (1995) and Kools et al. (1996), with the latter providing a detailed account of the processes which were used in one specific analysis. Ironically, it is possible to see how the procedures proposed by dimensional analysis, such as the use of the explanatory matrix, could themselves become prescribed practices in much the same way as has happened with the explicit formulations of grounded theory practices presented by Strauss and Corbin (1990). However, dimensional analysis does stipulate some functional practices for data analysis and theory development, and can be considered as essentially another variant of grounded theory.

Hence we can see that grounded theory methods, although essentially centred on a similar set of practices, are varied and contested. There is no one way or right way to conduct grounded theory analyses, but there are relatively clear guidelines as to what can be considered to constitute a grounded theory. As Charmaz has proposed, 'grounded theory methods provide a set of strategies for conducting rigorous qualitative research' (1995: 27).

Premises

Qualitative research, like all research, is not just about methods and techniques but is built on assumptions about ontology and epistemology. As there are debates about the correct practice of grounded theory, so too there are debates concerning the underlying assumptions on which grounded theory is based (for example, Annells, 1996; Lowenberg, 1993). Here we turn to a consideration of the premises which underlie grounded theory.

Post-positivist or Constuctivist

Henwood and Pidgeon propose that qualitative research can be classified into three different strands of inquiry, although they do note that this 'fixes a fluid set of possibilities' (1994: 228) and is essentially heuristic. They suggest that these three strands can be ordered by their epistemologies, which they label as empiricism, contextualism and constructivism. They argue that grounded theory should be located within the contextualism strand because it is concerned with generating theory which is grounded in the data, and is seeking to construct inter-subjective meaning. However, Henwood and Pidgeon go on to argue that the contextualist position is conflicted by a tension within grounded theory between realism and constructivism, a feature of grounded theory which also has been noted by others (Annells, 1996; Charmaz, 1990). Grounded theory attempts to be realist in reflecting participant accounts and contexts, but is constructivist at least in demanding that theory should emerge (be constructed) from data.

The nature of the assumptions underlying grounded theory have been discussed in detail by Annells (1996). She argues that it is this tension within grounded theory which has led to the development of different versions of grounded theory in practice. Annells draws on Guba and Lincoln's (1994) four basic paradigms of inquiry, positivism, post-positivism, critical theory and constructivism, to structure the field and concludes that the different versions of grounded theory are located in different paradigms. She considers that the classic view of grounded theory (for example, Glaser, 1978; Glaser and Strauss, 1967) is post-positivist, premised on a critical realist stance, which assumes that a reality does exist but can only be approximately known, and an objectivist epistemology with a detached observer seeking an objective view. However, she considers that the more recent developments in grounded theory (for example, Charmaz, 1990; Strauss, 1987; Strauss and Corbin, 1990, 1994) have moved away from this view and are more appropriately located within the constructivist paradigm of inquiry. Under this paradigm, 'reality' is constructed and grounded theory practice is accepted to be interpretive, with knowledge considered to be created rather than found, and to be provisional in the sense of being historically and contextually located. The constructivist approach has been presented most forcefully by Charmaz who argued that the outcome of any research using grounded theory was 'a social construction of the social constructions found and explicated in the data' (1990: 1165).

This division certainly contributed to the debate between Glaser and Strauss mentioned above, and Stern (1994) suggested that the dispute could be traced essentially to differences in the ontological and epistemological premises of the two proponents, with Glaser retaining a post-positivist view and Strauss and Corbin moving towards a more constructivist view. This epistemological conflict within grounded theory can be understood more clearly in the context of the historical background to the method. Grounded theory in its original form was influenced by Glaser's strong empirical quantitative background and Strauss's preference for symbolic interactionism. It was these premises, along with demands to provide more detailed elaboration of the technique, that ultimately led to the differences developing. Both Annells (1996) and Charmaz (1995) provide a concise overview of the historical development and influences on grounded theory.

Other Debates on Premises

Like any other research approach, grounded theory is subject to challenges and change over time, and the approach has experienced a number of challenges, both methodological and epistemological. It is not my intention to describe these in detail and attempt to draw a conclusion on each, but rather to indicate that they exist and offer some sources of reference where the debates may be pursued further.

For example, recent developments towards more post-modern perspectives in the social sciences offer challenges to our methods of inquiry, and grounded theory has not been exempted from these. Annells (1996) concludes her discussion of grounded theory premises with a brief consideration of post-modernism, and considers that some elements of post-modern thought have been influential on recent grounded theory developments. However, she also notes that grounded theory has difficulty in incorporating a critical theory perspective, and that some fundamental grounded theory issues, such as the evaluative criteria for theory and theory construction *per se*, raise considerable difficulties from a post-modern perspective. Lowenberg (1993) discusses some related issues and reaches similar conclusions, identifying how interpretive research approaches, in which she includes grounded theory, have developed in radical and less structured directions in response to influences from critical and feminist theory and post-modernism.

Feminism provides another potential challenge to grounded theory. Keddy, Sims and Stern (1996) and Wuest (1995) discuss the relationship of feminism to grounded theory, and conclude that research using grounded theory can be compatible with a feminist perspective, or as Wuest expresses it 'grounded theory is a method of knowledge discovery that can be conducted from a feminist perspective' (1995: 135). Kearney, Murphy and Rosenbaum (1994), in a study of mothering on crack cocaine, provide an example of this in practice. Although Wuest (1995) considers grounded theory primarily from a methodological perspective, she does comment specifically on the epistemological issues and tensions that emerge in the conjunction of grounded theory and feminism. However, the emphasis for our purposes in these discussions is on the fact that grounded theory is not a static method of analysis but an evolving one, which can be adapted to feminist concerns such as participant involvement, respect for subjective experience as a source of data, the utility and political implications of findings, and the ideology of the researcher. Grounded theory methods do present some difficulties for feminist research practice, but Wuest (1995) and Keddy, Sims and Stern (1996) see the method as flexible enough to be accommodated within a feminist perspective. Although this discussion is ostensibly about methods, it is actually more concerned with assumptions underlying the grounded theory approach and how compatible they are with feminist research.

Although I have focused here necessarily on grounded theory, it is worth noting that these issues are part of more general trends influencing social science methodology. Lowenberg (1993) provides an extensive account of the historical and disciplinary pressures on interpretive research methods in general, among which she locates grounded theory. She argues that these pressures arise from the development and adoption of ideas from the philosophical perspectives of existentialism and phenomenology, and from feminism, post-modernism and critical theory. These lead to an emphasis on the importance of everyday experience, the multiple con-struction of 'reality', and the ambiguity and complexity of the research process, as well as concerns about the assumptions, location and power of the researcher, and associated issues about the interaction between the researched and the researcher and reflexivity in research processes. Further discussion of many of these issues can be found in Denzin and Lincoln (1994).

All this means that grounded theory, like all other qualitative approaches, cannot simply be adopted as just a method of analysis. The premises underlying various approaches to grounded theory vary, and researchers need to be clear about which of these they subscribe to or reject. Ontological, epistemological and methodological issues are not separate from each other, and the assumptions about reality and how it can or should be known have important implications for the methods and findings of research. As Lowenberg (1993) has argued, it is important to be clear and explicit about our underlying assumptions if we want to improve the quality of our research and to take part in the continuing debate on these issues.

Potential

So what does all this mean for researchers who wish to use grounded theory? Does grounded theory have anything to offer health psychology research? I believe the answer is yes, and that grounded theory has much to offer as a qualitative research technique. In this section I want to draw out and comment on the potential of this approach for health psychology research.

First, it can be noted that grounded theory has been used successfully to investigate many topics of relevance to health psychology, covering such diverse issues as how general practitioners discuss psychosocial issues with their patients (Aborelius and Österburg, 1995); how smokers redefine themselves as non-smokers (Brown, 1996); the experience of recovery after liver transplantation (Wainwright, 1995); parents' reactions to cancer recurrence in a child (Hinds et al., 1996); transformation of the self in accident victims (Morse and O'Brien, 1995); modelling young children's pain experience (Woodgate and Kristjanson, 1996); and the experience of parents with HIV positive sons (Siegl and Morse, 1994). However, it is notable that almost all of these studies have been conducted by nurses, and it is rare to locate published research using grounded theory methods in health psychology journals. However, the topics listed here are ones in which psychological processes are intimately involved and in which psychologists have a direct interest.

A further argument in favour of grounded theory could be that it can accommodate many different epistemological and ontological positions. As we have seen, it can be utilized from a post-positivist (Glaser, 1992) or a constructivist perspective (Charmaz, 1995), it can be adapted to be compatible with a feminist perspective (Wuest, 1995), it can be combined with other approaches like phenomenology (Strauss and Corbin, 1994), and it can be open to incorporating an analysis of power relationships and a critical perspective (Lowenberg, 1993). This makes grounded theory a very flexible approach for qualitative researchers with different epistemological orientations. However, given the debates within grounded theory, labelling some of these approaches as grounded theory is likely to be contested. This means that researchers must be clear about their orientation, and should argue its relevance and make the assumptions and premises for their research explicit.

Related to this is the tension between grounded theory as a prescriptive method and an evolving methodology. As noted previously, many accounts of grounded theory method are presented quite prescriptively, and researchers are warned of the dangers of 'muddling methods' (Wilson and Hutchinson, 1996) or 'eroding methods' (Stern, 1994). In contrast, Keddy, Sims and Stern argue that grounded theory is an evolving methodology and suggest that 'the re-definition of grounded theory is ours for the doing' (1996: 450). This appears a more reasonable position and I believe that we should recognize that no research technique can be completely codified and structured. In fact, it is my view that research techniques should never be like this, but rather should be adaptable so as to be maximally useful for the particular research study being conducted. From this position, grounded theory has considerable potential for adaptation and I believe that health psychologists could utilize this method more widely, adapting it to suit their particular needs for specific research projects.

What this means is that grounded theory is available to be used by health researchers in a number of ways. It can be adopted and used as 'correct' grounded theory, or it can be adapted and used as a (justified) development of grounded theory. Beyond that, it offers a number of relevant qualitative research practices and techniques which can be selectively drawn on to improve qualitative research generally. In the following I comment on some specific grounded theory issues and practices that I believe can contribute to qualitative research generally, whether used within a 'strict' version of grounded theory, an adaptation of grounded theory, or in conducting research that would not seek to claim the grounded theory label.

Theory and Process

The grounded theory approach has two central premises which qualitative health psychology researchers could benefit from taking more strongly into account in their research: the focus on theory and the attempt to capture process. The focus on theory requires us to move beyond a descriptive account of the data. Merely categorizing and describing what participants said in an interview is not sufficient; we must go beyond this to develop an interpretive or theoretical account of the phenomena of interest. As noted earlier, theory can be developed at several levels, from substantive to formal, and grounded theory promotes theory development through its analytic procedures, from the initial categorizing of the data (open coding) to deriving more abstract categorical codes (axial coding) through to developing conceptual or theoretical codes (selective coding). For example, Olshansky (1996) describes the development of a formal theoretical frame-work accounting for how infertility becomes a defining aspect of life for persons experiencing it, and how this is reflected in the construction of their identities. Her account also reveals how successive grounded theory studies can function to elaborate and enhance theory. In spite of theorizing being a primary tenet of grounded theory, however, many studies which purport to be grounded theories do not achieve this, and suffer from 'premature closure' where they 'fail to move beyond the face value of the content in the narrative data' (Wilson and Hutchinson, 1996: 123). The emphasis on theory promoted by grounded theory is particularly pertinent for health psychology, which has been criticized for the inadequacies of its entrenched ways of theorizing as well as for its failure to go beyond an individual perspective and incorporate social context in theory (for example, Spicer and Chamberlain, 1996).

Further, developing grounded theory is frequently about theorizing process, and the analytic procedures of grounded theory facilitate consideration of the processes involved in the phenomena under investigation. Many issues of interest to us as health psychologists involve process – coping with chronic pain, adjusting to a diagnosis of chronic illness, dealing with aversive medical treatment, changing identities as a consequence of chronic illness or surgical procedures – and these aspects of grounded theory provide potential for advancing understandings of process in our research. In their study of cancer recurrence in children for example, Hinds et al. (1996) present an analysis of the coping process that parents experience, from initial attempts to regulate the shock through to preparing for loss and considering care-limiting decisions. Their account makes it clear how this is neither a linear nor a staged process, but an interactive set of adaptive coping strategies that parents utilize as they deal with this situation. Frequently, process is glibly held as able to be captured by conducting longitudinal research, usually at the conclusion to a cross-sectional study. Seed (1995) offers some interesting insights into the complexities of researching in the shifting context which marks longitudinal research and of attempting to develop a grounded theory of the processes involved. Focusing on process issues in this way can be highly salient for health psychology researchers who, in spite of examining issues that involve process (such as recovery from surgery), often limit themselves to documenting outcomes (such as days in bed or number of complications).

Specific Practices

Apart from these issues, there are several other specific techniques that can be drawn from grounded theory and usefully applied in much qualitative research.

SAMPLING   Grounded theory has some particularly valuable practices to offer in the area of sampling. Too often, qualitative researchers overlook or avoid issues of sampling, and simply choose an opportunistic sample of relevant respondents. In grounded theory, the premises for sampling are explicit, and researchers can offer a clear rationale for sample selection. The use of variational sampling to obtain diverse data, and discriminate sampling to ensure saturation are techniques that deserve wider application in qualitative research. The use of theoretical sampling, and the emphasis on seeking data which will extend, or contradict rather than merely replicate, existing data can be a powerful technique for developing understandings and strengthening the trustworthiness or credibility of the conclusions drawn from research. Taking a theoretical approach to sampling may also serve to extend the focus from the limited individualized context in which health psychologists all too often locate their research. Illness is social as much as individual, and sampling diverse participants (such as family, friends, and treatment providers) offers one way to explore and incorporate this context.

SATURATION   This concept, promoted strongly in grounded theory writing, also deserves more attention from qualitative researchers. Saturation is concerned with analysing sufficient data to be sure that we have a full and detailed understanding of the phenomenon and can present a full account of it. Morse (1995) notes that this is a difficult concept for new researchers and offers some principles for assuring saturation: select a cohesive sample; use theoretical sampling; value variation and examine negative instances; and ensure that data are rich, full and complete. She also offers the important caution that saturation is not about the frequency with which a category appears, and comments on how in practice 'it is often the infrequent gem that puts other data into perspective, that becomes the central key to understanding the data and for developing the model' (1995: 148). Saturation receives only lip service in many grounded theory research reports, but attending carefully to this issue can enhance the quality of research and facilitate the development of theory.

DATA COLLECTION AND ANALYSIS The deliberate intertwining of data collection and analysis is another important characteristic of grounded theory, and raises several general issues for research practice. Frequently qualitative researchers opt to gather all their data before commencing analysis, following the traditional positivist research model. However, by commencing analysis before all the data is collected, the researcher can identify areas which may have been missed and use subsequent data collection to include these, as well as follow up new insights and clarify the emerging theory. Data collection can become more focused and directed to analytic concerns as the research proceeds. Charmaz (1995) provides some specific examples of this, describing how attending to issues that were felt to be important by her research participants led her to redirect the focus of her research. Initially she was concerned with the sense of time and self-concept for chronically ill people but she moved to include issues around disclosure of illness and how this was managed over time as a result of attending to early analysis outcomes. This intertwining also has benefit in allowing analysis strategies to change in style and focus as the data collection and analysis proceeds, and for the analysis to progress from an emphasis on 'what is happening here?' to a concern with 'what does this mean?', thereby promoting theoretical development.

CONSTANT COMPARATIVE METHOD Perhaps the practice most commonly adopted from grounded theory is its analytic method of constant comparative analysis. It is not uncommon to find research stating that data 'were analyzed according to a method influenced by the constant comparative method for grounded theory' (Brydolf and Segesten, 1996: 39). As discussed earlier, this procedure involves systematic comparisons for similarities and differences at all levels; between data codes within and between cases, between incidents, between contexts, and between categories as they are developed. This procedure can provide a constructive means of initiating data analysis in many qualitative projects, regardless of whether formal grounded theory procedures are involved.

EMERGENT THEORY A further key feature of grounded theory is the demand that theory be emergent from data. In grounded theory, this has two implications for practice; a broad variety of data resources should be consulted to ensure that theory is comprehensive, and researchers are encouraged to avoid literature review in advance of data collection so as to avoid contaminating their analyses with pre-existing understandings. As I have argued already, the notion of avoiding the literature as an influence on what should be researched and what directions are interesting is both unavoidable and undesirable to some degree. As Morse and Field (1995) recommend, the best approach is critically to examine previous research and use it selectively. However, this guideline does draw attention to the need for caution in dealing with expectations of what will be found in the research. Unlike positivist research, we are not trying to test hypotheses, but aiming to allow findings to emerge. Finding a balance between having some (preconceived) directions and ideas and allowing the research process to be open to unanticipated directions and findings can be difficult, but grounded theory makes a strong case for the latter and reminds us of its utility.

MULTIPLE DATA SOURCES Collecting data from multiple sources is intended to ensure that emergent findings are comprehensive. In a study of young children's pain experience (Woodgate and Kristjanson, 1996) for example, data were collected through formal interviews, informal interviews, play interviews, hospital chart records, and participant observation. Once again this reflects an ideal, and most published grounded theory studies are based on analysis of interview transcripts. Obviously this guideline needs to be related to the objectives and research perspective of the study; for instance, conversation analysis requires samples of talk, for discourse analysis relevant texts are pertinent, and for phenomenology, accounts of personal experience are appropriate. In grounded theory, where the objective is to provide a comprehensive account of the phenomenon, this can be facilitated by drawing data from multiple sources. As already noted, health psychologists too frequently restrict their focus to the individual and neglect the social context (Chamberlain, Stephens and Lyons, 1997), and this grounded theory practice can serve to modify this tendency.

Conclusion

In this chapter I have argued that grounded theory is a methodology with considerable potential for qualitative health researchers. Because its techniques are often presented in a prescribed manner, there is a danger of method reification, with the expectation that researchers must conduct 'correct' grounded theory research. However, I have tried to show that there is considerable debate between researchers using the method, and that many of its directions and premises are contested. I concur with the view that regards grounded theory as a set of strategies (Charmaz, 1995) which are widely applicable in qualitative research. This leads me to argue that it can be best thought of as a rich store of resources and practices for qualitative health research that can be drawn on in two different ways. It offers, on the one hand, the procedures of an established and recognized qualitative method, adaptable for research from a variety of epistemological perspectives (although not all). On the other hand, it offers a range of practices which have the potential to improve the conduct and quality of our qualitative research, and which may be drawn on in many different research applications (although again not in all). Whichever way it is employed, researchers should be prepared to make the premises for their research explicit, and to argue in support of the specific practices they use. In doing so, they will be promoting the wider utilization of grounded theory, and advancing the case for rigorous qualitative practice in health psychology research.

Acknowledgements

I would like to thank Antonia Lyons for constructive comments on an earlier draft of this chapter.

References

Aborelius, E. and Österburg, E. (1995) How do GPs discuss subjects other than illness? *Patient Education and Counseling*, 25: 257–268.

Annells, M. (1996) Grounded theory method: philosophical perspectives, paradigm of inquiry, and postmodernism. *Qualitative Health Research*, 6: 379–393.

Barclay, L., Donovan, J. and Genovese, A. (1996) Men's experiences during their partner's first pregnancy: a grounded theory analysis. *Australian Journal of Advanced Nursing*, 13 (3): 12–24.

Becker, P.H. (1993) Common pitfalls in published grounded theory research. *Qualitative Health Research*, 3: 254–260.

Brown, J.M. (1996) Redefining smoking and the self as a nonsmoker. *Western Journal of Nursing Research*, 18: 414–428.

Brydolf, M. and Segesten, K. (1996) Living with ulcerative colitis: experiences of adolescents and young adults. *Journal of Advanced Nursing*, 23: 39–47.

Chamberlain, K., Stephens, C. and Lyons, A. (1997) Encompassing experience: meanings and methods in health psychology. *Psychology and Health*, 12: 691–709.

Charmaz, K. (1990) 'Discovering' chronic illness: using grounded theory. *Social Science and Medicine*, 30: 1161–1172.

Charmaz, K. (1995) Grounded theory. In J. Smith, R. Harré, and L. Van Langenhove (eds), *Rethinking Methods in Psychology*. London: Sage, pp. 27–49.

Chenitz, W.C. and Swanson, J.M. (eds) (1986) *From Practice to Grounded Theory: Qualitative Research in Nursing*. Menlo Park, CA: Addison-Wesley.

Denzin, N.K. and Lincoln, Y.S. (eds) (1994) *Handbook of Qualitative Research*. Thousand Oaks, CA: Sage.

Donovan, J. (1995) The process of analysis during a grounded theory study of men during their partners' pregnancies. *Journal of Advanced Nursing*, 21: 708–715.

Glaser, B.G. (1978) *Theoretical Sensitivity: Advances in the Methodology of Grounded Theory*. Mill Valley, CA: Sociology Press.

Glaser, B.G. (1992) *Basics of Grounded Theory Analysis: Emergence Versus Forcing*. Mill Valley, CA: Sociology Press.

Glaser, B.G. and Strauss, A.L. (1967) *The Discovery of Grounded Theory: Strategies for Qualitative Research*. Chicago: Aldine.

Guba, E. and Lincoln, Y.S. (1994) Competing paradigms in qualitative research. In N.K. Denzin and Y.S. Lincoln (eds), *Handbook of Qualitative Research*. Thousand Oaks, CA: Sage, pp. 105–117.

Henwood, K. and Pidgeon, N. (1994) Beyond the qualitative paradigm: introducing diversity within qualitative psychology. *Journal of Community and Applied Social Psychology*, 4: 225–238.

Hinds, P., Birenbaum, L., Clarke-Steffen, L., Quargnenti, A., Kreissman, S., Kazak,

A., Meyer, W., Mulhern, R., Pratt, C. and Williams, J. (1996) Coming to terms: parents' response to a first cancer recurrence in their child. *Nursing Research*, 45: 148–153.

Kearney, M., Murphy, S. and Rosenbaum, M. (1994) Mothering on crack cocaine: A grounded theory analysis. *Social Science and Medicine*, 38: 351–361.

Keddy, B., Sims, S.L. and Stern, P.L. (1996) Grounded theory as feminist research methodology. *Journal of Advanced Nursing*, 23: 448–453.

Keller, C. (1991) Seeking normalcy: the experience of coronary artery bypass surgery. *Research in Nursing and Health*, 14: 173–178.

Kools, S., McCarthy, M., Durham, R. and Robrecht, L. (1996) Dimensional analysis: broadening the conception of grounded theory. *Qualitative Health Research*, 6: 312–330.

Leininger, M. (1994) Evaluation criteria and critique of qualitative research studies. In J.M. Morse (ed.), *Critical Issues in Qualitative Research Methods*. London: Sage, pp. 95–115.

Lowenberg, J.S. (1993) Interpretive research methodology: broadening the dialogue. *Advances in Nursing Research*, 16: 57–69.

Melia, K.M. (1996) Rediscovering Glaser. *Qualitative Health Research*, 6: 368–378.

Morse, J.M. (1995) Editorial: The significance of saturation. *Qualitative Health Research*, 5: 147–149.

Morse, J.M. and Field, P.A. (1995) *Qualitative Research Methods for Health Professionals* (2nd edn). Thousand Oaks, CA: Sage.

Morse, J.M. and Johnson, J.L. (1991) Towards a theory of illness: the illness-constellation model. In J.M. Morse and J.L. Johnson (eds), *The Illness Experience: Dimensions of Suffering*. Newbury Park, CA: Sage, pp. 315–342.

Morse, J.M. and O'Brien, B. (1995) Preserving self: from victim, to patient, to disabled person. *Journal of Advanced Nursing*, 21: 886–896.

Olshansky, E.F. (1996) Theoretical issues in building a grounded theory: application of an example of a program of research on infertility. *Qualitative Health Research*, 5: 394–405.

Robrecht, L.C. (1995) Grounded theory: evolving methods. *Qualitative Health Research*, 5: 169–177.

Schatzman, L. (1991) Dimensional analysis: notes on an alternative approach to the grounding of theory in qualitative research. In D.R. Maines (ed.), *Social Organization and Social Process*. New York: Aldine, pp. 303–314.

Seed, A. (1995) Conducting a longitudinal study: an unsanitized account. *Journal of Advanced Nursing*, 21: 845–852.

Siegl, D. and Morse, J.M. (1994) Tolerating reality: the experience of parents of HIV positive sons. *Social Science and Medicine*, 38: 959–971.

Spicer, J. and Chamberlain, K. (1996) Developing psychosocial theory in health psychology: problems and prospects. *Journal of Health Psychology*, 1: 161–171.

Stern, P.N. (1994) Eroding grounded theory. In J.M. Morse (ed.), *Critical Issues in Qualitative Research Methods*. Thousand Oaks, CA: Sage, pp. 212–223.

Strauss, A.L. (1987) *Qualitative Analysis for Social Scientists*. New York: Cambridge University Press.

Strauss, A. and Corbin, J. (1990) *Basics of Qualitative Research: Grounded Theory Procedures and Techniques*. Newbury Park, CA: Sage.

Strauss, A. and Corbin, J. (1994) Grounded theory methodology: an overview. In N.K. Denzin and Y.S. Lincoln (eds), *Handbook of Qualitative Research*. Thousand Oaks, CA: Sage, pp. 273–285.

Wainwright, S.P. (1995) The transformational experience of liver transplantation. *Journal of Advanced Nursing*, 22: 1068–1076.

Wilson, H.S. and Hutchinson, S.A. (1996) Methodological mistakes in grounded theory. *Nursing Research*, 45: 122–124.

Woodgate, R. and Kristjanson, L.J. (1996) 'Getting better from my hurts': toward a model of the young child's pain experience. *Journal of Pediatric Nursing*, 11: 233–242.

Wuest, J. (1995) Feminist grounded theory: an exploration of the congruency and tensions between two traditions in knowledge discovery. *Qualitative Health Research*, 5: 125–137.

13

Action Research

Changing the Paradigm for Health Psychology Researchers

Sue Curtis, Helen Bryce and Carla Treloar

Research in health psychology seeks, ultimately, to improve health. For example, Anderson and colleagues (1997) sought to change the supermarket food purchases of shoppers to improve nutritional outcomes. Shoppers were offered a multi-media education package covering various aspects of nutrition and their supermarket dockets were used to assess pre–post differences in measures such as fibre and fat content of food and purchases of fruit and vegetables. In this example, the researcher has defined the problem, designed the intervention and determined the indicators of effective change. In other words, the research activities and outcomes were totally researcher driven and controlled.

This type of intervention is typical of research in health psychology. Knowledge about health, illness and disease risk factors from the bio-medical literature is combined with understandings of the influences on behaviour to produce an intervention to bring about change in individuals' behaviour (for example, Ingham and Bennett, 1990). This model requires that the researcher is the key to, or the expert in, understanding the behaviour of the study participants, that the researcher is outside the change process, that the measures of programme effectiveness relate solely to the pre-designated goals of the programme, that the measures of change are 'scientifically' validated and that the findings can be generalized to an appropriately defined reference population. The limitations of this approach are that research activities and research tools are restricted to already existing theory.

Just as qualitative researchers seek a different way of knowing from quantitative researchers, those involved in action research seek different ways of approaching change from those who conduct traditional intervention programmes. In an action researching methodology, the researcher does not seek to control. Rather the role of researcher is to participate meaningfully and productively in the knowledge-generating processes of the group. The development of options for change and definitions of effective change are products of collaborative action, reflection and negotiation. In action researching approaches, the participants are themselves taken to be the experts in their own lived experience.

The 'data' sought in action research are the meanings and values that participants attribute to activities and social relations in which they are involved. The researcher is not outside the dialogue process that is used to generate 'data', but is a participant in generating and critically examining information about the meaning and value of action. Measures of *effective* action are generated from and grounded in this data. The validity of these measures is guaranteed by the integrity of their relationship to the documented lived experience of participants. Finally, it is unlikely that the word 'data' will be found in action researching literature. This is simply because of the power relationship that is both implied and enacted in traditional experimental, scientific research practice.

You will see that the differences between action research and traditional interventionist research are fundamental to every aspect of the research process. Specifically we will focus on the differences between action research and traditional intervention studies in:

- ways of *knowing* and the *language* used to describe the research process;
- the *activities* and *goals* of research;
- the *role* of the researcher and the *relationship* between the researcher and study participants.

The language, activities and social relations of action research are introduced here in the form of a dialogue between three researchers experienced in action research. Both the questions and answers are indications of their respective pathways and journeys in action research. The question-and-answer format has been used as a way of focusing on concepts and tools that we have found to be most relevant to researchers in making the shift from experimental science to action research for everyday practice in the medical and health sciences.

Action research differs according to the purposes or interests that are served by the inquiry activity (Habermas, 1971). *Technical action research* is concerned primarily with the efficacy of purposeful action in achieving intended outcomes. This is the type of research that most closely resembles traditional scientific research because practitioners are co-opted, and the researcher plays the major role in facilitating the process and determining the intended outcomes (Carr and Kemmis, 1986). *Practical action research* is always oriented towards enhancing understanding of practical action. *Emancipatory action research* serves specifically to analyse critically and to change conditions of everyday practice so that these are fairer and more equitable. The case study presented in this chapter is aiming towards the more demanding levels of action research, the *practical* and *emancipatory*.

Question 1: How do I deal with my dissatisfaction with the
traditional experimental scientific method of research?

The action researcher recognizes that the type of knowledge generated in the experimental scientific paradigm is not the only way to generate theory for explanation and action (Bernstein, 1983). There are different, but equally legitimate ways of knowing, acting and being when it comes to research practice. The purposes served by scientific paradigm research are those of control over the physical world and accurate prediction of events. Validity of knowledge generated by this type of research is guaranteed by internal and external validity, reliability, reproducibility and generalizability of findings.

The paradigm in which action research is located is called the constructivist paradigm. In this paradigm it is assumed that there are multiple, socially constructed realities. If you want to know more about the constructivist paradigm, read Guba and Lincoln's, *Fourth Generation Evaluation* (1989). The constructivist paradigm has a very long history. It is a paradigm that serves to explain the *meaning* and *value* in action.

Question 2: Why is the constructivist paradigm better suited than the
scientific paradigm to researching the meaning and value in action?

Meaning and value do not exist outside human understanding, so the research methods in the constructivist paradigm have to enable us to understand *understanding* itself (Bernstein, 1983). It would be of little use to fragment 'meaning' or 'value' into component parts. Meaning is socially constructed through action – physical, conceptual and/or social action (Kemmis and McTaggart, 1988). It is the meaning and value inherent in what people do, in what they think and say and in the ways they interact socially that constitute the type of knowledge generated in this alternative paradigm. If you would like to know more about these concepts, read Bernstein's *Beyond Objectivism and Relativism: Science, Hermeneutics, and Praxis* (1983). Historically, the philosophy and practice associated with inquiry into meaning is that of hermeneutics. In hermeneutic philosophy and practice, understanding of understanding is derived by a continuous dialectical tacking between the most local detail and the most global structures so that both can be brought into view simultaneously (Bernstein, 1983). For example, in action research for health psychology, the local detail would be the individual's lived experience, and the global structures the broader health systems.

If you are clear about the purposes that are to be served by your research, then you are in a position to choose which paradigm is most appropriate for your needs and to justify your choice.

Question 3: How can I do research that is in the interests of the people
concerned and not just for myself, my discipline or my organization?

In any area of social life, there are aspects of everyday activities that people find problematic, disturbing or disruptive. Often, the concerns that people have about their everyday practices are shared concerns. In other words, there exists a community of interest in relation to the concern. Kemmis and McTaggart (1988) have described this as a thematic concern. Researchers do not have to generate artificial research topics because, with sensitivity to the needs of individuals and social groups, both the concerns and the questions are already always there.

The role of the researcher with an interest in social action is to facilitate collaborative reflection and action among those with the shared concern. Once shared interests and mutual benefit of research and action have been identified, those who have indicated their interest will be the ones who provide or seek out and acquire resources needed for research activities. Usually a core group of about six individuals, who share the same concern, form an action researching group.

Question 4: How can I do research in a way that doesn't exploit and further entrench unequal power relationships that so often occur in researcher/subject interactions?

Although well-intentioned, much research, particularly in the medical and health sciences, can unintentionally disempower and therefore serve to oppress research subjects. This is because the researcher comes to the research process as the expert and therefore has power over what is said and the way it is said, over what is discussed, what is recorded and what count as inquiry outcomes. In these circumstances, unequal power relationships are unavoidable.

In an action researching approach to inquiry, those who share the concern or who are likely to be affected by research outcomes, decide collaboratively what will be researched. Research methods are participatory and those who have responsibility for implementing research outcomes are the very ones who decide what will happen with the knowledge that they generate. Full participation in inquiry processes is, however, only possible where power is shared equally among all participants. This is not just power in relation to what is done in the name of research activities, but also in determining the language that is used to describe and justify what is being done and what counts as valid knowledge.

The researcher's voice is subject to the same critical review as are all others, so is only one among the group and therefore not in a position of privilege. Through systematic, collaborative, critical reflection, congruency between recorded information and emerging shared understanding about the meaning and value of action is assured at the level of information collection, interpretative analysis, critical analysis and reporting. The measures of success of social action are determined collaboratively and reporting formats are geared to the information needs of the different interest groups.

Question 5: How do I do action research?

The process of action research is conceptualized as a spiral of 'collective, self-reflective inquiry' (Kemmis and McTaggart, 1988). In the action

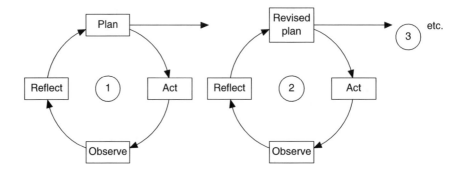

Figure 13.1   *The Traditional Spiral of Action Research Cycles (Zuber-Skerritt, 1992: 13)*

researching spiral, those with a shared concern are directly involved in planning for and implementing a plan of action to bring about social change. When the planned action is implemented, observation of and reflection on what happened provides the basis for better informed and more effective action. An interpretation of the researching spiral by professional development researcher and practitioner Zuber-Skerritt (1992), illustrates the cyclical nature of learning in action that defines an action researching inquiry.

The essential element of the action researching spiral is collective critical reflection on practical action where the problem or concern is taken as the vehicle for learning (Pedler, 1991). In the action researching process, both the problem and those reflecting on the problem are changed.

If you would like to know more about the process, then refer to Kemmis and McTaggart's *The Action Research Planner* (1988). This book provides a comprehensive guide for anyone wishing to be involved in action research. The work of Guba and Lincoln (1989), with their explanation of the hermeneutic circle, examines the concept of an inquiry circle in the much broader stream of thinking that is hermeneutic philosophy.

Question 6: What is my role in an action researching study?

The research processes have to be integral to the everyday lives of people. The people themselves have to become a self-critical community (McTaggart, 1991; Prideaux, 1995). Action researchers bring their skills, capabilities and knowledge for supporting effective reflective practice to the planning, acting, observing and replanning cycles. This will mean bringing to the process their own personal knowledge, their interests and their energy as well as relevant theoretical and methodological information to which they have access. Zuber-Skerritt (1992) explains how the researcher's role revolves around in-depth dialogue or 'learning conversations' with participants about their experiences and interpretations of experience. Critique and negotiation among equals are crucial to these conversations. Above all, involvement of the researcher will mean respecting the fact that there are as many ways of interpreting experience as there are individuals to interpret it. For this reason, one of the most important contributions a researcher can make to the inquiry process is to support those involved in developing a critical attitude (Habermas, 1982). The information generated in this dialogue process can contribute to both the knowledge base and everyday practices of the wider professional community.

Question 7: What is a critical attitude?

The critical attitude of action research is grounded in two levels of inquiry. At the first level, it is only possible to understand the meaning of what someone says or does to the extent that there is understanding of the reasons behind what they say or do. Inquiry methods have to make explicit the logic behind the action. The basic aim of this practical reflection is to build shared understanding of the *meaning* of social action. The term used to describe this type of reflective inquiry is *practical action research* (Smyth, 1986). At the second level, collective, critical reflection is used to determine the *value* of action. In order to judge the value of action, inquiry activities have to go beyond description to *critical analysis* of the purposes served by the action. This second level of action research serves to emancipate people from the conditions that oppress them, so, for this to occur, critical reflection must take place in conditions free from coercion (Smyth, 1986).

While practical action research assures valid understanding of action, *emancipatory action research* assures that broader institutionalized practices do not frustrate or distort intended meaning in the activities of individuals or groups (McTaggart, 1991). Inherent in both practical and critical reflection are the moral and ethical aspects of what is considered to be 'effective' action (Bernstein, 1983). The most important aspect of this action researching approach is the opening up of possibilities that new questions – questions outside current frameworks of thinking – can be asked of the situation. New questions give rise to new options for effective action.

Question 8: What information do I collect and how?

The type of information collected in action research is that which describes people's lived experience of an activity or circumstance. However, this is not a one-off information collection. As in other forms of qualitative inquiry, action research employs flexible, iterative and holistic information collection, analysis and interpretation practices. Any number of information sources are possible and could include, for example, written records, tape-recorded interviews, videos, diaries, field notes, documents, mental models or photographic records (Fiol and Huff, 1992). Basically, anything that people can use to reflect on the activities that they and others are involved in is useful information. The preferred information for action research is qualitative. Quantitative records, however, are also used to the extent that they contribute to a deeper understanding of lived experience for those involved in a particular activity or circumstance. Whatever the form of recorded information, the action researcher's interest is in the *language* that is used to identify or describe and justify what is happening; the *activities* that are taking place; and the *social relations* involved in these activities.

The type of information collected will depend on just who is doing the collecting and whether the research is serving primarily technical, practical or emancipatory action researching purposes. If a researcher is participating as facilitator and inquirer, the main source of information will be open-ended interviews or interviews based on focus questions. The role of the researcher will be to record and to confirm with participants the accuracy of the record of their lived experience. Recorded information, or 'talk' in the form of 'text', will be used as a resource for developing shared under-standing of the meaning and value of currently used language, activities and social relations.

Question 9: What do I do with the information when I have it?

Basically, you start asking questions of the recorded information. The central question will always be, 'What is this telling me about effective or ineffective action in relation to the thematic concern?' Coding of the information according to the shared concern will be greatly assisted by an initial sorting into generic action categories of language, activities and social relations. Within each of these generic categories the researcher and/ or participants look for themes. These themes form the sub-categories of the three main types of action. The *sub-category labels* determine the structure of knowledge generated. This structure is specific to the participants and their concerns. In other words, the information will be organized by practical theory (Polkinghorne, 1983; Schön, 1983) rather than by formal theory.

Strauss and Corbin (1990) provide a method of open coding based on the constant comparative method of data analysis (Glaser and Strauss, 1967). In this method, each statement is compared with the one before and with all others that have been read. Just like the action researching cycle, this process is repeated many times until the groups of statements become stable. The aim of the constant comparative method of analysis is to find look-alike clusters of statements that represent a theme that has emerged in the reading of the recorded statements. It is also possible for participants to attribute a numerical value to each statement according to its importance for effective action (Curtis, 1996).

Question 10: What does the process of an action researching study look like?

Action research proceeds in phases of information building and the study is written up in a way that mirrors these phases. In effect, anyone interested in the study should be able to follow the same logical processes as those involved in the theory building. These phases represent the traditional action researching cycle beginning with observation and reflection on practice. While the phases will be repeated a number of times, the generic types of action include:

PHASE 1   PRACTICAL REFLECTION – ESTABLISHING THE FOCUS AND THE BOUNDARIES

The activities of Phase 1 are concerned primarily with practical reflection on the part of inquiry participants. The aim is to build a rich picture, from the perspective of all stakeholders, about the inquiry focus. This means capturing action related to the inquiry focus in as effective, efficient and meaningful a way as possible. The information is recorded in a meaningful way if it is readily accessible and usable by all participants for enhancing their understanding of everyday action. The meanings that are captured in the recorded information are confirmed as accurate by those involved. The function of Phase 1 is the development of shared understanding about the focus and the boundaries of the study.

PHASE 2   DEVELOPING A SHARED LANGUAGE FOR UNDERSTANDING AND VALUING ACTION

Phase 2 focuses on the development and refinement of categories of activity that emerge from the collected information. The important function of Phase 2 is the generation and confirmation of a knowledge structure that is grounded in shared understanding about the meaning of everyday action.

PHASE 3   CRITICAL REFLECTION – ON THE MEANING AND VALUE OF ACTION

Participants use the information generated in Phases 1 and 2 as a resource for critical reflection on current practices. This phase is particularly important in emancipatory action research. Those directly involved in the action step back and analyse how and in what ways accepted practices may be constraining, distorting or controlling the meaning and value of their activities and the outcomes that are possible. Phase 3 also involves critical reflection on the efficacy and usefulness of the action researching process itself.

PHASE 4   REPORTING AND PLANNING – FOR MORE EFFECTIVE ACTION

While reports serve to document and communicate the outcomes of action researching studies, new practices will, as a rule, have already been implemented. In this type of study, enhanced understanding leads inevitably to changed practice. Reports are still important, however, because they serve to assure accountability and to disseminate inquiry findings to all stakeholders. They provide a useful resource for planning more effective action and for the next cycle of inquiry into the effectiveness of any changes that have been implemented.

Question 11: How do I ensure the quality of the outcomes?

The following methodological options are modelled on the work of Lincoln and Guba (1985) and Guba and Lincoln (1989) because these evaluation researchers have directly addressed the need for inquiry rigour appropriate to a constructivist paradigm. The selection of tools for action research is more of a personal choice. These will be determined primarily by the type of information that is being collected and the information needs of participants.

If you want to ensure the legitimacy of knowledge generated in this paradigm then you have to demonstrate that meaning and value have been recorded and analysed holistically and interpreted in context. The type of theory generated is grounded in the practical theory of everyday action and this is what is needed for more effective practical action. It is important that information is collected, recorded and analysed either by the researcher as facilitator or by participants themselves, and that all participants are actively involved in the inquiry processes. For example, any information collected should be stored in such a way that an audit trail for confirmability and dependability is easily accessible and publicly inspectable. Recorded information should be returned to those who generated it for confirmation, correction or clarification where necessary (member checking). Themes identified by either the researcher or collaboratively by the group must be subjected to debriefing and critical analysis, first with disinterested peers (peer debriefing), and then among participants themselves. Categories generated to explain the meaning and value of action should be subjected to critical analysis in the same way that themes were. Case reports should be the product of group collaboration and 'owned' by participants.

There is a range of quality assurance measures that can be used in action research. While some of these have already been mentioned, others noted by Guba and Lincoln (1989) include:

- prolonged engagement – to overcome the effects of misinformation and to build trust;
- persistent observation – to identify those characteristics and elements most relevant to the concern;
- negative case analyses – for revising working hypotheses until they account for all known cases;
- progressive subjectivity – a record of the researcher's developing construction to provide a check on the degree of privilege as well as increasing understanding of the concern;
- transferability – extensive and careful description of the context of the concern so that the degree of transferability of findings to another setting can be judged.
- the fairness and trustworthiness of the action researching process itself confirmed by all participants.

Case Study: A Researcher's Experience of Participatory Action Research – Women who Live in Caravan Parks and Cervical Cancer Screening

The principles and practice described in this chapter are being implemented by one of us, Helen Bryce. She is involved in a study of cervical cancer screening for women who live in caravan parks. Caravan parks are defined areas of land, either private or council owned, where people live in caravans or mobile homes, generally with shared amenities. Caravans were designed primarily for holiday accommodation but in the case of many people in parks, they serve as *de facto* housing or long-term accommodation.

In this case study, the researcher's own reflections on an inquiry in progress are used as a narrative to describe action research in practice. When the term 'construction' is used here, it is in terms of Guba and Lincoln's (1989) constructivist paradigm.

What do we 'know' about cervical screening and women who live in caravan parks?

Caravan parks in our region are involved in a community development project called the Hunter Caravan Project. Project staff visit the caravan parks on a regular basis to conduct craft groups for women and after-school activities for children. It is at these craft groups that women talk about their lives, their hopes and disappointments. During one of these craft sessions, a woman mentioned that she was due for a pap smear. The discussion that followed illustrated the distaste that these women had towards cervical cancer screening. They *knew* that 'everyone' should have a pap smear, yet many of them were not adequately screened.

Much research has already been conducted to explore the reasons why women are not attending for regular pap smears (Adamson, 1991; Adamson and Taylor, 1991; Bowman, 1991; Peters, Bear and Thomas, 1989; White, 1995). None of these studies, however, has explored the reasons that are specific to caravan park communities. The methodologies used in these inquiries have been located in the scientific paradigm, where the researchers have asked women why they don't like having a pap smear. The researchers have maintained control over what questions are asked, how they are asked, and what counts as relevant.

Numerous intervention strategies have been devised from this knowledge base and all have achieved limited success. For example, Byles and her colleagues explored the effectiveness of direct-mail interventions in increasing women's participation in cervical cancer screening (Byles et al., 1995). Two strategies were used: a first letter which gave simple information about pap smears, and a second letter which was more informative, providing information on strategies women could utilize to help them overcome barriers to screening. The types of strategies discussed in the second letter evolved from research located in the scientific paradigm.

Interestingly, the second approach did not achieve any greater success than the first. A conclusion drawn from this study is that 'reported barriers may not have any functional significance, and women may remain unscreened even when these barriers have been removed' (Byles et al., 1995: 13). What is needed is research that can explore not only what constitutes a 'barrier' to these women but also the relative importance of what they define as barriers to attending cervical screening.

Why did I choose an action researching process?

Through consultation with community workers who visit the caravan park, we decided that an action research approach was essential to the success of this project. If anything was to come of my involvement in the park, then it had to be through sharing responsibility for the inquiry and the changes it generated with the women in the park and their service providers.

How did I do it?

Research on the health needs and practices of caravan park communities is almost non-existent. The research that has been conducted used traditional scientific methodology and has not received the support of the community whom it was designed to assist (Eddy, 1993). The project I envisaged needed a methodology that would support the women in identifying their own constructions of what it is like to have a pap smear. I did not want to impose my construction, nor the construction of other researchers onto the women's understandings of cervical cancer screening. I wanted a methodology that would encourage the development and implementation of effective strategies for change by the women themselves. After all, these women are the best informed on what is effective action for them.

I chose Guba and Lincoln's (1989) fourth-generation method of research. This methodology fits neatly into the realms of participatory action research. Fourth-generation evaluations are based on the constructivist paradigm and require all key stakeholding groups to participate. Participants are encouraged to explore their understanding of the world. The information collected is grounded in how the women see and interact with the world around them. Implementing this methodology has proved challenging and rewarding. Below is a brief overview of the major challenges that I have overcome. Some others I have yet to attempt, but my plan of action is presented.

Challenge Number 1: Developing a shared understanding of participatory research

When I first talked to the women about the project they were happy to participate but they had difficulty understanding the extent of their involvement in the project. They tended to think of it as a 'survey', where I would make up the list of questions and they would dutifully answer them. This would result in information that was grounded in my construction of cervical cancer and screening practices, not theirs. My first interview took place in a participant's caravan. I began with a couple of introductory questions that were designed to open the focus of the conversation. But it didn't work. My participant held her construction under wraps, while I pleadingly offered questions, hoping she would open up. Her answers were direct and to the point. What went wrong . . . why didn't she talk about it? I had learnt more listening in at the craft group than I had here. Then it dawned on me. This woman thought that I was the expert; she thought that I knew all there was to know and that I just needed her to validate my construction. I realized that I had failed to let her, and probably the other women, know what was expected of them. Back to the craft groups, and a new introduction. This time I spelled it out more clearly. I told them that this was their project, that they were the experts. We talked about how they could use the project to help themselves, and other women like them.

During the next set of interactions with each of the women they willingly shared their own constructions of cervical cancer screening. By reflecting on their own understandings and experiences, the women were able to identify and communicate their construction of how they felt about pap smears. Each had her own understanding of what encouraged and discouraged her from attending for a pap smear. As they talked the women became more confident in their understanding of the issues surrounding cervical cancer screening. So much so, that in the course of the dialogue they began suggesting strategies that they thought would have the potential to improve the participation of women who live in caravan parks in cervical cancer screening.

Challenge Number 2: Putting the women's construction into a format that can be used to generate change

The women have identified many things that encourage and discourage them from having a pap smear. But from the information, I am still unsure of *how important* these factors are, and what effect they have on women's practice. To address this problem a weighting scale (Curtis, 1996) will be used to analyse critically what counts as effective and ineffective action. The practical knowledge that is gained through this critical reflection will form the basis on which the women generate change strategies.

The women's recorded statements will be categorized according to the type of action they represent. The three types of action are: language, activity and social relations. Sorting their understandings in this way should tell us how the women describe and justify what counts as effective action, what action is effective and what type of social interactions are involved in action that is effective.

Thematic statements that emerge from what the women say will be listed on the weighting grid. The women will be asked to weight how important each statement is in either encouraging or discouraging them from cervical cancer screening. The results of this weighting procedure will be used as a resource by the women and by the professionals with whom the women decide they would like to work to negotiate strategies for improved screening.

Challenge Number 3: Involving key stakeholders in the development of change

The women will indicate their preference for the type of health professional they would like to take part in this project. They may choose to include general practitioners or women's health nurses. Local members of the chosen profession will be invited to participate in collaborative problem-framing and problem-solving workshops. Understandings about cervical screening from both stakeholding groups will be shared amongst those who have indicated their intention to participate in the workshops. In this way, all participants will have a greater understanding of the claims, concerns and issues that are relevant to each of them.

My role at the workshop will be to facilitate and mediate information-sharing and negotiations between the women and the service providers. It is of the utmost importance that all voices be heard and that the strategies developed satisfy both stakeholding groups. The issues for each group will be reframed by participants as an action plan for improved cervical screening practices. Through group brainstorming, strategies will be devised that have the potential to help women overcome the barriers to screening. Group members will take responsibility for specific aspects of each strategy and a time frame will be agreed upon. My involvement in this part of the project is guided by the writings of Guba and Lincoln (1989) who believe that strategies for change are most likely to be supported by the people who are most affected by them, if they are given the responsibility for devising and implementing them.

Challenge Number 4: Finding out if I have done the right thing by the participants

The participants will be asked to evaluate the success of this project by commenting on the authenticity criteria established by Guba and Lincoln (1989). These criteria are designed to assess the extent to which the project has valued the construction of each woman. Participants will also assess the extent to which their construction has been expanded upon and the level to which they have become more aware and understanding of the attitudes and behaviours of those who differ from themselves. Finally, participants will be asked to assess the extent to which they have been stimulated and empowered to act on the recommendations that they have generated. This should not be the end of the action research process. The women should continue to evaluate their action and implement change to fit their needs.

Conclusions

Already, I have learnt so much from my experiences with the women in the park. They are the experts in their own realities, they know what works for them and what doesn't. They have demonstrated that simply by tapping into their own knowledge and experiences they are able to generate strategies for improving their participation in cervical cancer screening.

For me, I enjoy working with these women as an equal. I like the feeling of energy that is generated when we all work together for the good of the group. I don't feel drained by having to find solutions that will work for these people. We are doing it together, and by sharing the responsibility we are sharing in the successes.

Conclusion

In summary, then, this chapter illustrates that there are a number of key elements of research practice of which health psychologists need to be aware if they are to organize their interventions around action research (Fine and Vanderslice, 1992).

1. Action research requires a shift from the scientific paradigm to the constructivist paradigm. These paradigms are based on different understandings about the nature of knowledge, what constitutes research practice and what research outcomes are valued.
2. The different language used in action research reflects the shift that is required to work in this paradigm. Underlying assumptions and traditions of the scientific paradigm can no longer provide certainty about what constitutes effective research practice.
3. The knowledge generated in action researching methodologies is mutually shaped by the relationship which exists between the researcher as facilitator and research participants.
4. The researcher does not hold the position of expert. Action research involves members of key stakeholders in the community of interest, as equal partners. The researcher's voice is only one of many in the construction of knowledge.
5. All participants involved in an action researching study play an active role in identifying the problem to be researched, in constructing the reality that is taken to be the problem, in identifying strategies for change, in implementing agreed-upon strategies and in evaluating the effectiveness of these strategies.
6. Action research is based on an iterative spiral of practical and critical reflection.
7. The desired outcomes of an action researching project will be determined by participants and may generate outcomes that are markedly different from those of traditional scientific research projects.

Given these principles, some researchers will find themselves better suited to this method than others. This is because action research embraces a world where control of variables and outcomes is no longer possible. The action researcher must employ iterative, collaborative processes in order to generate precise knowledge in a specific setting (Banister et al., 1994). As the case study researcher in this chapter has demonstrated, there are, however, significant benefits in changing the paradigm for research in health psychology. The action researching cycle of planning, acting, and then observing and reflecting as a basis for replanning provides an opportunity for health psychologists to make an important contribution to continuous improvement processes in health-care practice.

Banister and colleagues (1994) acknowledge that there is a 'paucity' of action research conducted in psychology departments. Whether this indicates that there exist significant institutional, financial and organizational obstacles to action research, that lack of mentors impedes promotion of this method or that the conceptual leap from experimental research is too difficult or unattractive, is not known.

For health psychologists working in established health systems, institutionalized ways of acting and thinking about health and illness are an important consideration in the choice of inquiry paradigm. Health systems are complex social constructions of institutionalized action. This chapter presents a strong argument for health psychologists to embark on practical and, in particular, emancipatory action research. Knowledge generated in an action researching inquiry serves as both a motivation and a resource for action against inequitable systems that disadvantage, disenfranchise or oppress particular social groups. The possibility of a methodology that can bring into question accepted practices that erect barriers to effective health-care practice is an exciting challenge.

References

Adamson, B. (1991) *Young Women's Knowledge of Cervical Cancer Screening.* (Women's Health Studies Discussion Papers and Research Reports No. 5). Sydney: University of Sydney.

Adamson, B. and Taylor, R. (1991) *A Cross Cultural Study of Older Women's Knowledge, Attitudes and Practices Regarding Cervical Cancer Screening.* (Women's Health Studies Discussion Papers and Research Reports No. 7). Sydney: University of Sydney.

Anderson, E.S., Winett, R.A., Bickley, P.G., Walberg-Rankin, J., Moore, J.F., Leahy, M., Harris, C.E. and Gerkin, R.E. (1997) The effects of a multimedia system in supermarkets to alter shoppers' food purchases. *Journal of Health Psychology,* 2: 209–223.

Banister, P., Burman, E., Parker, I., Taylor, M. and Tindall, C. (1994) *Qualitative Methods in Psychology: A Research Guide.* Buckingham: Open University Press.

Bernstein, R.J. (1983) *Beyond Objectivism and Relativism: Science, Hermeneutics, and Praxis.* Oxford: Basil Blackwell.

Bowman, J. (1991) *Screening for Cancer of the Cervix: Barriers to Utilization and*

Strategies for Promotion. Unpublished doctoral dissertation, University of Newcastle.

Byles, J., Redman, S., Sanson-Fisher, R. and Boyle, C. (1995) Effectiveness of two direct-mail strategies to encourage women to have cervical (pap) smears. *Health Promotion International*, 10: 5–16.

Carr, W. and Kemmis, S. (1986) *Becoming Critical: Education, Knowledge and Action Research.* London: Falmer Press.

Curtis, S. (1996) *Quality Appraisal of Higher Education Research: An Action-oriented, Process-based Alternative to Performance Indicators.* Unpublished doctoral dissertation, Centre for Research Policy, University of Wollongong.

Eddy, G. (1993) *Health and Social Needs Survey.* Newcastle: University of Newcastle, Family Action Centre.

Fine, M. and Vanderslice, V. (1992) Qualitative activist research: reflections on methods and politics. In F.B. Bryant, J. Edwards, R.S. Tindale, E.J. Posavac, L. Heath, E. Henderson and Y. Suarez-Balcazar (eds), *Methodological Issues in Applied Social Psychology.* New York: Plenum Press, pp. 199-218.

Fiol, M.C. and Huff, A.S. (1992) Maps for managers: Where are we? Where do we go from here? *Journal of Management Studies*, 29: 267–285.

Guba, E. and Lincoln Y. (1989) *Fourth Generation Evaluation.* Newbury Park, CA: Sage Publications.

Habermas, J. (1971) *Knowledge and Human Interests.* Boston: Beacon Press.

Habermas, J. (1982) A reply to my critics. In J.B. Thompson and D. Held (eds), *Habermas: Critical Debates.* London: Macmillan, pp. 219–283.

Ingham, R. and Bennett, P. (1990) Health psychology in community settings: models and methods. In P. Bennett, J. Weinman, P. Spurgeon (eds), *Current Developments in Health Psychology.* London: Harwood Academic Publishers, pp. 35–61.

Kemmis, S. and McTaggart, R. (eds) (1988) *The Action Research Planner* (3rd edn). Geelong: Deakin University Press.

Lincoln, Y. and Guba, E. (1985) *Naturalistic Inquiry.* Beverly Hills, CA: Sage Publications.

McTaggart, R. (1991) *Action Research: A Short Modern History.* Geelong: Deakin University Press.

Pedler, M. (1991) *Action Learning in Practice* (2nd edn). Aldershot: Gower.

Peters, R., Bear, M. and Thomas, D. (1989) Barriers to screening for cancer of the cervix, *Preventive Medicine*, 18: 133–146.

Polkinghorne, D. (1983) *Human Action in Methodology for the Human Sciences: Systems of Inquiry.* Albany, NY: State University of New York Press.

Prideaux, D. (1995) Beyond facilitation: action research as self-research and self-evaluation. *Evaluation Journal of Australasia*, 7: 3–13.

Schön, D.A. (1983) *The Reflective Practitioner: How Professionals Think in Action.* New York: Basic Books Inc.

Smyth, W.J. (1986) *Educational Leadership in Schools: Reflection-in-action.* Geelong: Deakin University Press.

Strauss, A. and Corbin, J. (1990) *Basics of Qualitative Research: Grounded Theory Procedures and Techniques.* Newbury Park, CA: Sage Publications.

White, G. (1995) Older women's attitudes to cervical screening and cervical cancer: a New Zealand experience. *Journal of Advanced Nursing*, 21: 659–666.

Zuber-Skerritt, O. (1992) *Action Research in Higher Education: Examples and Reflections.* London: Kogan Page.

14

Doing Interpretative Phenomenological Analysis

Jonathan A. Smith, Maria Jarman and Mike Osborn

This chapter introduces one particular form of qualitative analysis, interpretative phenomenological analysis (IPA) and takes the reader through the stages of conducting studies employing IPA, with illustrations taken from the authors' own research in health psychology.[1] The main aim is to provide the reader with detailed descriptions of the analytic process, and therefore the theoretical orienting material is kept to a minimum. Readers interested in knowing more about the theoretical underpinning and rationale of IPA are referred to Smith (1996). After a brief introduction, the bulk of the chapter is taken up with two extended examples of IPA in practice. In the first, an idiographic, case-study approach is outlined, where the analysis slowly builds from the reading of individual cases to claims for a group. This procedure is illustrated with material from a project on patients' perceptions of chronic back pain. In the final section of the chapter, a more exploratory method is outlined; here the focus shifts to the theorizing of themes at the group level and is illustrated with data from a project concerned with health professionals' experiences of working with patients with anorexia nervosa.

What is Interpretative Phenomenological Analysis and why is it Useful to Health Psychology?

The aim of interpretative phenomenological analysis (IPA) is to explore in detail the participant's view of the topic under investigation. Thus the approach is phenomenological in that it is concerned with an individual's personal perception or account of an object or event as opposed to an attempt to produce an objective statement of the object or event itself. At the same time, IPA also recognizes that the research exercise is a dynamic process. One is trying to get close to the participant's personal world, to take, in Conrad's (1987) words, an 'insider's perspective' but one cannot do this directly or completely. Access depends on, and is complicated by, the researcher's own conceptions and indeed these are required in order to make sense of that other personal world through a process of interpretative activity. Hence the term interpretative phenomenological analysis is used to signal these two facets of the approach.

It is important to distinguish IPA from discourse analysis (for example Potter and Wetherell, 1987).[2] While IPA shares with discourse analysis (DA) a commitment to the importance of language and qualitative analysis, where IPA researchers would typically differ from discourse analysts is in their perception of the status of cognition. DA, as generally conceived of in contemporary social psychology, is sceptical of the possibility of mapping verbal reports on to underlying cognitions and is concerned with attempting to elucidate the interactive tasks being performed by verbal statements and the pre-existing discourses which speakers draw on in this process. Thus, Potter and Wetherell's DA regards verbal reports as behaviours in their own right which should be the focus of functional analyses. IPA by contrast *is* concerned with cognitions, that is, with understanding what the particular respondent thinks or believes about the topic under discussion. Thus, IPA, while recognizing that a person's thoughts are not transparently available from, for example, interview transcripts, engages in the analytic process in order, hopefully, to be able to say something about that thinking.

Why is IPA relevant to health psychology? It can be argued that health psychology is generally premised on the belief that people think about their bodies and that their talk about these bodies in some way relates to those thoughts. So for example if considering a questionnaire completed by a patient about their illness, a health psychologist usually assumes there is a chain of connection between verbal response, cognition and physical problem. Many of the assumptions underlying this approach draw directly from the social cognition paradigm in social psychology (Smith, 1996).

For IPA, the existence of real entities such as bodies and illnesses provides a useful backdrop against which to consider personal accounts of physical processes. So, for example, an IPA researcher may choose to explore how two patients diagnosed with the same illness may talk very differently about the condition, precisely because this may help to illuminate the subjective perceptual processes involved when an individual tries to make sense of his or her health condition. Thus a dialogue between IPA and health psychology seems possible. While IPA may see the nature of the links in a particular way, it shares with the social cognition paradigm a belief in, and concern with, the chain of connection between verbal report, cognition and physical state.

The aim of this chapter is to provide for the reader new to this way of working a detailed presentation of interpretative phenomenological analysis. Smith (1995) gives an overview of conducting a study in this way, from constructing an interview schedule through to writing it up. However, that chapter had only limited space to discuss analysis. We therefore decided to devote this whole chapter to the business of doing analysis once one is confronted with transcripts of semi-structured interviews with participants.[3] We give details of each stage involved in the process and illustrate it with examples taken from health psychology. At the same time it should be recognized that there is no single definitive way to do qualitative analysis. We are offering suggestions, ways we have found have worked for us. We hope these will be useful in helping the newcomer to IPA to get under way with analysis, but remember that, as you proceed, it is likely that you will find yourself adapting the method to your own particular way of working. Moreover, qualitative analysis is inevitably a personal process and the analysis itself is the interpretative work which the investigator does at each of the stages.

An Idiographic, Case-study Approach

The next part of the chapter will give a basic outline of one form of such analysis using examples of its application to the study of people in chronic pain, as illustration. Chronic pain is particularly suitable for qualitative study as it is widely recognized that it is the meaning of the experience to the sufferer that mediates the relationship between their pain, distress and disability (Skevington, 1995).

A project may take the form of a single case design or involve a larger group of participants. Either way it is advisable to begin by looking in detail at the transcript of one interview before incorporating others. This follows an idiographic approach to analysis, beginning with particular examples and only slowly working up to more general categorization or theory (see Smith, Harré and Van Langenhove, 1995).

Looking for Themes in the First Case

Read the transcript a number of times, using one side of the margin to note down anything that strikes you as interesting or significant about what the respondent is saying. It is important in the first stage of the analysis to read and re-read the transcript closely in order to become as intimate as possible with the account, as each reading is likely to throw up new insights. Some of your comments may be attempts at summarizing, some may be associations or connections that come to mind, others may be preliminary interpretations. In the following example the notes in the left margin focus on how the participant, who is identified as Linda,[4] struggled to understand the chronic nature of her pain, and how the implications for her self-concept began to emerge:

	I.	Do you know why you have pain?
wants to know	L.	No. I just keep asking myself why the pain is there and I
disbelief		haven't got an answer. I don't know how I should feel really,
uncertain astonished		it's just that I don't think it should be there. Why should I have
needs an answer – but has none		it? I would have thought that after all this time it should have
pain – unpredictable/unusual/		eased up and gone away but it hasn't.
inexplicable		

	I. So how does that make you feel?
self-critical	L. I'm sort of mad at myself. I start banging things and getting
aggressive	so aerated with myself that it's there and I can't get it to go
frustrated	away.

The other margin is used to document emerging theme titles, that is, using key words to capture the essential quality of what you are finding in the text. At this preliminary stage the key words need not be definitive but should enable you to articulate something about the concept you have identified. From Linda's account, the following themes emerged and were noted:

I. Do you know why you have pain?	
L. No. I just keep asking myself why the pain	uncertainty
is there and I haven't got an answer. I don't	
know how I should feel really, it's just that I	trying to make sense
don't think it should be there. Why should I	
have it? I would have thought that after all this	searching for an explanation
time it should have eased up and gone away	
but it hasn't.	
I. So how does that make you feel?	
L. I'm sort of mad at myself. I start banging	implications for the self
things and getting so aerated with myself that	
it's there and I can't get it to go away.	

Generally one would go through the whole interview making preliminary notes in the left margin first, and then proceed to abstract theme titles afterwards. To illustrate further how this process works here is another section of the transcript, showing first initial notes and then the emergent themes:

shoulds, ideals, expectations	I. What's it like being in pain?
frustration, other people	L. I'm only 50, and I should be doing this and
	that and the other 'cos they say life begins at 40
	but I can't and I suppose it does bother me. It's
	frustrating that people of my own age are, you
mobility restriction	can see them flying their kite and you feel as if
trapped	you can't, well you can't.
	I. You can't.
	L. No which is so stupid, I just think I'm the
	fittest because there are three girls [she and her
compared to sisters	sisters] and I'm the middle one and I thought
	well I'm the fittest and I used to work like a
compared to past when fit/strong	horse and I thought I was the strongest and then
ideal past/doubt, 'I thought' not 'I was'	all of a sudden it's just been cut down and I
adjustment, shock	can't do half of what I used to do.
loss/change	

The emergent themes noted in the right-hand margin were:

I. What's it like being in pain?

L. I'm only 50, and I should be doing this and
that and the other 'cos they say life begins at 40
but I can't and I suppose it does bother me. It's   loss
frustrating that people of my own age are, you   social comparison – others
can see them flying their kite and you feel as if
you can't, well you can't.

I. You can't.

L. No which is so stupid, I just think I'm the
fittest because there are three girls [she and her   social comparison – family
sisters] and I'm the middle one and I thought
well I'm the fittest and I used to work like a   nostalgia – selective recall
horse and I thought I was the strongest and then
all of a sudden it's just been cut down and I   sense of self
can't do half of what I used to do.

Of course, as one moves through the transcript, some of the notes will reflect connections with previous sections of the interview – pointing to similarities and differences in what the participant is saying. At this stage all of the transcript is treated as potential data and no attempt is made to omit or select particular passages for special attention.

Looking for Connections

On a separate sheet, list the emerging themes and look for connections between them. Thus you may find that some of them cluster together and that some may be regarded as superordinate concepts. Do some of the themes act as a magnet, seeming to draw others towards them and helping to explain these others? You may also find that during this process you come up with a new superordinate theme that helps to pull together a number of the initial categories you had identified.

The preliminary list of themes which emerged from Linda's transcript and were noted in the right-hand margin was:

- trying to make sense
- searching for an explanation
- uncertainty

- lack of understanding
- frustration
- confusion and anger
- implications for the self-concept
- sense of self
- self-critical

- social comparisons with others
- social comparison within family
- social comparison with self before the pain
- loss
- bereavement and shock
- mobility/physical restrictions
- adjustment
- nostalgia/selective recall of the past
- planning activity

- self-doubt
- social problems
- social withdrawal

These were clustered in the following way:

- trying to make sense/searching for an explanation
- uncertainty/lack of understanding
- frustration
- confusion and anger

- implications for the self-concept
- self-critical/self-doubt
- loss and bereavement/shock/adjustment
- social comparison   – with others
                       – within family
                       – with self before the pain
- nostalgia/selective recall of the past

- mobility/physical restrictions/planning activity
- social/identity problems and withdrawal

   As new clusterings of themes emerge, check back to the transcript to make sure the connections work for the primary source material – what the person actually said. This form of analysis involves a close interaction between you and the text, attempting to understand what the person is saying but, as part of the process, drawing on your own interpretative resources. You are now attempting to create some order from the array of concepts and ideas you have extracted from the participant's responses.

A Table of Themes

The next stage is to produce a master list or table of the themes, ordered coherently. Thus the process outlined above may have identified a certain number of major themes which seem to capture most strongly the respondent's concerns on this particular topic. Care must be taken at this point to ensure that each theme is represented in the verbatim transcript and not to let the researcher's own bias distort the selective process. Where appropriate, the master list will also identify the sub-themes which go with each superordinate theme.

   At this point certain themes can be dropped – for example the theme related to 'planning activity' which was present in the first theme list was deleted as it neither fitted well into the structure of themes and sub-themes nor was it very rich in evidence within the transcript. It is useful to add an identifier to each instance. Alongside each theme you should indicate where in the transcript instances of it can be found. This can be done by giving key words from the particular extract plus the page and line number of the transcript. It may also help to code the instances in the transcript itself in some way. For Linda, the final table of major themes becomes:

1. *Searching for an explanation*
- lack of understanding   'no idea' $(2.9)^5$
- frustration   'can't do it'   (4.15)
- anger and self-criticism/doubt   'mad at myself'   (2.20)

2. *Self-evaluation and social comparison*
- with others   'other people'   (10.12)
- within family   'fittest of all'   (11.3)
- nostalgic recall of self before the pain   'like a horse'   (11.7)
- as an index of loss and bereavement/shock 'used to be'   (16.20)

3. *Social problems*
- withdrawal   'stay in'   (24.7)

Some of the themes you elicit will be governed by and follow closely the questions on your schedule, but others may be completely new. The respondent could well have tackled the subject in a way different from how you had anticipated. Other themes may be at a higher level, acting as pointers to the respondent's more general beliefs or style of thinking and talking. For example, in the chronic pain study the topic under discussion was the participants' attitudes toward their chronic pain. One theme, however, that emerged from the transcripts but was not anticipated as strongly was a broader exploration of the utility of social comparison in self-appraisal and evaluation. These emergent themes may force you to think about the focus of your project and take it in a slightly different direction. Again, remember analysis is a cyclical process – be prepared to go through the stages a number of times, dropping a superordinate theme if a more useful one emerges.

Continuing the Analysis with Other Cases

A single respondent's transcript may be written up as a case study in its own right, or you may move on to analyse interviews with a number of different individuals. If you do have a number of individuals' transcripts to analyse, then you can proceed in a number of ways.

One possibility is to use the master-theme list from the first interview to begin your analysis of the second one, looking for more instances of the themes you have identified from the first interview but being ready to identify new ones that arise. Or you can begin the process anew with the second interview, going through the stages outlined above and producing a master list for this second interview. If this alternative route is followed, the master lists for each interview could then be read together and a consolidated list of master themes for the group produced. Again, the process is cyclical. If new themes emerge in subsequent interviews, they should be tested against earlier transcripts. Perhaps the new themes can enlighten, modify or become either subordinate or superordinate to a previously elicited one.

This system works well with studies which employ a small sample size of up to about ten participants, such as the one that has been presented here of women with chronic pain. The number of participants is small enough for one to retain an overall mental picture of each of the individual cases and the location of themes within them.

For this study the master list from Linda's account was used to inform the analysis of the other transcripts. By remaining aware of what had come before it was possible to identify what was new and different in the subsequent transcripts and at the same time to find responses which further articulated the extant themes.

Evidence of the themes 'searching for an explanation' and 'social comparison' emerged in each of the following participants' transcripts in ways which helped to illuminate them further. For example, other participants also used social comparison, but it was often employed in different ways and for different reasons. One participant, Dottie, compared herself with those whom she felt were in a worse situation than herself, not better off as in Linda's case:

	I. What kind of things do you think about?
social comparison	D. I've done heaps more things than other
nostalgia as compensation?	people have done, so I think well, I would, you
	always think well there's loads of people far far
downward comparison as coping strategy	worse off than you, you know so you try to
	think of other people who are permanently in
	wheelchairs, and it's supposed to make you feel
equivocal effect	better, which in a way it does. But basically it's
fear	frightening.

As the analytic process continued, a new theme emerged, 'being believed', which although it was implicit in Linda's account, was not as rich in evidence as in those of the subsequent participants and it was therefore added to the master list for the group. It was during the analysis of Alice's account that the difficulties of 'being believed and being judged' achieved prominence:

	I. What does it feel like?
frustration/anger	A. It's like anger building up in you. It's like
	if you're talking to people you're forever, it's as
defensive re:	though you've got to try and convince them
credibility	that there's something wrong with you, that
legitimacy	gets you down. You feel as though no one
being disbelieved	believes you, unless people who have got bad
pain identity	backs, it's only them who'd believe you.

A Master List of Themes for the Group

As you proceed through each transcript following the interpretative process, a final master list of themes should emerge. Deciding upon which themes to focus upon requires the analyst to be selective. The themes are not selected purely on the basis of their prevalence within the data. Other factors, including the richness of the particular passages which highlight the themes, and how the theme helps illuminate other aspects of the account, are also taken into account. From the analysis of this group of nine women who suffered chronic pain, four superordinate themes emerged. The master list below shows these four themes with identifiers from the first two women in the study. The full matrix for the study indicated the instances for each woman to support each theme:

		Linda	Dottie
1.	*Searching for an explanation*		
	• response to uncertainty	(2.9)	(3.15)
	• participants' explanatory models	(3.8)	(5.9)
	• biomedical dominance		(9.17)
	• self-criticism	(2.20)	
2.	*Comparing this self with other selves*		
	• with others	(10.12)	(7.12)
	• with self in the past		(7.15)
	• with self in the future		(12.3)
	• nostalgic recall of self	(11.7)	
	• upward and downward comparison		(14.18)
	• equivocal coping strategy	(12.11)	
	• index of loss and threat	(16.20)	
3.	*Not being believed*		
	• invisibility of chronic pain		(31.15)
	• assumptions of others about pain	(10.4)	
	• understandings/expectations of others		(31.21)
	• implications for identity/pain roles	(22.13)	(34.12)
	• judgements of others		(33.2)
4.	*Withdrawing from others*		
	• private experience vs social appearance		(11.12)
	• shame and embarrassment	(23.14)	(28.6)
	• misunderstandings		(30.17)
	• fear of rejection	(24.7)	
	• stigma		(34.18)
	• self-regard/concept	(26.12)	

Writing Up

This section is concerned with moving from the master themes to a write-up, in the form of a report for publication or submission for a degree. In one sense the division between analysis and writing up is a false one, in that the analysis continues during the writing phase.

We are now concerned with translating the themes into a narrative account. What are the interesting or essential things to tell our audience about the respondents and how can we present this in a compelling way? How does what we have found illuminate the existing work? There is more flexibility to writing up a qualitative study than a psychological experiment. This section points to some of the options within the analysis/results/discussion section.

The analysis section of a report is the most important part. This is where you will try to convince your reader of the importance of your respondents' stories and your interpretative analysis of them. What you are doing here is using the table or index of themes as the basis for an account of the participants' responses which should take the form of your argument interspersed with verbatim extracts from the transcripts to support your case. Good qualitative work clearly distinguishes between what the respondent said and the analyst's interpretation or account of it. Again the process is iterative. Keep thinking as you write, because your interpretation is likely to become richer as you look at the respondents' extracts again.

The type of results section you write will obviously be influenced by the level of analysis you have adopted. Thus the results may take the form of a presentation of the typology of responses that emerged during the analysis or may represent your attempt to theorize or explain your respondents' answers. The level of detail and structure of the results or analysis section can also vary. Usually the thematic account is prioritized and uses the verbatim extracts to elucidate or exemplify each theme, as part of a clearly constructed narrative argument. Sometimes, however, you may wish to present a closer textual reading of certain extracts. This may be particularly appropriate if the analysis is mainly concerned with complexity or ambiguity. In this case it may be that key extracts will be more foregrounded in the organization of the write-up and will be followed by sections of detailed interpretative reading.

Qualitative reports have considerable flexibility in the relationship between results and discussion. Sometimes the themes are presented together in one analysis section while a separate section is devoted to exploring their implications in relation to the existing literature. In other cases each theme is taken in turn and linked to the existing work at the same time.

The chronic pain study used as an example in this section was intended as a reconnaissance of the area. The final write-up employed a discrete analysis section followed by a discussion relating the findings to the extant literature. During the analysis a wide range of themes emerged which highlighted the multi-dimensional nature of the participants' experience. The write-up focused on relating the breadth of the various theme typologies. One theme which was not anticipated was the tremendous variety and contradictory nature of the participants' use of social comparison, and it was this complexity that was the focus within that particular theme section.

To finish, here is the beginning of the analysis write-up from the back pain project, to illustrate how the narrative account unfolds. Clearly there is only space to provide a short passage here. See Osborn and Smith (1998) for the full account:

The first theme 'Searching for an Explanation' sets the scene for those which follow as it articulates the participants' attempts to understand what is happening to them and is a prerequisite for the subsequent self-reflection. Because such questioning recurs throughout the analysis, it is only presented briefly at the outset.

Participants were not asked specific, closed questions but simply to describe their pain and the various ways it had affected them. They showed a strong motivation to understand and explain their situation, to know 'why?':

> I just keep asking myself why the pain is there and I haven't got an answer. I don't know how I should feel really, it's just that I don't think it should be there. Why should I have it? I would have thought that after all this time it should have eased up and gone away but it hasn't. (Linda)

Participants regularly stated they simply could not 'believe' that nothing more could be done to relieve their pain. There was a marked contrast between their pre-occupation with their pain and their inability to account for its chronic presence. Despite their long history of pain and extensive contact with the health service they neither felt informed about their condition, nor able to influence it. Their pain was often felt to act of its own volition. 'It just comes and goes when it wants really' (Alice).

Linda's account of her situation suggested that despite wanting to understand why she had chronic pain, she could not; to her it was 'unbelievable really'. This was not a simple account of ignorance but a profound state of bewilderment as she failed consistently to understand why she should be suffering, or being punished despite not having done anything wrong. As the best efforts of others had failed, she felt she could only blame herself:

> I'm sort of mad at myself. I start banging things and getting so aerated with myself that it's there and I can't get it to go away.

Exploring and Theorizing Shared Experiences

The next part of this chapter illustrates how IPA was used in a study examining shared experiences of a larger number of participants, in this case fourteen paediatric nurses involved in caring for patients with anorexia nervosa (though the method also lends itself to larger numbers). This example is considered particularly useful as it provides a focus on the health-care provider, rather than the patient or client, a focus which is still relatively rare in psychological health-related research.

In contrast to the previous section, which outlined a specific, sequential process for analysing individual cases, this section is providing a more exploratory account, and aims to illustrate *one* way in which IPA techniques have been used to facilitate the identification of shared experiences across a group of participants.

Initial Coding

When trying to identify shared experiences across a relatively large number of participants, a too detailed examination of one person's account would not be cost-effective. Therefore, although the primary concern was still with personal perceptions and understandings of phenomena, there was a need to distinguish one or more themes, mutually relevant to all participants, at an early stage so that these could form the focus of a subsequent, more detailed analysis, where personally distinct experiences could then be considered.

Keeping in mind that the initial concern was the identification of shared themes across participants' accounts, the first step of the analytic process nevertheless involved spending some time analysing each individual transcript, in turn. The procedure was similar to that described for the case-study method illustrated earlier. The first transcript was read through a number of times, with initial thoughts, possible codes and anything of particular interest noted in the left-hand margin. Then, the interview was worked through more closely, the interviewer writing down themes, as they emerged, in the right-hand margin. However, this early coding was kept at a much broader level than in the case-study approach. Many codes related to large parts of the interview extracts, although some were more specific, referring to one or two sentences. An example of an extract with fairly specific coding, from an interview with a nurse we have called Pam, is given below. It can be seen that, at this early stage of analysis, the actual codes are at a fairly broad, unrefined level:

You grow very emotionally involved. You get to know	relationship
this child so intimately that you grow close to the child	involved
and you know you despair, you're frustrated. You feel	
angry – I feel anger a lot of the time.	emotions

When the whole transcript had been coded in this way, the codes were then examined to see if there were ways in which they could be meaningfully grouped together. As this process was going to be repeated for a relatively large number of accounts the aim was not to develop 'higher-order' themes as one would do with the case-study method, but rather to identify some groupings which collected together the codes generated in meaningful ways. Themes emerging from the analysis of Pam's account were grouped into five clusters as follows:

– organizational issues	– trust	– emotional impact
– ward/team	– responsibility	– emotions
– information cascade	– barrier	– anger
– hierarchy	– involvement	– distrust
– support		– frustration

– partnership	– manipulation
– mothering	– disobedience

Once clusters of themes had been produced for the first interview, the coding process was then repeated for each interview in turn, until clusters of themes were generated for all the participants. During this process attempts were made to look at each interview afresh, and, in particular, to keep the coding emergent from the interview text. However, the sequential nature of this stage of the analytic process meant that when examining the latter transcripts the researcher was oriented or primed to certain aspects of the data.

Identifying Shared Themes

When this process had been completed for each transcript, the next stage of analysis moved to the search for themes reflecting shared aspects of experience for all the participants, which could then be intensively examined. As stated previously, there is no definitive or prescribed way in which the 'discovery' of shared themes will be achieved. What follows is a detailed outline of the process and techniques used to identify and intensively analyse shared themes across participants' accounts in the nursing study. What is important to keep in mind is that the aim of IPA is to develop an understanding of participants' experiences, with the themes that are identified considered to come from your *personal* interaction with, and interpretation of, the interview data, regardless of the particular strategy you choose to employ.

To begin the search for shared themes, all the clusters of themes previously identified for each of the participants were collected together and examined to see if any general categories could be created that aggregated seemingly disparate themes across the accounts. These general categories needed to be relatively broad as it was important that they were relevant to *all* the participants.

After some reflection it was determined that a substantial proportion of the themes identified could be subsumed within a general category of 'relationships'. For example, some themes related to *types* of relationships (mothering; partnership); others to *processes* of the relationships (involvement; trust), or to *emotional reactions* to relationships with anorexic patients (anger; frustration). In this instance, the theme of 'relationships' was considered particularly important because although the interviews had covered various aspects of the nurses' experiences of working with the anorexic patient, the topic of relationships had not been a pre-determined area for specific exploration. Rather it had been identified as important through the analytic process. While you may similarly identify one salient theme across all the participants' accounts, you may alternatively find that it is possible to distinguish several different general themes. If you do identify a number of such themes it is probably best to select one for further analysis, at least in the first instance, as the interpretative work that follows can be both lengthy and demanding.

Analysing Shared Themes

Once the general theme of 'relationships' had been selected for more intensive analysis the next stage involved going back to the transcripts to make sure that a 'complete' corpus of data on relationships was available for further examination. Many extracts concerning relationships had already been identified through the previous coding process, but it was possible that other extracts could have been previously overlooked. Therefore the transcripts were examined again through a more focused 'lens', to produce a comprehensive collection of extracts concerning relationships.

To facilitate this process, a word-processed file of each transcript was searched on a computer screen and segments relating to relationships were 'copied' and 'pasted' into a new composite file. First, the transcript was carefully examined to make sure that all the extracts identified as being associated with the general category of 'relationships', through the previous coding process, were selected. Then, the remaining text was examined to try and identify any further examples of relationship-related extracts, not previously selected. When making decisions about whether or not an extract referred to the general category of relationships, it was important to keep in mind the diverse concepts that had come together to produce 'relationships' as the shared theme to be explored in the previous instance. Also, at this stage, one errs on the side of over- rather than under-inclusion to make sure all potentially relevant data is incorporated.

Once all the transcripts had been examined in this way, a new, more focused corpus of data was then available to be intensively examined. The next stages of analysis were all directed to the central aim of determining what exactly constituted the *shared* aspects of the participants' experience in relation to this general theme.

The first step involved coding the extracts that had been selected in more detail. A printed version of the text was used in this instance but this procedure could alternatively be undertaken on the computer screen. First the printed text was divided up into the individual extracts and each extract was labelled with the name of the participant. Most extracts were fairly short (one to two sentences long), though some extracts were longer (up to a page in length). Then, each extract was examined in turn and a provisional code was generated for each, for example:

Carol: I just feel frustrated I think. I just wish that I could help 'em
         more and you know sort out what's happened. I could   wanting to help
         become more involved actually if I let myself.

Once the extracts had been examined in this way, a list of all the provisional codes that had been generated was produced. This list was then
examined to see if these codes in turn could be grouped together in
meaningful ways (see Table 14.1).

Once this coding scheme had been created, each extract was then re-
labelled, giving it a numerical code. Most extracts tended to retain their
original codes; however many were also given additional codes because of
their association with more than one category. For example:

Carol: I just feel frustrated I think. I just wish that I could help 'em   emotions 1.3.5.
         more and you know sort out what's happened. I could   wanting to help 1.2.5.
         become more involved actually if I let myself.   involvement 1.3.3
                                                                                resistance 1.3.2

The next stage of the analysis was to group the extracts according to
these new coding categories to produce collections of extracts all relating to
similar concepts. Again, this could have been be done on the computer or
with a hard copy. In this case the latter was considered advantageous,
enabling groups of extracts to be collected together in quick succession. As
many of the extracts had multiple labels, a system had to be developed to
enable cross-category coding. In this instance, a fairly complex grouping
system was developed, creating many new cross-category groups. An
alternative strategy would have been to make photocopies of extracts with
multiple labels and then have copies of the same extracts in different
groupings.

Searching for Patterns, Connections and Tensions

While it would be possible to write up an account of the separate clusters
of themes, and the sub-themes of which they are comprised, the approach
outlined here is concerned with exploring patterns and relationships
within and between the conceptual groups, thinking about how different
themes come together to help us understand further the participants'
experiences. Exploring the relationships between the different conceptual
groupings involves a sustained interaction with the text, and a number of
techniques, commonly associated with grounded theory (Strauss and
Corbin, 1990), can assist the process of moving from the fragmented text to
a more holistic perspective on the data.

One option is to use diagrams to capture the relationships between
emergent themes. Diagrams are useful as they enable the temporary
movement away from the data to more abstract thinking, and because they
facilitate the identification of new, implicit or undeveloped relationships

Table 14.1 *Coding scheme for the nursing study*

1.1 Types of Nurse–patient Relationship	1.2 The Nursing Role	1.3 Features of Relationship	1.4 Relationship process	1.5 Aspects of Anorexic Patient Affecting Relationship
1.1.1 parental	1.2.1 caring – loving	1.3.1 trust	1.4.1 forming a relationships	1.5.1 age
1.1.2 partnership	1.2.2 responsibility	1.3.2 resistance	1.4.2 getting involved	1.5.2 psychological vs. physical problem
1.1.3 supervisory	1.2.3 human – nursing	1.3.3 involvement	1.4.3 changes in relationship over time	1.5.3 manipulative
1.1.4 friendship	1.2.4 demanding – tiring	1.3.4 distance	1.4.4 ending the relationship	1.5.4 disobedient
	1.2.5 wanting to help	1.3.5 emotions		1.5.5 deceitful
		1.3.6 anger		1.5.6 secretive
				1.5.7 clever

between thematic categories. Other useful techniques include keeping notes or memos to yourself about your thoughts and interpretations of the data. This provides a useful way of recording how the analysis develops over time. Another useful strategy is to discuss your emerging analytic ideas with another researcher. Once you verbally articulate your ideas about the data it may then be easier to identify the relationships between the various themes. Audio-taping the conversation may be useful so that you have a complete record of your ideas which can be written up later as a memo.

Before moving to diagrammatic representations of the relationships between concepts, some time was spent exploring the inter-relationships between the categories that had emerged through the analysis. This involved a process of taking different categories in turn and reflecting on how they related to other categories. This comparison process indicated that a number of the most salient relationships between categories were signalling conflicts. For example, the themes of 'involvement' (1.3.3.) and 'wanting to help' (1.2.5.) both conflicted with those of 'distance' (1.3.4.), and 'resistance' (1.3.2.).

A closer examination of the extracts within the categories linked by 'conflicts' was then undertaken to enable the inter-relationships between them to be explored further. For example, the two extracts below were seen as illustrating the conflicts nurses experienced regarding their wanting to trust the anorexic patient and the perception of the anorexic patient as dishonest and untrustworthy. However, the second extract also captured a connection between the categories of 'trust' and distrust' and those of 'involvement' and 'distance':

> *Anna*:   And she used to promise me these things, and perhaps
>   I were taken in. You know were I taken in or? But I wanted
>   to trust her whereas nobody else did. Perhaps I'm too soft.   trust
>   But I'd say 'why have you lost weight?' 'I haven't been doing
>   'owt I promise you.' And she sort of pleads, you know. She
>   can, you can really feel sorry for 'em, you can. But they're
>   manipulative aren't they, kids. But of course you want to   distrust
>   give them benefit of the doubt.
> *Emma*:   It's difficult sort of like er you build a relationship with them
>   because you're closely involved with them and, but yet you   involved
>   know you can't get that close to them if you like.   distance
>   You couldn't get that close to them because you knew you
>   weren't on the same wavelengths 'cos most of the time I knew
>   that they weren't actually honest with me, telling the truth
>   type of thing.   distrust

The salience of these and other conflicts in the data resulted in 'conflicts in relationships' becoming the central organizing construct for building up the analysis. Three particularly salient conflicts were identified in the nurses' accounts, relating to: (a) emotional involvement versus emotional distance in the nurse–patient relationship; (b) trusting versus distrusting the anorexic patient; and (c) nurses' feelings of anger toward the anorexic patient being viewed as either appropriate or inappropriate. Each conflict linked together different conceptual categories which had been identified earlier, and diagrams were used to illustrate these conflicts. See Figure 14.1 for an example.

Further reflection on these conflicts suggested that they were all under-pinned by an ongoing tension of maintaining simultaneous connection and separation in the nurse-patient relationship. 'Conflicts of connection and separation in the nurse-patient relationship' subsequently became the superordinate, organizing device of the analysis, with this considered to be an important 'shared-experience' of the nurses in this study. This was then illustrated in a final diagram (Figure 14.2).

Writing Up

Once overall diagrams had been created, the final stage was to translate the analytic themes into a narrative account. Although the emphasis was on conveying the shared experiences across the participants, it was at this stage that the unique nature of each participant's experience could re-emerge. The shared themes across the participants' accounts became the structure to the write-up, with the conflicts summarized in the diagrams forming the three sections of the results; the different participants' experiences in relation to these themes formed the basis of the narrative account.

The section of analysis below is from the write-up, focusing on the conflicts that nurses experience in relation to issues of trust and distrust in their relationships with the anorexic patient, illustrating the link between this conflict and the ongoing tension around issues of separation and con-nection in the nurse–patient relationship. The full account can be seen in Jarman, Smith and Walsh (submitted for publication) from which this extract is taken. A related paper employing IPA is Jarman, Smith and Walsh (1997):

Neil's account indicated the conflict he experienced in relation to issues of trust and distrust in his encounters with the anorexic patients on the ward. Neil had established a close relationship with a young male anorexic (Stuart) during the course of his stay on the ward, but after some time an incident occurred which challenged Neil's perception of the relationship he had formed with Stuart:

> It were an incident over this paper towel thing. Well up to this point I'd been really close to him, I'd really trusted him etc., or so I thought.

Neil relates how his discovery of Stuart trying to hide a paper towel into which he had vomited challenged the trusting aspect of their relationship. Although Stuart's behaviour could have been viewed as an aspect of his 'disorder' or 'eating problem', signifying distress and a

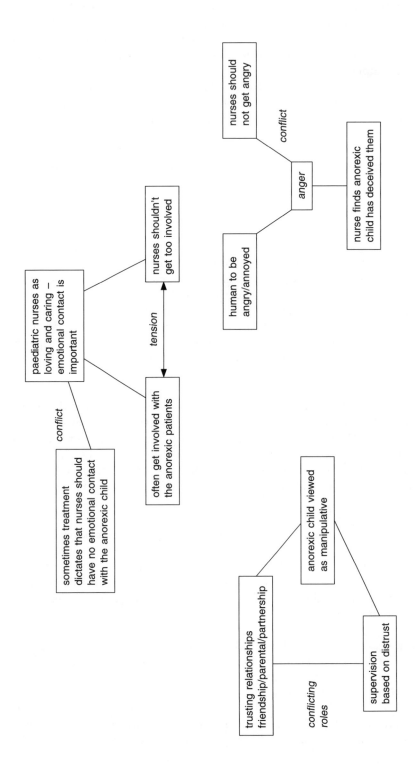

Figure 14.1 *Examples of Conflicts in Nurses' Relationships with Patients with Anorexia Nervosa*

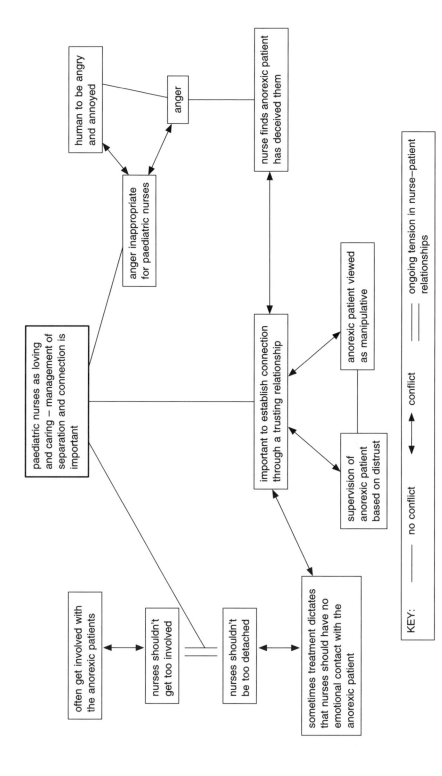

Figure 14.2 *Conflicts of Connection and Separation in Nurses' Relationships with Patients with Anorexia Nervosa*

problematic relationship with eating (Garfinkel et al., 1985), Neil took Stuart's behaviour more personally, interpreting it in terms of the lack of closeness and trust, on the part of Stuart, in their relationship.

Neil illustrates the centrality of trust to maintaining a close, connected relationship with the anorexic patient, and goes on to describe how the loss of trust impacted on his experience:

> I sat down that night, er, I were still thinking about it. So I had a drink and I phoned the staff nurse that were with me, that went in. And she said 'I'm glad you phoned me' 'cos she couldn't get it off her mind that I'd been conned. I said 'What's he playing at, how could he, how could he con me when he's taken me into his trust like this.' And you want, and you're thinking all bad things like, well that's it, totally cut myself off, don't want any more trust. I want to get on with my job. But it's so difficult when you come back to work.

Neil's continuing to dwell on what happened into the evening, his contacting of another colleague to discuss the incident, and his considering keeping more 'detached' in his relationships despite regarding 'separation' as a 'bad thing', all signify the personal impact of this encounter on Neil. However, the last of these illustrates how the 'betrayal' of trust by the anorexic leads Neil to reconsider the close aspect of their relationship and contemplate a distanced one, despite his view that this would be a 'bad' and difficult thing to do.

Concluding Word

Increasing numbers of health psychologists are interested in qualitative approaches. It is important therefore that guides are provided to help encourage them to translate their interest into action by carrying out qualitative research studies. In this chapter we have outlined one particular qualitative approach, IPA, and given a detailed description of how it works in practice.[6] We hope this will indeed encourage readers who are enthusiastic but new to the approach to have a go at conducting projects using this method. At the same time we would hope it is apparent that this is not a prescriptive methodology. However systematically a qualitative method is presented, the crucial part of the analysis remains the particular interpretative analysis the investigator brings to the text. That makes doing qualitative research difficult and demanding. It is also what makes it creative, exciting and, ultimately, marks its potential to make a significant and distinctive contribution to health psychology.

Notes

1. While this chapter is concerned with IPA and health psychology, IPA can also be employed in other areas of psychology.

2. DA is not a unitary phenomenon. See Parker (1992) for another account of DA. The purpose of this section is not to describe DA in detail but merely to help position IPA in contrast to a different qualitative approach.

3. While the main form of data collection for IPA studies so far has been semi-structured interviews, there is no reason why other sources, for example diaries or personal accounts, cannot be employed in IPA studies.

4. Names of all participants in this chapter have been changed to protect confidentiality.

5. (2.9) = page 2, line 9 of the interview transcript.

6. At appropriate points in this chapter, reference has been made to further IPA papers. Additional examples of studies employing IPA can be found in Flowers et al. (1997); Smith (1994); and Smith, Flowers and Osborn (1997).

References

Conrad, P. (1987) The experience of illness: recent and new directions. *Research in the Sociology of Health Care*, 6: 1–31.

Flowers, P., Smith, J.A. Sheeran, P. and Beail, N. (1997) Health and romance: understanding unprotected sex in relationships between gay men. *British Journal of Health Psychology*, 2: 73–86.

Garfinkel, P.E., Garner, D.M. and Kennedy, S. (1985) Special problems of in-patient management. In D.M. Garner and P.E. Garfinkel (eds), *Handbook of Psychotherapy for Anorexia Nervosa and Bulimia Nervosa*. London: Guildford Press, pp. 344–359.

Jarman, M., Smith, J.A. and Walsh, S. (1997) The psychological battle for control: a qualitative study of healthcare professionals' understandings of the treatment of anorexia nervosa. *Journal of Community and Applied Social Psychology*, 7: 137–152.

Jarman, M., Smith, J.A. and Walsh, S. (submitted for publication) Conflicts of connection and separation: a qualitative study of nurses' experiences of their relationships with anorexic patients.

Osborn, M. and Smith, J.A. (1998) Personal experiences of chronic pain: an interpretative phenomenological analysis. *British Journal of Health Psychology*, 3: 65–84.

Parker, I. (1992) *Discourse Dynamics*. London: Routledge.

Potter, J. and Wetherell, M. (1987) *Discourse and Social Psychology: Beyond Attitudes and Behaviour*. London: Sage.

Skevington, S. (1995) *The Psychology of Pain*. Chichester: Wiley.

Smith, J.A. (1994) Reconstructing selves: an analysis of discrepancies between women's contemporaneous and retrospective accounts of the transition to motherhood. *British Journal of Psychology*, 85: 371–392.

Smith, J.A. (1995) Semi-structured interviewing and qualitative analysis. In J.A. Smith, R. Harré, R. and L. Van Langenhove (eds), *Rethinking Methods in Psychology*. London: Sage, pp. 9–26.

Smith, J.A. (1996) Beyond the divide between cognition and discourse: using interpretative phenomenological analysis in health psychology. *Psychology and Health*, 11: 261–271.

Smith, J.A., Harré, R. and Van Langenhove, L. (1995) Idiography and the case study. In J.A. Smith, R. Harré and L. Van Langenhove (eds), *Rethinking Psychology*. London: Sage, pp. 59–69.

Smith J.A., Flowers, P. and Osborn, M. (1997) Interpretative phenomenological analysis and the psychology of health and illness. In L. Yardley (ed.), *Material Discourses of Health and Illness*. London: Routledge, pp. 68–91.

Strauss, A. and Corbin, J. (1990) *Basics of Qualitative Research: Grounded Theory Procedures and Techniques*. London: Sage.

15

Shaping Health Psychology: Qualitative Research, Evaluation and Representation

Antonia Lyons

The use of qualitative research in health psychology has a number of functions. Most obviously, it can be used to address specific research questions posed by health psychologists. However, more generally, it can also function to radically reshape the nature and orientation of the field. After briefly outlining the underlying perspectives dominating health psychology to date, in this chapter I will outline some of the major alternative contributions offered by qualitative research. I will illustrate various schools of thought which underlie a range of qualitative methods, using research examples from areas of women's health. In exploring the impact of qualitative research on the field of health psychology, I will consider how the field is affected by the use of a diverse range of qualitative research, and what this means for issues of evaluation, views on the production and legitimation of knowledge, and perspectives on language and representation. It will be evident from this discussion that certain qualitative approaches, namely those from the more recently developed paradigms, have potentially radical implications for the field of health psychology.

The Nature of Health Psychology

The study of health and illness has been dominated by the biomedical model, which assumes that all diseases and physical disorders can be explained by disturbances in physiological processes, and that the body is separate from psychological and social processes of the mind. This view is coupled with a dominant investigative framework based in the positivist paradigm. Disease is perceived to be a result of particular cause and effect relationships which can be examined and revealed through the use of empiricist methods. This has led to a way of thinking about health that is linear and causative, and also to a study of health and illness that has emphasized measurement of persons, comparisons of groups, counting events and statistical analyses.

Health psychology is located alongside physical health disciplines which are steeped in this biomedical model. As a field of study, it has a broad mission which involves all branches of psychology in almost all aspects of the health enterprise (Taylor, 1990). Health psychologists strive to include the individual in the health equation, and advocate the biopsychosocial model of health and illness. In practice, however, very little attention has been given to the integration of the social, psychological and biological in health psychology (Chamberlain, Stephens and Lyons, 1996). Research has drawn almost exclusively on the hypothetico-deductive approach (Stainton Rogers, 1996) in which complex psychological, social and behavioural phenomena are conceptualized as separate, and often isolated, variables. These variables are then 'measured, manipulated and analysed to reveal some generalizable truth' (Zyzanski et al., 1992: 244). Theories and research methods have tended to focus on the individual as a rational decision-maker who is often stripped of social context. This is most apparent in models of health behaviour, such as the health belief model (Rosenstock, 1974) and the theory of reasoned action (Fishbein and Ajzen, 1975). Despite the relative abundance of literature in the area of health behaviours, it has been noted that our understanding remains largely fragmented (Conrad, 1990).

The Qualitative Research Endeavour in Health Psychology

The individualistic nature of the health psychology field has recently been strongly criticized (Marks, 1996), and there has been a call for an integration of the psychological and the social in health psychology theories and methods (Chamberlain, Stephens and Lyons, 1996; Spicer and Chamberlain, 1996; Stainton Rogers, 1996). In general, qualitative research is concerned with explanation and understanding, and its primary aims are to elicit meaning and to gain understanding (rather than to predict and control). These aims introduce a different kind of research question into health psychology. Rather than comparing groups or categorizing behaviours, questions can be asked about the personal context of health and illness, the meanings of health, illness and disease for individuals, and their lived experience of these constructs. Qualitative research methods enable an incorporation of the social world into health research (Chamberlain, Stephens and Lyons, 1996), and in this way allow insights into individuals' perspectives that are rendered invisible in quantitative methods (Griffin and Phoenix, 1994).

Although qualitative methods have long been used in other forms of health research (for example areas such as nursing), they have been somewhat slower to gain acceptance in health psychology. There are a number of reasons for this resistance to qualitative research, including historical efforts by the discipline of psychology to be aligned with 'hard' sciences such as physics (and separate from philosophy). These sciences work within a positivist paradigm, where research is value-free and 'truth' achievable through the use of particular research methodologies. As the work is said to be objective, there is no need to examine its political and moral commitments. Qualitative research has often been called 'soft' because much of it does not begin with the assumptions made by positivist scientists, and as such has been viewed as an attack on reason and truth (Denzin and Lincoln, 1994). Employing qualitative research methods in health psychology can broaden the subject area of the field by incorporating social and cultural aspects into theory, simultaneously redressing concerns that health psychology has been overly individualistic.

Qualitative Research: Paradigms and Perspectives

For some researchers, the term 'qualitative research' simply refers to a particular way of gathering data (i.e. carrying out interviews) or to a particular type of data (i.e. non-numeric). However, as Henwood and Pidgeon (1992: 98) have argued, 'method is more than data alone'. Qualitative research refers to a diverse range of methods with varying approaches and assumptions. These methods are amalgamated under this title as they are all concerned with an emphasis on meanings and processes rather than on measurement and causal relationships. Qualitative researchers vary in their ontologies, epistemologies and methodologies, or more simply, in the set of beliefs that they bring to the research endeavour. This set of fundamental beliefs is termed a paradigm, and represents a world view – a way of seeing the world, our place in it, and the relationships we can have with it (Guba and Lincoln, 1994). There are a number of paradigms that have been identified as governing different kinds of qualitative research (see Denzin and Lincoln, 1994; Guba and Lincoln, 1994), three of which I would like to discuss here in relation to health psychology, namely the post-positivist paradigm, the critical paradigm and the constructivist-interpretive paradigm. To provide a contrast, I will begin this discussion with a brief overview of the positivist paradigm. It is worth noting that with the exception of positivism, the paradigms are still in formative stages and there are tensions and disagreements within paradigms as well as between them (Guba and Lincoln, 1994). Specific examples of women's health research (primarily regarding menopause) will help to illustrate distinctions within and between paradigms.

Positivist Perspectives

As already noted, the positivist paradigm assumes that there is a reality 'out there' that can be fully apprehended, objectively and free of individual bias (i.e. a realist ontology). This can be achieved through the proper techniques of control and manipulation. The emphasis is on measurement and cause–effect relationships (thus, these criteria generally exclude qualitative research as irrelevant). Holte and Mikkelson (1991) provide a good example of positivist research in their study of psychosocial determinants of menopausal complaints. The first aim of the study was to 'test the validity of an association between menopausal development and climacteric complaints' (Holte and Mikkelson, 1991: 206) – in other words, to see if such a relationship exists in 'reality' in the population. A large sample (n = 1,886) was used so results could be more reliable and generalizable. Constructs such as complaints, menopausal development, coping style and social network were quantified through questionnaire responses, providing variables which were subjected to statistical analyses to identify relationships among them. The assumption is that if a relationship exists, the 'truth' of that relationship will be apparent in this sample, given the methods employed. Results are viewed as objective and value-free.

Post-positivist Perspectives

For post-positivists, the reality 'out there' can never be fully apprehended, only approximated (a critical realist ontology) (Guba, 1990). Multiple methods are employed to capture as much of this reality as possible, including the use of qualitative methods in more natural settings. For example, a recent exploratory study (Salazar and Carter, 1994) used in-depth interviews to examine women's beliefs about breast self-examination (BSE). Nineteen women (from a total group of fifty-nine) were selected on the basis of age, race and self-reported frequency of BSE (to include a range of respondents). However, the group of participants was still fairly homogeneous, being mainly white, middle-class and relatively well-educated. The aims of the study were to explore the women's beliefs and attitudes regarding BSE, and to develop a 'hierarchy of attributes related to BSE performance' (Salazar and Carter, 1994: 344). The second phase of the study involved the construction of a survey based on the information provided in the interviews, and the use of quantitative methods. As the authors point out, presenting results of their qualitative research provides a 'more complete description of the phenomena' (ibid.) identified in the interviews, and gets closer to the 'real' concerns of women. The small size of the sample and its homogeneity are viewed as limitations to the study, which is consistent with a post-positivist perspective where the aim is to generalize results to populations.

Critical Perspectives

The critical paradigm encompasses Marxist, feminist, ethnic and cultural studies traditions. Critical theorists hold a view of reality as something that, over time, has been shaped by social, political, cultural, economic, ethnic and gender forces into a set of structures that, although historically constructed, are now taken as 'real' and 'natural' (Guba and Lincoln, 1994). As Denzin and Lincoln (1994) point out, the real world is viewed as making a material difference in terms of race, class and gender (hence this paradigm assumes a material-realist ontology). The values of the researcher are brought to the fore in this paradigm and knowledge is seen as value-dependent. In addition, there is a political intervention/action orientation to a critical approach, with a need to make a difference through research (Seibold, Richards and Simon, 1994). Naturalistic methodologies are usually employed (particularly ethnographies) by researchers in this paradigm.

Drawing largely on the ideas of Foucault, Sybylla (1997) has carried out a critical feminist analysis of the menopause. Her starting assumption is that the knowledge and practices surrounding menopause today are more to do with historical circumstance and much less to do with progress. Her analysis focuses on discourses of the menopause over the previous two centuries, and through this genealogy her aim is to show how ideas and knowledge concerning menopause have changed 'in keeping with wider changes in the coalitions and oppositions in the complex network of power relations between institutions, businesses, diverse groups, and individuals' (p. 202). The conclusions of the study revolve around the implications of identifying the so-called 'truth' concerning menopause that has been *created* by the medical profession. By showing that these 'truths' are in fact the creations of those claiming expert knowledge, Sybylla encourages the idea that women can participate actively in these power games by producing their own truth regarding menopause, women's bodies and women themselves.

Constructivist Perspectives

The constructivist paradigm can be said to include radical constructivism, social constructionism and feminist standpoint epistemologies (Schwandt, 1994). It assumes that there are multiple realities (a relativist ontology) which are sometimes conflicting, and these realities may change as reconstructions and understandings shift. Further, constructivist researchers assume that the knowledge derived through research is created by both the researcher and the researched, and they tend to employ a range of naturalistic methods. Social constructionists, in particular, focus on language as a functional system which does more than transparently reflect reality – rather, it functions to create social reality through the process of social exchange and shared meanings (Gergen, 1985).

From this viewpoint Martin (1997) has carried out an analysis of the construction of the menopausal body in medical texts. She shows how the metaphor of the factory is used in describing physiological events (for example DNA communicating with RNA, producing proteins) as well as in discourse on the menopause. Applied to menopause, however, the metaphor of the factory constructs events as failing in their purpose. For example, 'the fall in blood progesterone and estrogen *deprives* the *highly developed* endometrial lining of its hormonal support' (Martin, 1997: 240). Terms such as 'degenerate', 'decline', 'withdrawn', 'deteriorate' are frequent, and Martin points out the negative image of aligning menopause with one of the horrors of our late capitalist society, namely the lack of production. She also examines another metaphor used in medical discourse, that of the body as an information-processing system (with a hierarchical structure). Within this discourse, any change to the system is perceived as negative, and this is obvious with descriptions of menopause (for example, ovaries become 'unresponsive' and 'regress'). Martin argues that the propensity of the medical profession to view menopause as a pathological state comes in part from its construction in medical textbooks – 'as a logical outgrowth of seeing the body as a hierarchical system held rigidly in order by its central control system in the first place' (ibid.: 245). At the end of her analysis, Martin provides alternative, more positive medical constructions of menopause.

Multiple Paradigms, Multiple Methods

The different assumptions and perspectives brought to the research endeavour by qualitative methods explicitly influence theory and evaluation in health psychology. For example, in the positivist framework, theory is developed prior to the empirical study, and is assumed to guide the way in which data are gathered, analysed and interpreted. In contrast, in many qualitative methods, theory is unspecified in advance of a study; the aim is to develop theory from within the data (for example grounded theory) (Henwood and Pidgeon, 1992). Researchers working within critical or constructivist perspectives in particular draw explicitly upon the assumptions of their paradigms to develop theory. For example, constructionist researchers use methods which have been generated by a discursive perspective. From this perspective, concepts such as the self, identity and other psychological phenomena are assumed to be products of discursive practices which cannot be separated from social position and socio-historical location (for example Davies and Harré, 1990; Frazer, 1989; Sampson, 1993). Therefore, any examination of individual beliefs, attitudes and behaviour must take the wider social and cultural context into consideration. Researchers in health psychology have begun to use these ideas in their own theorizing about particular health issues (see Yardley, 1997), such as AIDS (Joffe, 1997), pregnancy and childbirth (Woollett and Marshall, 1997), and dieting behaviour (Ogden, 1997). Further, Levin and Solomon (1990) have examined the discursive formation of the body in the history of medicine, and conclude that the body is more than a physical substance; it is an ongoing process of socialization and acculturation. This socialization interacts with the biological nature of the body to develop it and permanently shape and transform it. Thus, the body can be viewed simultaneously as a biological entity, the site of the experience of pain, and also a discursive formation. This discursive view allows theory to be developed about the body as the site of meaningful experience.

However, problems emerge with the use of a multiplicity of qualitative methods and competing paradigms. One problem occurs when research carried out in different paradigms results in contradictory findings. Levine-

Silverman (1991) has noted this in relation to menopause research. While one paradigm views this stage of life as a subjective, experiential life event, the more reductionist scientific model views it as a biological state. Findings from the research across these two paradigms are often inconclusive and contradictory, and Levine-Silverman points out that to deal with these inconsistent results health-care professionals selectively use findings consistent with their own ideologies. Similarly, how a health psychologist integrates research findings from various perspectives will depend on their own views regarding knowledge and its production. Despite this problem, there is much to be said for approaching the same problem in health research from different theoretical and methodological angles, while maintaining an awareness of the disciplinary traditions and the assumptions and rationales of different approaches (Lupton, 1994).

Further, there is a problem with the evaluation of findings from a diverse range of qualitative methods. The diversity of methods reflects several different research paradigms, necessitating various criteria for evaluation. Thus, effective evaluation of qualitative research requires explicit consideration of ontological, epistemological and methodological issues, as I will discuss in the following section. For the researcher, the requirement to understand various sets of evaluation criteria (and corresponding jargon) can be paralysing, particularly when there are debates raging within and between different paradigms about the use of specific evaluation criteria.

Evaluation and Legitimation

The use of qualitative methods in health psychology affects the criteria by which we assess pieces of research. In quantitative research, a well-defined set of criteria is applied to all research findings to evaluate the goodness of a particular study and its results. If we begin with the positivist assumption that there is a 'truth' out there that is defined as having some form of correspondence with reality, then questions about whether the research yields an accurate account of this reality can be asked (Smith, 1990). For example, questions about the adequacy of the measurement process (is this a valid measure of construct X?) and the results (do they provide a valid picture of what is really going on out there?) can be posed, as can questions about the reliability of the measurement process and the results. Further, assuming there is a reality out there that can be depicted (or at least approached), then research findings should be generalizable across different settings.

Concepts such as reliability, validity and generalizability are often irrelevant in the evaluation of qualitative research as they are based on assumptions central to a positivist perspective. Qualitative research often concerns itself with meaning, and because meaning in human experience is not likely to be universal, generalization from qualitative research findings is not relevant (Zyzanski et al., 1992). Evaluation criteria depend on the epistemological assumptions of the particular research paradigm (that is, what can we know about the world?) so any evaluation questions must take into account the paradigm within which the research was carried out. For example, researchers working within the post-positivist framework also have a view of a reality 'out there', although they believe that this reality cannot be fully apprehended. Therefore, the evaluation criteria employed in this paradigm are the conventional benchmarks of rigour (reliability, validity, objectivity), which are often redefined slightly to encompass non-numeric data.

Within the critical paradigm, researchers look to aspects of the work such as credibility, dependability, transferability, and confirmability (Denzin and Lincoln, 1994). These evaluation criteria do not decontextualize the data – indeed, a good quality inquiry will be historically situated (taking account of the social, political, cultural, economic and gender antecedents of the situation). Additionally, the extent to which the findings stimulate action and change existing structures may also be examined (Guba and Lincoln, 1994). For research findings to be dependable, then, it is expected that different investigators using similar procedures will perceive similar meanings. In addition, by following what is known as 'decision trails' the inquiry can be audited, and other investigators can assess whether interpretations are generally supported by the data (Seibold, Richards and Simon, 1994). For example, in a critical study of the menopause, teams could be set up to ensure the 'constant comparison of analyses and rigorous explanations of different interpretations' (ibid.: 399).

According to Guba and Lincoln (1994), researchers working within the constructivist paradigm have two sets of criteria. One surrounds the *trustworthiness* of the work and the other its *authenticity*. From this perspective an interview study on menopause may emphasize women's understandings of menopause and their interpretations of the menopause experience. The starting assumption is that there are multiple realities so no one true description will exist. Further, it is explicitly acknowledged that the researcher and the researched co-produce any findings that are derived within the context of the research process, and the results provide a new (and hopefully useful) 'construction' of the menopause experience. This construction can be evaluated for its trustworthiness, in terms of its credibility (to researchers or other women), whether it is dependable (would a similar construction be produced in similar contexts?), transferable (would a similar construction be produced in different contexts?), and also whether it is confirmable (do similar others have similar constructions?). To establish the authenticity of the results, the researchers could examine whether the construction produced leads to improved understandings of other women's constructions of the menopause experience, whether it empowers action among women and researchers, and also whether it stimulates action.

No one set of evaluation criteria exist to evaluate all qualitative research. It has been argued, however, that there are a few common criteria which can be used to judge the goodness of different kinds of qualitative studies, although these will be weighted differently by different paradigms

(Marshall, 1990). In many qualitative methods the concepts of credibility, dependability and confirmability are applied (Zyzanski et al., 1992), and are examined with the use of triangulation, reflexivity and independent audits (Banister et al., 1994). Triangulation involves approaching the data from different perspectives to gain a richer and more illuminating interpretation (Banister et al., 1994). There are different levels of triangulation (such as data, investigator and method triangulation), and this technique highlights the notion that there are various ways of 'knowing', all of which can contribute to building a body of knowledge. However, the value of this concept for evaluation has been contested among qualitative researchers, with some arguing that it rings too many 'positivist criteria' bells (attempting to close in on the one 'true' picture). There has also been a call for new labels to describe the combinations of evaluations triangulation is now representing (for example Blaikie, 1991).

What do these evaluation issues mean for the field of health psychology? First, any evaluation of qualitative research in health psychology requires an awareness that alternative research paradigms exist outside the dominant, positivist paradigm. If such an awareness is not achieved, traditional evaluation concepts such as reliability, validity and generalizability will be erroneously applied to qualitative findings. Given where health psychology is located, alongside medicine and other physical sciences, and the subject matter it concerns itself with (physical health), legitimation claims have primarily been in the form of the traditional criteria used for evaluating research. Some critical theorists argue that the application of traditional evaluation concepts to qualitative studies means that this kind of research is never legitimized (Denzin and Lincoln, 1994). Readers who are ignorant of shifts in paradigms when considering qualitative research will regard any materials that have been produced by qualitative health researchers as unreliable and not objective, thus denying them any status and therefore also simultaneously reinforcing traditional ways of producing knowledge (ibid.). In this sense evaluation criteria can be seen to legitimate a piece of research.

In addition, consideration of evaluation issues in qualitative research in health psychology may increase awareness that validation and methodology are inherently linked, and work together to produce knowledge claims (Smith, 1990). It is clear that method affects the production of knowledge (Hollway, 1989), and post-modern theorists strongly criticize the idea that method can be used as a generator of truth (Chaiklin, 1992). According to Mishler (1990), evaluation criteria such as reliability and falsifiability are simply ways to warrant validity claims, rather than abstract guarantors of truth, and further, they are strategies that only fit one scientific paradigm. He defines validation as the 'process through which we make claims for and evaluate the trustworthiness of reported observations, interpretations and generalizations' (p. 419). Whether or not these claims are upheld is tested through researchers' ongoing discourses and consensus in the research community. In this way what is counted as scientific knowledge can be seen to be produced, or constructed, socially.

In evaluating qualitative research in health psychology, researchers are invited not only to investigate various research paradigms and appropriate evaluation criteria, but to consider the broader implications of qualitative research for power and legitimacy issues inherent in methodology and the production of knowledge. With the use of qualitative methods from various paradigms comes an acceptance of the diverse ways of producing knowledge (Kvale, 1992), which further expands the area of health psychology, increasing the kinds of research that are able to make valuable contributions to the field. Using qualitative methods in health psychology and evaluating them appropriately will also legitimate the use of these methods in producing knowledge within the domain of health and illness.

Consideration of evaluation criteria from the newer critical and constructivist perspectives does therefore have an impact on health psychology, for they require that health psychologists are flexible in their perspectives and understandings. This research acknowledges explicitly that all research is interpretive and political, guided by the beliefs and perspectives of the researcher. Researchers in these traditions have particular perspectives on how to gain knowledge and what knowledge is, views that reflect the current *Zeitgeist*, with its encouragement of diversity and critique of truth, and a focus on language and representation.

Language and Representation

The increasing interest in qualitative research using critical and constructivist perspectives reflects what has come to be known as the 'linguistic turn' in the philosophy of science (Kvale, 1992), and this has seen a change in emphasis in the research endeavour. Kvale succinctly summarizes this change in emphasis as from a confrontation with nature to a focus on conversation, and from a correspondence with an objective reality to the negotiation of meaning. The linguistic turn has also altered the way in which language is viewed. There is a focus on the power of language to create: to organize our thoughts and experiences, and to influence conceptual boundaries. There is also a focus on the power of research language to construct: to legitimate power relations, to develop multi-centred discourse, and to produce the very objects of the research investigation (Lather, 1992). In the latter case, ideas and concepts used in the research endeavour become reified through their description, investigation and interpretation.

Researchers investigate language as the representational system through which participants' realities are constructed, yet must then use this system to *make sense* of qualitative data, and to write the results of qualitative research (Stainton Rogers, 1996). Sense-making involves a number of processes. How the researcher makes sense of the qualitative data and the meaning that they extract from it depends upon their own experiences, and location in the social 'seascape', as Shotter (1993) calls it. This reflexive aspect of qualitative research is often acknowledged explicitly and the researcher and the researched are seen as collaborators in constructing and producing research findings (Banister et al., 1994). In any research interview, accounts are given that depend not only on the questions asked and the characteristics of the researcher, but also on his/her mere presence as an interviewer. For example, how ill people talk about health and illness in an interview is influenced by the interviewer, who is understood as being 'healthy' by virtue of carrying out a task of their employment (the interview itself) (Radley and Billig, 1996). Thus their talk can be seen as warranting or legitimizing accounts of their own 'normalcy', constructed for, and as a consequence of, the interview situation (ibid.).

Any analysis and interpretation of qualitative data will be shaped by conventions of language and conventions of narrative. Narrative analysts highlight the pervasiveness of stories in all human thought and action, and point out that our experiences and memories are organized in the form of narrative (Bruner, 1991). Therefore, a researcher is guided by stories and during any qualitative analysis will begin to construct a new story, one which is acceptable to his/her audience (Murray, 1997). Throughout this process, s/he makes decisions about what should and should not be included, how it should be included and what kind of form the writing should take (Denzin, 1994). The researcher must also rely on conventions of narrative and other conventions of language when writing reports of qualitative research. In the qualitative report, the author is providing a text of their interpretations of other people's meanings for an audience. The text, in turn, is read by members of an audience who will derive their own meanings or readings of it based on their own sense-making capacities (Schwandt, 1994).

How the author chooses to write for an audience in the health field, therefore, and what s/he includes in the report, depends upon assumptions made about this audience in terms of what its members accept as knowledge and what they believe constitutes good inquiry. For example, although many qualitative health researchers work within the more recent critical and constructivist paradigms, some choose to use the evaluation terms of the more dominant positivist paradigm, such as reliability and validity, because they write for readers who are health workers embedded in the quantitative framework (Appleton, 1995; Brink, 1991). However, this can be misleading and confusing (Leininger, 1994), even when the terms are redefined to make them appropriate for the methods that have been employed (for example Lather, 1993).

For many qualitative researchers the qualitative report is not seen as a reproduction of what is going on in the data, or what is going on with the participants involved in the research, but a *representation* of what is going on (or the *activity* of representing what is going on). The role of the researcher/author becomes crucial in creating knowledge (and reality) through the processes of writing and interpretation. Social constructionists accept that knowledge is constructed in the social realm, and that what is written and how the author has made sense of their data is just one of many possible versions of reality. A number of writers have readily acknowledged that academic discourse itself is a form of rhetoric (see Billig, 1994; Gergen, 1992), in which a researcher makes a claim to moral and scientific authority (Denzin and Lincoln, 1994).

According to Lupton (1994), being aware of the assumptions on which any research analysis is founded is almost mandatory at the present time. However, this has not been the case in health psychology. In being reflexive about our own research and writing, health psychologists can reflect not only on what they have produced and their part in it, but on the endeavour of the health psychology field as a whole. Their writings work to simultaneously shape and construct the field as one that is legitimate and important. Further, an awareness that all knowledge, and claims to knowledge, depend upon the assumptions, location, history and context of the researcher and the wider scientific community, permits consideration of issues of power, particularly about the legitimation and distribution of knowledge (Stainton Rogers, 1996). Some of the disciplines that are concerned with physical health have considerable power over this domain, and are subject to ideological, political and economic forces (Spicer, 1995). The use of certain qualitative methods in health psychology (such as action research and feminist research) makes these forces explicit, and enables an examination of the wider political context in which the research is occurring.

Conclusion

The current age has been termed 'post-modern', and has been characterized by a move from an intra-individual perspective to a focus on text and discourse. According to Kvale (1992), the post-modern era has seen a shift from inside to outside and from psyche to text. Ironically, health psychology has been said to be paying more attention to intra-individual processes (Ogden, 1995) and has been criticized for its over-emphasis and concern with the individual, despite its claim to be working within a biopsychosocial model of health and illness. Focusing on discourse and constructions of reality through the use of qualitative methods and theorizing may enable health psychologists to transcend the psychosocial distinction (Spicer and Chamberlain, 1996) and allow an incorporation of the socio-cultural aspects of health into research and theory (Chamberlain, Stephens and Lyons, 1996). This can occur at a number of levels, from eliciting individual participants' interpretations and meanings, to a focus on text and discourse as social constructors of reality, to an analysis and critique of power structures in society that affect individuals.

Qualitative research findings contribute to the accumulation of health psychology knowledge and serve to construct and reinforce the field as legitimate and valid. In particular, the critical and constructivist nature of many qualitative methods has the potential to shape the domain of this field of research by incorporating and emphasizing the inherent socialness of our accounts and understandings. This shifts the location of key concepts (such as self, mind and body) into the social realm and can function to blur the boundaries of the health psychology field while encouraging a more interdisciplinary approach to the study of health and illness. With their visions of what expert knowledge is and how it comes to be constructed, these methods also have the potential to radically transform the nature of health psychology itself.

References

Appleton, J.V. (1995) Analysing qualitative interview data: addressing issues of validity and reliability. *Journal of Advanced Nursing*, 22: 993–997.

Banister, P., Burman, E., Parker, I., Taylor, M. and Tindall, C. (1994) *Qualitative Methods in Psychology*. Buckingham: Open University Press.

Billig, M. (1994) Repopulating the depopulated pages of psychology. *Theory and Psychology*, 4: 307–335.

Blaikie, N.W.H. (1991) A critique of the use of triangulation in social research. *Quality and Quantity*, 25: 115–136.

Brink, P.J. (1991) On issues of reliability and validity. In J.M. Morse (ed.), *Qualitative Nursing Research: A Contemporary Dialogue*. Newbury Park, CA: Sage, pp. 164–186.

Bruner, J. (1991) The narrative construction of reality. *Critical Inquiry*, 18: 1–21.

Chaiklin, S. (1992) From theory to practice and back again: what does postmodern philosophy contribute to psychological science? In S. Kvale (ed.), *Postmodernism and Psychology*. London: Sage.

Chamberlain, K., Stephens, C. and Lyons, A.C. (1996) Encompassing experience: meanings and methods in health psychology. *Psychology and Health*, 12: 691–709.

Conrad, P. (1990) Qualitative research on chronic illness: a commentary on methods and conceptual development. *Social Science and Medicine*, 30: 1257–1263.

Davies, B. and Harré, R. (1990) Positioning: the discursive production of selves. *Journal for the Theory of Social Behavior*, 20: 43–63.

Denzin, N.K. (1994) The art and politics of interpretation. In N.K. Denzin and Y.S. Lincoln (eds), *Handbook of Qualitative Research*. London: Sage, pp. 500–515.

Denzin, N.K. and Lincoln, Y.S. (eds) (1994) *Handbook of Qualitative Research*. London: Sage.

Fishbein, M. and Ajzen, I. (1975) *Belief, Attitude, Intention and Behaviour*. Reading, MA: Addison-Wesley.

Frazer, E. (1989) Feminist talk and talking about feminism: teenage girls' discourses of gender. *Oxford Review of Education*, 15: 281–290.

Gergen K.J. (1985) The social constructionist movement in modern psychology. *American Psychologist*, 40: 266–275.

Gergen, K.J. (1992) Toward a postmodern psychology. In S. Kvale (ed.), *Psychology and Postmodernism*. London: Sage, pp. 17–30.

Griffin, C. and Phoenix, A. (1994) The relationship between qualitative and quantitative research: lessons from feminist psychology. *Journal of Community and Applied Social Psychology*, 4: 287–298.

Guba, E.G. (1990) The alternative paradigm dialog. In E.G. Guba (ed.), *The Paradigm Dialog*. Newbury Park, CA: Sage, pp. 17–27.

Guba, E.G. and Lincoln, Y.S. (1994) Competing paradigms in qualitative research. In

N.K. Denzin and Y.S. Lincoln (eds), *Handbook of Qualitative Research*. London: Sage, pp. 105–117.

Henwood, K.L. and Pidgeon, N.F. (1992) Qualitative research and psychological theorizing. *British Journal of Psychology*, 83: 97–111.

Hollway, W. (1989) *Subjectivity and Method in Psychology*. London: Sage.

Holte, A. and Mikkelson, A. (1991) Psychosocial determinants of climacteric complaints. *Maturitas*, 13: 205–215.

Joffe, H. (1997) The representational and materialist perspectives: AIDS and 'the other'. In L. Yardley (ed.), *Material Discourses of Health and Illness*. London: Routledge, pp. 132–149.

Kvale, S. (1992) Postmodern psychology: a contradiction in terms? In S. Kvale (ed.), *Psychology and Postmodernism*. London: Sage, pp. 31–57.

Lather, P. (1992) Postmodernism and the human sciences. In S. Kvale (ed.), *Psychology and Postmodernism*. London: Sage, pp. 88–109.

Lather, P. (1993) Fertile obsession: validity after poststructuralism. *The Sociological Quarterly*, 34: 673–693.

Leininger, M. (1994) Evaluation criteria and critique of qualitative research studies. In J.M. Morse (ed.), *Critical Issues in Qualitative Research Methods*. London: Sage, pp. 95–115.

Levin, D.M. and Solomon, G.F. (1990) The discursive formation of the body in the history of medicine. *The Journal of Medicine and Philosophy*, 15: 515–537.

Levine-Silverman, S. (1991) Commentary on 'Women's decisions about estrogen replacement therapy' by M.L. Logothetis. *Western Journal of Nursing Research*, 13: 469–470.

Lupton, D. (1994) *Medicine as Culture*. London: Sage.

Marks, D.F. (1996) Health psychology in context. *Journal of Health Psychology*, 1: 7–21.

Marshall, C. (1990) Goodness criteria: are they objective or judgment calls? In E.G. Guba (ed.), *The Paradigm Dialog*. London: Sage, pp. 188–197.

Martin. E. (1997) The woman in the menopausal body. In P.A. Komersaroff, P. Rothfield and J. Daly (eds), *Reinterpreting Menopause: Cultural and Philosophical Issues*. London: Routledge, pp. 239–254.

Mishler, E.G. (1990) Validation in inquiry-guided research: the role of exemplars in narrative studies. *Harvard Educational Review*, 60: 415–442.

Murray, M. (1997) *Narrative Health Psychology*. Visiting Scholar Series No. 7, Department of Psychology, Massey University, New Zealand.

Ogden, J. (1995) Changing the subject of health psychology. *Psychology and Health*, 10: 257–265.

Ogden, J. (1997) Diet as a vehicle for self-control. In L. Yardley (ed.), *Material Discourses of Health and Illness*. London: Routledge, pp. 199–216.

Radley, A. and Billig, M. (1996) Accounts of health and illness: dilemmas and representations. *Sociology of Health and Illness*, 18: 220–240.

Rosenstock, I.M. (1974) The Health Belief Model and preventive health behaviour. *Health Education Monographs*, 2: 354–386.

Salazar, M.K. and Carter, W.B. (1994) A qualitative description of breast self-examination beliefs. *Health Education Research*, 9: 343–354.

Sampson, E.E. (1993) *Celebrating the Other: A Dialogic Account of Human Nature*. San Francisco: Westview Press.

Schwandt, T.A. (1994) Constructivist, interpretivist approaches to human inquiry. In N.K. Denzin and Y.S. Lincoln (eds), *Handbook of Qualitative Research*. London: Sage, pp. 118–137.

Seibold, C., Richards, L. and Simon, D. (1994) Feminist method and qualitative research about midlife. *Journal of Advanced Nursing*, 19: 394–402.

Shotter, J. (1993) *Cultural Politics of Everyday Life*. Buckingham: Open University Press.

Smith, J.K. (1990) Alternative research paradigms and the problem of criteria. In E.G. Guba (ed.), *The Paradigm Dialog*. London: Sage, pp. 167–187.

Spicer, J. (1995) Individual discourses in health psychology. *Psychology and Health*, 10: 291–294.

Spicer, J. and Chamberlain, K. (1996) Developing psychosocial theory in health psychology: problems and prospects. *Journal of Health Psychology*, 1: 161–171.

Stainton Rogers, W. (1996) Critical approaches to health psychology. *Journal of Health Psychology*, 1: 65–78.

Sybylla, R. (1997) Situating menopause within the strategies of power: a genealogy. In P.A. Komersaroff, P. Rothfield and J. Daly (eds), *Reinterpreting Menopause: Cultural and Philosophical Issues*. London: Routledge, pp. 200–221.

Taylor, S.E. (1990) Health psychology: the science and the field. *American Psychologist*, 45: 40–50.

Woollett, A. and Marshall, H. (1997) Discourses of pregnancy and childbirth. In L. Yardley (ed.), *Material Discourses of Health and Illness*. London: Routledge, pp. 176–198.

Yardley, L. (1997) *Material Discourses of Health and Illness*. London: Routledge.

Zyzanski, S.J., McWhinney, I.R., Blake, R. Jr., Crabtree, B.F. and Miller, W.L. (1992) Qualitative research: perspectives on the future. In B.F. Crabtree and W.L. Miller (eds), *Doing Qualitative Research*. Series in research methods for primary care, vol. 3. Newbury Park, CA: Sage.

Name Index

Subject Index